olam ha-zeh v'olam ha-ba: This World and the World to Come in Jewish Belief and Practice

Studies in Jewish Civilization
Volume 28

Proceedings of the Twenty-Eighth Annual
Symposium of the Klutznick Chair
in Jewish Civilization,
the Harris Center for Judaic Studies,
and the Schwalb Center
for Israel and Jewish Studies

October 25–26, 2015

Other volumes in the
Studies in Jewish Civilization Series
Distributed by the Purdue University Press

2010 – Rites of Passage:
How Today's Jews Celebrate, Commemorate, and Commiserate

2011 – Jews and Humor

2012 – Jews in the Gym:
Judaism, Sports, and Athletics

2013 – Fashioning Jews:
Clothing, Culture, and Commerce

2014 – Who Is a Jew?
Reflections on History, Religion, and Culture

2015 – Wealth and Poverty in Jewish Tradition

2016 – Mishpachah:
The Jewish Family in Tradition and in Transition

olam ha-zeh v'olam ha-ba:
This World and the World to Come in Jewish Belief and Practice

Studies in Jewish Civilization
Volume 28

Editor:
Leonard J. Greenspoon

The Klutznick Chair in Jewish Civilization

Purdue University Press
West Lafayette, Indiana

Copyright © 2017 by Creighton University
Published by Purdue University Press
All rights reserved
Manufactured in the United States of America

Library of Congress Cataloging-in-Publication Data

Names: Greenspoon, Leonard J. (Leonard Jay), editor.
Title: olam ha-zeh v'olam ha-ba : this world and the world to come in Jewish belief and practice / edited by Leonard Greenspoon.
Description: West Lafayette, Indiana : Purdue University Press, [2017] | Series: Studies in Jewish Civilization | Includes bibliographical references.
Identifiers: LCCN 2017031449 | ISBN 9781557537928 (pbk. : alk. paper) | ISBN 9781612495132 (epdf) | ISBN 9781612495149 (epub)
Subjects: LCSH: Future life—Judaism—History of doctrines. | Eschatology, Jewish—History of doctrines. | Immortality—Judaism—History of doctrines. | Resurrection (Jewish theology)—History of doctrines.
Classification: LCC BM635 .O43 2017 | DDC 296.3/3—dc23 LC record available at https://lccn.loc.gov/2017031449

No part of *Studies in Jewish Civilization* (ISSN 1070-8510) volume 28 may be reproduced or transmitted in any form or by any means, electronic or mechanical, including photocopying, recording, or any information storage and retrieval system, without permission in writing from the publisher, except in the case of brief quotations embodied in critical articles and reviews.

In Memory of
Moshe Gershovitz

With deep affection and warm memories, we dedicate this volume to our colleague Moshe Gershovitz, who directed the Schwalb Center at the University of Nebraska at Omaha. His death earlier this year saddened us all. May his life inspire us to be and to do the very best we can.

Table of Contents

Acknowledgments ix

Editor's Introduction. xi

Contributors xix

"The End of the World and the World to Come": What
Apocalyptic Literature Says about the Time After the End-Time 1
Dereck Daschke

Warriors, Wives, and Wisdom: This World and
the World to Come in the (So-Called) Apocrypha 17
Nicolae Roddy

The Afterlife in the Septuagint 29
Leonard Greenspoon

Rabbi Akiva, Other Martyrs, and Socrates: On Life, Death,
and Life After Life. 49
Naftali Rothenberg

Heaven on Earth: The World to Come and Its (Dis)locations. 69
Christine Hayes

Olam Ha-ba in Rabbinic Literature: A Functional Reading. 91
Dov Weiss

Dining In(to) the World to Come. 105
Jordan D. Rosenblum

What's for Dinner in *Olam Ha-ba*? Why Do We Care
in *Olam Ha-zeh*?: Medieval Jewish Ideas about Meals in the World
to Come in R. Bahya ben Asher's *Shulhan Shel Arba*. 115
Jonathan Brumberg-Kraus

The Dybbuk: The Origins and History of a Concept. 135
Morris M. Faierstein

Tasting Heaven: Wine and the World
to Come from the Talmud to Safed. 151
Vadim Putzu

Worlds to Come Between East and West: Immortality
and the Rise of Modern Jewish Thought. 171
Elias Sacks

Emmanuel Levinas's Messianism and the World to Come:
A Gnostic-Philosophical Reading of Tractate *Sanhedrin* 96b–99a 197
Federico Dal Bo

Acknowledgments

The 28th Annual Symposium on Jewish Civilization took place on October 25 and October 26, 2015, in Omaha and Lincoln, Nebraska. The title of the symposium, from which this volume also takes its name, is "*olam ha-zeh v'olam ha-ba*: This World and the World to Come in Jewish Belief and Practice."

Anyone who reads carefully and has a phenomenal memory (that sounds a lot like me!) will observe that the symposium has formally changed its name yet once again. Rather than take its name from the expanding list of academic sponsors, the symposium now proclaims in its title what it does—and has always done: provide an opportunity for the exchange and interchange of information about a different aspect of Jewish civilization each year.

Thankfully, our major sponsors remain: the Klutznick Chair in Jewish Civilization at Creighton University; the Kripke Center for the Study of Society and Religion, also at Creighton; the Harris Center for Judaic Studies at University of Nebraska-Lincoln; the Schwalb Center for Israel and Jewish Studies at the University of Nebraska at Omaha; and the Jewish Federation of Omaha.

As in past years, much of the success of this symposium is due to the unwavering support of colleagues: Dr. Ronald Simkins, of the Kripke Center; Drs. Jean Cahan and Sidnie White Crawford, of the Harris Center; and Drs. Moshe Gershovitz and Curtis Hutt, of the Schwalb Center. Colleen Hastings, administrative assistant for the Klutznick Chair and the Kripke Center, continues her invaluable contributions at all stages in the planning and implementation of the symposium and in preparing this volume for publication. I also offer warm thanks to Kasey De Goey, staff assistant for the Schwalb Center, who ensures, among many other things, that the Sunday morning symposium session at University of Nebraska at Omaha runs smoothly. Equally efficient and dependable is Mary Sue Grossman, who is affiliated with the Jewish Federation of Omaha.

With this volume, we are completing eight years in our ongoing relationship with the Purdue University Press. Its staff, under the previous director Charles Watkinson and his successor Peter Froehlich, continues to make us feel welcome in every possible way. We look forward to many more years of collaboration with the press.

Additional generous support is provided by:

Creighton University Lectures, Films and Concerts
The Creighton College of Arts and Sciences

The Ike and Roz Friedman Foundation
The Riekes Family
The Henry Monsky Lodge of B'nai B'rith
Gary and Karen Javitch
The Drs. Bernard H. and Bruce S. Bloom Memorial Endowment
And others.

Leonard J. Greenspoon
Omaha, Nebraska
March 2017
ljgrn@creighton.edu

Editor's Introduction

When I was growing up in the 1950s and 1960s (chronological point of reference: I celebrated my bar mitzvah in January 1959), I was regular and punctual in my attendance at Junior Congregation on Saturday mornings and religious school on Sunday mornings and twice during the weekday. (Yes! They worked us hard in those days.) I attended Beth El, the Conservative synagogue in Richmond, Virginia.

I remember a lot of what I heard (well, that's undoubtedly something of an exaggeration), mostly about Israel and the Holocaust. Later on, I found out that my experience in this regard was typical. What I do not remember hearing about was *olam ha-ba*, the world to come.

Fast forward to the mid-1990s. I was still attending Congregation Beth El, but now in Omaha, Nebraska. It was a Saturday morning, and our younger daughter was attending services along with her teenaged friends. At some point in the D'var Torah [sermon], the rabbi mentioned hell.

Immediately after the service (or was it mid-sermon?), my daughter and her friends rushed over to me: "Jews don't believe in hell, do we?" By then, she surely knew that she was not likely to get a quick yes/no answer from me. (If that was true when she wanted to borrow the car, how much more so in this instance?)

In all fairness to everyone involved, there is almost never a simple answer to a question that begins with "[All] Jews" and continues with "believe [and/or practice]." And so it was on this occasion. Her question was followed by several of my own: "Which Jews?" "When? "What do you/they mean by hell?" And so on.

The theoretical goal of such queries on my part was to point to the chronological, historical, and theological nuances of defining or describing beliefs and practices of "Jews." I suspect that the practical consequence of my strategy was to lead my daughter, along with her cohorts, to Google.

In some sense, then, we can view the present volume as an extended answer—or, more properly, partial answer—to my daughter's question of almost twenty years ago. But the present volume is also an extended answer to a query (or set of queries) that goes back well beyond two decades, to at least two millennia: How do beliefs about the afterlife, or world to come, affect the way we lead our lives in this world?

Beliefs have consequences. As a general observation, I know this to be true. Beliefs about the world to come have this worldly consequences. If I didn't know that before hearing and later editing the papers in this volume, I know this now, as will those who read the chapters in this collection.

As is true with earlier volumes in the Studies in Jewish Civilization Series, the goal here is not comprehensive coverage of a given field. If it were, we would determine which topics or subtopics were essential and seek out experts in each. But we operate in reverse order. First, we seek out experts in a general field or area of study and then allow them to determine what topic they wish to address in their oral and written presentations.

So, for example, it is axiomatic among almost all mainstream Jewish thinkers that those who are rewarded in the afterlife neither eat nor drink. In this volume we have three papers that are based on the continuation (with important variations) of prandial and oenological activities after death. Whether correct or incorrect (and who really knows for sure?), these beliefs have had an impact in this world on those who accept them.

Don't like the way things are going in this world? Be patient (sometimes, very patient): it will all work out for the best, or better for perfection, in the world to come. Throughout history there have been those who have staked their lives, their very lives, on the bedrock truth of this proposition. Indeed, beliefs do have consequences.

The essays in this volume, all of which have their origins in the 28th Annual Symposium on Jewish Civilization, are arranged in roughly chronological order, beginning with accounts in the Hebrew Bible and continuing up to philosophical-theological thought of the twentieth century. That said, I hasten to add that this organization through chronology is inexact, inasmuch as many of our primary sources gather together material far older than the time of their publication. Further, several chapters range widely through hundreds if not thousands of years of thought and practice. Even so, I have confidence that this structure will prove valuable in situating the varied contents of this volume for careful readers. (Do we have any other kind?)

The first chapter is by Dereck Daschke, Truman State University. It is titled "'The End of the World and the World to Come': What Apocalyptic Literature Says about the Time After the End-Time." While Jewish speculation about *olam ha-ba*, either in the sense of personal eschatology (afterlife) or in the sense of the messianic age (cosmic eschatology), has largely been restrained, Daschke begins, in one area of theological imagination, such speculation has been persistent and insistent: apocalyptic literature. Almost all works in this literary genre, which encompasses works from roughly 400 B.C.E. to the second century C.E., give some indication as to what kind of existence shall follow. Frequently global and personal eschatology are linked together. Themes of individual sickness and healing underscore the healing of a corrupt world in the messianic age; individual fealty to Jewish law not only redeems the people but also restores the earth. Among the apocalypses he highlights are the books of Enoch, Daniel, 4 Ezra, 2 Baruch, and Revelation (a work composed well within the Jewish literary tradition).

Nicolae Roddy, Creighton University, is the author of the second chapter, "Warriors, Wives, and Wisdom: This World and the World to Come in the (So-Called) Apocrypha." He observes that the vast array of Jewish late Second Temple Period religious texts written under the pressures of imperial and Hasmonean domination presents almost as diverse an assembly of responses to the political as to the cultural challenges of the times. For some groups, the perceived hostilities of the Hellenistic world could not help but provoke the question of what it might mean ultimately to be a Jew. In this study, Roddy examines Jewish texts abandoned by the rabbis after the destruction of the Temple, while retaining quasi-canonical status in the Roman Catholic Church and remaining fully canonical throughout the Eastern Orthodox and Oriental Orthodox traditions. Although no longer part of the Jewish canon, the real value of these texts lies with the insight they provide into the minds of late Second Temple period Jews regarding the world in which they lived—as well as any world to come.

The third chapter, by Leonard Greenspoon, is titled "The Afterlife in the Septuagint." Greenspoon's survey of the relevant literature reveals that many claims have been made about the Septuagint's view of, or attitude toward, the afterlife, which is often seen as different from the Masoretic Text and reflective of distinctive beliefs among Hellenistic Jews. To counter such global descriptions, Greenspoon points out the diverse nature of the books that make up the Septuagint, the varying ways in which the translators reflected the Hebrew they were rendering, and the need to perform the hard work of textual criticism before asserting theological exegesis on their part. Only then can scholars make informed determinations about what the translators themselves (as opposed to later interpreters) intended.

The fourth chapter is titled "Rabbi Akiva, Other Martyrs, and Socrates: On Life, Death, and Life After Life." It was written by Naftali Rothenberg, Van Leer Jerusalem Institute. He begins by pointing to the transition between life and death as a major focus for discussion about life in this world and the next in talmudic literature. Here the focus for Rothenberg is a comparison of the discussion between Rabbi Akiva and his students during his execution and Socrates's discourse with his friends as the time approached for him to drink the cup of hemlock—in connection with the immortality of the soul. The equanimity with which both men accept their deaths stands in sharp contrast to the agitation of those around them. The similarity between the two stories ends, however, at the composure with which the protagonists accept their deaths. The two discussions regarding the meaning of death and the source of comfort are fundamentally different. Akiva cherishes the most terrible moments of his life, refusing to cease pursuing his moral objective in this world for even a single instant. For Socrates, immortality of the soul is the source of meaning; for Rabbi Akiva there exists only the moral dimension.

Christine Hayes, Yale University, was the keynote speaker at the 28th Annual Symposium on Jewish Civilization. Her chapter, titled "Heaven on Earth: The World to Come and Its (Dis)locations," is far-reaching. As she notes, ancient Jewish sources from the Bible to the Talmud contain a dizzying array of ideas about a better world to come (be it a messianic era in historical time, an eschatological end of days, or an afterlife). Some of these sources imagine such a deep disjunction between this world and the world to come that entry into the latter requires an escape from the former. But other sources imagine a conjunction between the two and apply themselves to the task of attaining a foretaste of the world to come in this world. Hayes explores the radically diverse strategies employed by ancient Jews to bridge this world and the world to come so as to locate "heaven on earth."

Dov Weiss, University of Illinois at Urbana-Champaign, is the author of the next chapter, titled "*Olam Ha-ba* in Rabbinic Literature: A Functional Reading." In his analysis, the rabbis sometimes express their moral discomfort with a biblical idea or received tradition by declaring it inoperative for the "future world." Whether it refers to the Messianic Era or a soul's existence after death (or both), eschatology provided the rabbis with a moral safe haven: although a troubling law or theology might not be eradicated in this world, it could be branded as such in the next. This ethical response does not solve the moral problem, but it does minimize it. Weiss presents three examples to highlight this rabbinic ethical hermeneutic. The first revolves around the biblical concept of the evil inclination; the second around the biblical doctrine of inherited punishment (Exod 20:5); and the third example, the case of *mamzer*, deals with a "bastard" child that is the product of incest or an extramarital affair. In each of these cases, the exegetical grounding is forced, highlighting the rabbinic agenda to minimize the theological irritant by distinguishing this world from the next.

Following Weiss is Jordan D. Rosenblum, University of Wisconsin–Madison, whose essay is titled "Dining In(to) the World to Come." Entrance into the world to come requires a proper rabbinic diet, he observes. Unlike this world, however, the world to come features a smorgasbord that would put the fanciest Las Vegas buffet to shame, including such mythical creatures as the famous Leviathan and Behemoth, as well as the lesser-known Ziz. Rosenblum examines classical rabbinic discussion about the diet that merits entrance into the world to come and about the menu that awaits therein. He concludes that such discussions are used to justify rabbinic dietary practices in this world. Included in this conversation are topics such as why non-Jews need not keep kosher and why nonkosher foods are prohibited for Jews only in this world (but not in the world to come).

Food continues to be on the table in the next chapter: "What's for Dinner in *Olam Ha-ba*? Why Do We Care in *Olam Ha-zeh*? Medieval Jewish Ideas about Meals in the World to Come in R. Bahya ben Asher's *Shulhan Shel Arba*" by Jonathan Brumberg-Kraus, Wheaton College (MA). He begins by pointing to the fact that rabbinic traditions about meals for the righteous in the world to come are contradictory. On the one hand, the righteous are promised a banquet of Leviathan, Bar Yochnai. But Rav says, "In the world to come, there is no eating and drinking." Rabbenu Bahya ben Asher, the fourteenth century Spanish biblical exegete and kabbalist, devotes the final "Gate" of his short treatise on Jewish eating practices, *Shulhan Shel Arba* [Table of Four], to address this apparent contradiction about meals prepared for the righteous in the world to come. Since R. Bahya wrote *Shulhan Shel Arba* as a guide for meals in this world, the question arises: how does talking about, imagining, and knowing about meals in the next world affect our practice and enjoyment of meals in this world? In Brumberg-Kraus's analysis, such talk about body- and soul-rewarding meals in the world to come while at meals in this world is intended to cultivate the transformation of our physical hunger for food from "*Fressen* to *Essen* . . . to sanctified eating."

Morris M. Faierstein, University of Maryland, is the author of the next chapter, titled "The Dybbuk: The Origins and History of a Concept." The concept of the dybbuk in contemporary Jewish culture is identified with S. Ansky's play, which has nothing to do with the historical concept of the dybbuk. As Faierstein explains, this has its roots in the concept of transmigration [*gilgul*] that is first mentioned in the *Sefer Bahir* and expanded in the *Zohar*. The first locus for an appearance and exorcism of a dybbuk is Safed and its kabbalistic circles. All later manifestations are built on these earliest models. In the eighteenth century, the motif of the dybbuk and exorcism becomes a literary genre that is not based on factual events, but is created as "folktales." Ansky took these folktales and wrote a play based on the style of late nineteenth century Russian literature (the so-called Silver Age). So, Faierstein determines, very little of Ansky's play is based on historical or cultural realities.

The next chapter is by Vadim Putzu, Missouri State University. It is titled "Tasting Heaven: Wine and the World to Come from the Talmud to Safed." Here Putzu investigates wine as it is represented and employed in relation to the world to come in rabbinic and kabbalistic literature. His analysis of the ways in which the rabbis and certain kabbalists pictured and/or used wine gives us an intoxicating taste of their perspectives on the present world and the hereafter alike. On the one hand, the rabbis' discussions of wine mirror their perspectives on *olam ha-zeh*. On the other hand, the wine of *olam ha-ba* is deprived of all of its negative aspects: it is easy to make, abundant, and gladdens without ever leading to sinful drunkenness—thus coming to represent the very delights that characterize existence in the world to come. Further, Joseph Karo's insistence on the importance of abstention and the Zoharic author's recommendation to imbibe the symbolic wine of Torah signal their negative perception of this world. Moses ben Jacob Cordovero's strategic emphasis on the significance of preserving wine from gentile contact for the sake of reaching *olam ha-ba* reveals much about his overall plan for *olam ha-zeh*.

Elias Sacks, University of Colorado at Boulder, is the author of the chapter titled "Worlds to Come Between East and West: Immortality and the Rise of Modern Jewish Thought." Sacks has determined that the concept of *olam ha-ba* is not generally taken to be central to modern Jewish thought. Here he challenges that view through exploring the neglected Hebrew works of two foundational figures: the German-Jewish thinker Moses Mendelssohn (1729-1786) and the Eastern European philosopher Nachman Krochmal (1785-1840). Krochmal casts belief in an afterlife as a product of fierce debates among ancient Jews who disagreed about whether the soul is immortal. This position is best read as a covert critique of Mendelssohn, whose Hebrew writings cast the doctrine of an immortal soul as a belief affirmed by the Hebrew Bible. This dispute is, in part, a dispute about the nature of Jewish tradition: whereas Mendelssohn's position implies that Judaism is a vehicle of timeless truths affirmed by the Bible, Krochmal's position entails that Judaism is a historically developing phenomenon whose content emerges through clashes among human beings. For these foundational philosophical voices, then, *olam ha-ba* becomes a crucial terrain for formulating—and contesting—theories of Jewish existence.

The last chapter in the volume is by Federico Dal Bo, Marie Curie Postdoctoral Fellow at the Universitat Autònoma de Barcelona. It is titled "Emmanuel Levinas's Messianism and the World to Come: A Gnostic-Philosophical Reading of Tractate *Sanhedrin* 96b–99a." According to traditional Jewish terminology, several pages from the Babylonian Talmud (*Sanhedrin* 96b–99a) specifically treat the notion of "messianism" and amplify the contrast between "this world" and "the world to come." As analyzed by Dal Bo, influential Jewish philosopher Emmanuel Levinas read these talmudic pages not according to, but rather in contrast with, the traditional notion of "religion." Levinas does not consider religion as a specific "belief" in a deity. Rather, he interprets religion fundamentally as a form of "ethical-moral association" between human beings. With respect to this, Levinas recasts the notion of "messianism" as well as its two correlated notions: "this word" and "the world to come." Yet these are not accounted for in their traditional religious sense, but rather under a different perspective: in an ethical-philosophical sense. This kind of "hyperphilosophy" actually neutralizes the cultural specificity of these notions with consequences, especially for so-called interreligious relationships.

As someone who is partial to eating and drinking in this world, I relish the thought of continuing these pursuits in the world to come—with or without condiments. I also like the idea of everyone getting his or her due. For sure, this is not happening in this world. It is reassuring to picture the proper allocation of reward and punishment in the world to come. In addition, I have come to understand that my beliefs about the afterlife are largely conditioned on what I have experienced and learned. More broadly, this has been true for Jews, as individuals and as members of a community, for at least two thousand years.

I invite all readers of this volume to interpret and interact with its contents in a variety of ways. And to recognize the inextricable bonds that unite beliefs about the afterlife with practices in this one.

Leonard J. Greenspoon

Contributors

Jonathan Brumberg-Kraus
Department of Religion
Wheaton College
26 E. Main Street
Norton, MA 02766
brumberg-raus_jonathan@wheatoncollege.edu

Frederico Dal Bo
Marie Curie Postdoctoral Fellow
ERC-Project "The Latin Talmud"
Institute of Medieval Studies
Mòdul de Recerca A
Universitat Autònoma de Barcelona
E-08193 Bellaterra (Cerdanyola del
   Vallès, Barcelona)
Spain
fdalbo@gmail.com

Dereck Daschke
Department of Philosophy & Religion
Truman State University
100 E. Normal
Kirksville, MO 63501
ddaschke@truman.edu

Morris M. Faierstein
1547 Templeton Place
Rockville, MD 20852
Kotsker@yahoo.com

Christine Hayes
Religious Studies
Yale University
451 College St.
New Haven, CT 06511-8906
christine.hayes@yale.edu

Vadim Putzu	Department of Religious Studies Missouri State University 901 S National Ave Springfield, MO 65897 VPutzu@missouristate.edu
Nicolae Roddy	Department of Theology Creighton University 2500 California Plaza Omaha, NE 68178 nroddy@creighton.edu
Jordan D. Rosenblum	Religious Studies Department University of Wisconsin-Madison 1404 Sterling Hall 475 North Charter Street Madison, WI 53706 jrosenblum@wisc.edu
Naftali Rothenberg	The Van Leer Jerusalem Institute 43 Jabotinsky Street P.O. Box 4070 Jerusalem 91040 Israel naftalir@vanleer.org.il
Elias Sacks	University of Colorado Boulder Department of Religious Studies 292 UCB Boulder, CO 80309 elias.sacks@colorado.edu
Dov Weiss	Department of Religion University of Illinois, Urbana-Champaign FLB 3021, 707 S. Mathews Urbana, Illinois 61801 dyweiss@illinois.edu

"The End of the World and the World to Come": What Apocalyptic Literature Says about the Time After the End-Time

Dereck Daschke

Olam ha-ba originated as a term designating the messianic age, the time after the end of time, but eventually it became more closely associated with one's personal disposition in the afterlife. While the term is likely first recorded in the early apocalyptic book of *1 Enoch*, later the rabbinic sages would highlight the meanings for personal eschatology that were originally bound up with biblical conceptualizations of cosmic eschatology, especially as found in the anticipation for the Day of the Lord and the messianic age. This tension and confusion between the two meanings of the concept is in large part at the heart of apocalyptic literature's presentation of the events of the end-time.[1]

Without a doubt, the eschatological framework within which Jewish apocalypse works derives directly from the prophets of the Hebrew Scriptures, in particular some of the passages that Paul Hansen termed "protoapocalyptic" in his classic study *The Dawn of Apocalyptic*.[2] Taken as a whole, the picture of the time after the end of time is the quintessential dream of restoration, healing, and rebirth in the individual, social, and even global realms. The individual experience of the restoration at the end of days is where personal and cosmic eschatologies intertwine, and this study will address this complex subject shortly. First, though, it is important to sketch the key ways in which the biblical sources anticipate the restoration of the people of Israel, individually and collectively, and even of the planet itself.

THE TIME AFTER THE END IN THE HEBREW BIBLE

The concept of the Day of the Lord in Hebrew prophecy, the anticipated end of history and time of judgment, establishes an apocalyptic scenario that foregrounds essentially all of the events prophesied for God's people.[3] God may chastise and pour out his wrath upon his beloved chosen (against Israel: virtually all of Amos and Hosea; against Judah: Isa 1:1–20, Mic 3:12, Jer 5:14–17) but there will come a day when He will turn his anger to the enemies of Israel (Zech 12:9, Isa 60:12). Once their foes are vanquished, the Jews shall be gathered back to the Land of Israel (Isa 11:11–12, Jer 23:8). Isaiah 4:2–4 describes how perfected the survivors already in Israel and Jerusalem will be: "In that day, the radiance of the Lord will lend beauty and glory, and the splendor of the land will give dignity and majesty, to the survivors in Israel. And those who remain in Zion and are left in Jerusalem—all who are inscribed for life in Jerusalem—shall be called holy." The Lord will wash away "the filth of the daughters of Zion, and from Jerusalem's midst [will rinse] out her infamy—in a spirit of judgment and in a spirit of purging."[4]

While the prophets Amos, Zephaniah, Habakkuk, Joel, and Malachi anticipated God returning the people to the land without reference to a human figure to do so, the expectation of "an ideal human leader possessed of lofty spiritual and ethical qualities" who will restore sovereignty to Israel and righteousness to the office of the king, as depicted by the prophets Isaiah, Micah, Jeremiah, and Zechariah, certainly became emblematic of Jewish hopes for the triumph of the future over the past, "based in part on visions of a past Golden Age."[5] The period that follows the return of the Davidic king concomitant with the restoration of the people to the land is known, of course, as the messianic age.[6]

To say that a full exploration of the roots and impact of the ancient Jewish belief in a messiah could—and do—fill volumes of critical study and theological exegesis is, even so, naught but an understatement. The meaning of "the messiah" is, perhaps, the question upon which Western history of the last two millennia hinges. That said, in order to anchor the appearance of this figure in association with *olam ha-ba* in the Jewish apocalyptic literature, it is worth very briefly establishing the biblical roots of this expectation. The prophets Isaiah (ch. 11) and Jeremiah (ch. 23) establish that he will be a devout and reverent king from the line of David who will reign wisely by the spirit of the Lord and will embody righteousness in his judgments.[7] Therefore, Jeremiah says, "In his days Judah shall be delivered and Israel shall dwell secure. And this is the name by which he shall be called: The Lord is our Vindicator" (Jer 23:6).

The ingathering of the Jews under the divine leadership of the Messiah culminates in the reuniting of Israel and Judah as one nation. This is depicted in Ezekiel's famous prophecy of Ephraim's hand and Judah's stick: "I am going to take the Israelite people from among the nations they have gone to, and gather them from every quarter, and bring them to their own land. I will make them a single nation in the land, on the hills of Israel, and one king shall be king of them all. Never again shall they be two nations, and never again shall they be divided into two kingdoms" (Ezek 37:21–22, see also Zech 11:12–14). This expectation is elaborated in Hosea 3:4–5: "For the Israelites shall go a long time without king and without officials, without sacrifice and without cult pillars, and without ephod or teraphim. Afterward, the Israelites will turn back and will seek the Lord their God and David their king—and they will thrill over the Lord and over His bounty in the days to come."

With the return of the people and their king to their land, the resumption of traditional Yahwistic worship must necessarily follow, which means the restoration of one essential thing: the Temple. The book of Isaiah throughout promotes the image of Jerusalem and its Temple "in days to come" as the cosmic center of the world, through which both Jew and Gentile will be enlightened and transformed.[8] It will be so glorious, it will become a beacon for the other nations: "In the days to come, the Mount of the Lord's house shall stand firm above the mountains. . . . [A]ll the nations shall gaze on it with joy. . . . For instruction shall come forth from Zion, the word of the Lord from Jerusalem" (Isa 2:2–3). The promise of the new Temple is most fully realized in the final chapters of the book of Ezekiel, which is detailed not only in its construction plans but also in its reestablishment of the roles and duties of individuals and tribes (Ezek 47:13).

Furthermore, this being an ideal "golden age," moral conditions that had not existed since the height of the United Kingdom, if ever, would remake the Jewish people: "My servant David shall be king, they shall faithfully obey my laws," promises Ezekiel 37:24. And Zephaniah 3:13 states that "[t]he remnant of Israel shall do no wrong and speak no falsehood; a deceitful tongue shall not be in their mouths," implying that finally all Israel will achieve the ideal state of religious practice and personal ethics that God has expected from them all along.[9] The transformation will not be limited to Israel, either. As the passage above from Isaiah indicates, all nations and peoples will recognize the true God and the religion of the Jews as the true religion—and this realization will bring about peace not only with Israel, but among the other nations as well (Isa 2:3–4, 17; 11:10; Mic 4:2–3; Zech 14:9, Zeph 3:18–20).

Even the very nature of the earth itself will be remade in the image of peace and prosperity (Isa 51:3: "He has made her wilderness like Eden, her desert like the Garden of the Lord"; see also Isa 6–8, Ezek 36:29–30, and Amos 9:13–15); and ultimately God will even end the threat of death once and for all: "He will destroy on this mount the shroud that is drawn over the faces of all the peoples and the covering that is spread over all the nations: He will destroy death forever. My Lord God will wipe the tears away from all faces and will put an end to the reproach of His people over all the earth" (Isa 25:7–8).

RESURRECTION OF THE DEAD AND FINAL JUDGMENT IN THE BIBLE

At this point, two major concepts associated with the biblical understanding of the messianic age and the end of days need to be addressed, but they are also the root source of the confusion between personal and cosmic eschatology in the apocalyptic literature (and indeed in the later rabbinic and even Christian traditions): the bodily resurrection of the dead and the final judgment. Simcha Paull Raphael writes in *Jewish Views of the Afterlife*:

> The notion of a divine postmortem judgment, which is central in rabbinic Judaism's teachings on life after death, has its roots in the collective eschatology of the biblical period. . . . In early prophetic literature, divine judgment is spoken of in national-political terms. . . . There is no sense of individual judgment; all the people of the nation [whether Israelite or Gentile] merit the punishment or reward collectively. [But an] important development . . . takes place in the Book of Zephaniah (1:2, 9) . . . [where] YHVH's judgment is universal." [10]

But the book of Ezekiel is where the eschatological picture gets really interesting—and complicated. Raphael writes:

> In Ezekiel, judgment is conceived of in a dual sense. . . . For the nations, judgment will be collective (Ezek 25:8ff). For Israel, however, judgment will be based on the merit of each individual. The sinful wicked will be annihilated by God's wrathful vengeance. The righteous Israelite will be saved, and thereby selected to participate in the coming kingdom of YHVH. (Ezek 11:17–21; 36:25–32 [the "new heart" passage]). With Ezekiel, an important and subtle philosophical transformation takes place: individual and collective conceptions of divine judgment merge for the first time. . . . The righteous individual Israelite will be awarded a share in YHVH's messianic collective. . . . Judgment takes place in the human realm and through the unfolding of history, not in an afterworld.[11]

Furthermore, the very next chapter in Ezekiel provides one of the most powerful images of bodily resurrection in the prophecy of the valley of dry bones, though in the context it is clearly a spiritual metaphor for the restoration of the political collective of the people of Israel. Yet the image itself seems deliberately intended to blur the line between the personal and the political, especially following from the "new heart" rhetoric of personal renewal and restoration—all but resurrection. Still, what can a new heart mean but a new life? It lies between the symbolic and the literal, between the prophetic (in the national-moral sense) and the apocalyptic (in the sense of future cosmic transformation).

However, it is in the next chapters, from 38 to 48, that Ezekiel is firmly in apocalyptic territory, and it is in these that readers get the first strong glimpse of the postapocalyptic *olam ha-ba*. Chapters 40–48 refer to the blueprint for the new temple-city, named "YWVH is there." But 38 and 39 depict the great eschatological war, which we might today call by its Judean place name: Armageddon. The aftermath of the defeat of the nations, represented by Magog, is depicted with relish: "Then the inhabitants of the cities of Israel will go out and make fires and feed them with the weapons—shields and bucklers, bows and arrows, clubs and spears; they shall use them as fuel for seven years. . . . They will despoil those who despoiled them and plunder those who plundered them" (Ezek 39:9–10). The chapter continues on in stark, bloody detail, leaving no doubt about how the fortunes of the people of Israel and the nations who oppressed them have turned.

THE TIME AFTER THE END IN THE APOCALYPSES

This theme of eschatological war is picked up in the one true canonical apocalypse of the Hebrew Scriptures, the book of Daniel. As it happens, Daniel is better known not for its depiction of the lives of those who prevail in this conflict but rather for those faithful who have died, in it and previously—namely, in the introduction of the idea of the resurrection of the dead at the end of times in chapter 12. Daniel is also very explicit that this resurrection is part and parcel of the final judgment: "At that time, the great prince, Michael, who stands beside the sons of your people, will appear. It will be a time of trouble, the like of which has never since the nation came into being. At that time, your people will be rescued, all who are found inscribed in the book [of life]. Many of those that sleep in the dust of the earth will awake, some to eternal life, others to reproaches, to everlasting abhorrence" (Dan 12:1–2).[12] This passage, as short as it is, is foundational for the understandings of *olam ha-ba* in Judaism—and Christianity—that will emerge in the centuries thereafter, and even until today.

Scholarly consensus holds that "the many" who awake from the dust does not refer to a universal resurrection, but only of the faithful Jews, likely specifically those who died in the second century B.C.E. resisting the forces of

Seleucid king Antiochus IV Epiphanes, which gave rise to the book and the *ex eventu* prophecies of chapters 7–11.[13] These multitudes of the dead will arise from their graves and face judgment on an individual basis, presumably due to their moral disposition toward or away from righteousness during their lives, and those who find favor with God will enjoy a new life without end. Those who do not apparently face eternal shame and contempt.

There is no specific indication what the moral measure that divides the one group from the other is. However, the overall presentation of resurrection in Daniel asserts a divine, cosmic morality by underscoring God's justice: "Resurrection becomes the means whereby God's justice will ultimately triumph. A new, revisionist, individualized eschatology is introduced to resolve the challenge of theodicy, the attempt to vindicate God's justice. The new doctrine of resurrection vindicates God."[14]

In the centuries that followed the exile, resurrection rapidly became part of mainstream Jewish thought and distinguished Pharisees from Sadducees, who rejected it for its lack of Torah support.[15] (In fact, the idea may originate in Persian Zoroastrianism, imported in the wake of the Persians' reign in the region after the exile.)[16] And it plays a particularly prominent role in *1 Enoch*, perhaps the most important extracanonical apocalypse and a text that reflected a great deal of theological speculation and creativity of the Second Temple period. Leila Leah Bronner states, "As a work of eschatology, [*1 Enoch*] ties together the notions of the soul's journey after death with an end-point in time, a day of judgment, and a spiritual messiah who presides over human destiny."[17]

As noted from the outset, *1 Enoch*, which R. H. Charles dates to between 105 and 64 B.C.E., appears to be the earliest textual source of the term *olam ha-ba*.[18] Genesis 5 tells us that Enoch was the great-grandfather of Noah and is one of two figures in the Hebrew Scriptures who do not die, the other being the messianic predecessor Elijah. Genesis 5:22–24 reports, "After the birth of Methuselah, Enoch walked with God 300 years. . . . All the days of Enoch came to 365 years. Enoch walked with God; then he was no more, for God took him." It is in this span of sixty-five years when Enoch "walks with God" that the accounts of the book of *1 Enoch* take place. These include a stunning variety of revelations of the nature of the heavens, history, the origin of sin, and, most significant for the purposes of this study, the final dispositions of the good and the wicked after the judgment. It is in one of these tours of heaven that the phrase meaning "eschatological world of the messianic age," equivalent to the Hebrew *olam ha-ba*, is first encountered in a Jewish text:

With them is the Antecedent of Time: His head is white and pure like wool and his garment is indescribable.... Then an Angel came to me and greeted me and said to me, "You, the Son of Man, who art born in righteousness and upon whom righteousness has dwelt, and the righteousness of the Antecedent of Time will not forsake you." He added and said to me: "He shall proclaim peace to you in the name of the world that is to become. For from here proceeds peace since the creation of the world, and so it shall be unto you forever and ever and ever" (*1 En* 71:10, 14–15).[19]

The Son of Man here is the Messiah, elsewhere called "the Elect One" in the translation from the Ge'ez language of the Ethiopic Church, which preserved the book and consider it canonical.[20] In clear contrast with the biblical Messiah, this one represents a supernatural, eternally anointed figure of perfect righteousness (*1 En* 48:2–7) who "would remove the kings and the mighty ones from their comfortable seats and the strong ones from their thrones" (*1 En* 46:4). Thereupon he will render judgment upon all mortals at the end of time: "Thenceforth nothing corruptible shall be found; for that Son of Man has appeared and has seated himself on the throne of his glory; and all evil shall disappear from before his face" (*1 En* 69:28–29).

Thus *1 Enoch* is clearly a critical source for the idea that the messianic age culminates a divine plan set into motion at the time of creation (as well as one source for the understanding of messianism that Christians would come to attribute to Jesus of Nazareth). This plan will rid the world of evil and restore the realm of perfect peace lost with the fall in the Garden of Eden.[21] Yet Enoch's tours of the heavens also reveal a complex system of personal eschatology at work, one that appears to elaborate on the postjudgment fates described in Daniel, wherein the souls of the dead are collected into hollow places in a heavenly mountain, with separate places for the righteous and the sinners, until the time of judgment. The angel Raphael tells Enoch, "[U]ntil the great day of judgment . . . to those who curse [there will be] plague and pain forever, and the retribution of their spirits. They will bind them there forever—even if from the beginning of the world" (*1 En* 22:11).[22] But regarding the righteous and elect among humanity, at the time of the great judgment:

In those days, Sheol will return all the deposits which she had received and hell will give back all that which it owes. And he shall choose the righteous and the holy ones from among (the risen dead), for the day when they shall be selected and saved has arrived. In

> those days, [the Elect One] shall sit on my throne, and from the conscience of his mouth shall come out all the secrets of wisdom, for the Lord of the Spirits has given them to him and glorified him. In those days, mountains shall dance like rams; and the hills shall leap like kids satiated with milk. And the faces of all the angels in heaven shall glow with joy, because on that day the Elect One has arisen. And the earth shall rejoice; and the righteous ones shall dwell upon her and the elect ones shall walk upon her. (*1 En* 51)

In both of these accounts of the fates of the righteous and the wicked, their personal dispositions are also rendered as part and parcel of the events of the end-times, and the righteous anticipate as part of their reward continued existence on earth but in a time of perfect peace and cosmic joy.[23]

Of course, the national sovereignty and security—let alone perfect peace and cosmic joy—of the messianic age continued to elude the Jewish people even during the Second Temple period, and the destruction of that temple by the Romans in 70 C.E. underscored for many Jews both how far off the promise of the messianic age was in the current era and, at the same time, how necessary divine intervention would be to put things right. Two apocalypses, *4 Ezra* and *2 Baruch*, written in the wake of the Temple's destruction and the Jewish Diaspora, capture the mingling of dread of history and hope for cosmic redemption in the future that the messianic promise in the aftermath of another such disaster surely evoked.

With an apparent reference in chapter 12 to the Flavian emperors of Rome, scholars generally believe that *4 Ezra* (*2 Esdras* 3–14 in the Apocrypha) reflects the situation in Palestine circa 100 C.E.[24] However, the narrative is set in the aftermath of the Babylonian destruction of the first Temple, some seven centuries earlier, and consists mainly of the figure of Ezra, that great hero of the restoration of Jewish society after the exile, interrogating a divine interlocutor regarding the meaning of the devastation to which he was now witness. The tension in this line of questioning is broken by a spectacular vision of a woman in mourning who becomes the New Jerusalem on Earth. Unlike Ezekiel's vision, however, the reader is not permitted to tour the divine city with the seer. Still, following this revelatory encounter, the focus of the dialogues with the angel shifts from past and present to future, and there are extensive presentations of what the surviving Jews may expect of the end-times and thereafter.

4 Ezra 6 contains this spooky glimpse of the time just before the judgment:

> Infants a year old shall speak with their voices, and women with child shall give birth to premature children at three and four months, and these shall live and dance. . . . At that time friends shall make war on friends like enemies, and the earth and those who inhabit it shall be terrified, and the springs of the fountains shall stand still, so that for three hours they shall not flow. (6:21, 24)

Those who are alive to witness these events will also bear witness to God's salvation and the return of "those who did not die," presumably Enoch and Elijah but possibly including other apocalyptic seers such as Baruch and Ezra himself.[25] As a result, their hearts will be fundamentally transformed away from evil (6:25–28).

4 Ezra 7:26–44 lays out a timeline of the world to come; the length of the messianic age, after which the return to primeval creation both mirrors and presages the final judgment (the common apocalyptic trope of *Urzeit wird Endzeit*, "the beginning time becomes the end-time"). Specifically, the Messiah will be revealed, and he will live for four hundred years, bringing joy to those who live among him. Then the Messiah will die, as will all humanity. The world will be returned to primeval silence, as at the time prior to creation; and after seven days will be reawakened, and "that which is corruptible shall perish" (7:31). The dust shall yield the dead, God will then begin His judgment without mercy, and the places of reward and torment will appear. And God will speak to the nations on the day of judgment, and his determination of their fates "will last for about a week of years" (v. 43). *4 Ezra* 13:39–50 also indicates that in the last days, the lost tribes of Israel shall return from the land of Arzareth, where they had hidden themselves since the Assyrian conquest. In all, *4 Ezra* gives the most complete account of the events, timeframe, and disposition of the events of *olam ha-ba* of any apocalypse, and it appears equally focused on the personal and collective eschatology of the Jews.

The final major Jewish apocalyptic text to address the nature of the end-times is *2 Baruch*. Also known as the *Syriac Apocalypse of Baruch*, its seer is the faithful scribe of the prophet Jeremiah. It is likely of Palestinian provenance from the early second century, roughly contemporaneous with *4 Ezra*. Like Ezra in *4 Ezra*, Baruch begins the narrative amid the ruins of the first Temple, lamenting all that has beset his people. And while a dialogue ensues with an *angelus interpres* [interpreting angel] that echoes that of *4 Ezra*, the emotional tenor is not as palpable. In fact, relatively quickly, a very clear idea emerges of what a future without a Temple looks like for the Jews: in a word, the law. Bronner states, "The author of the book appears to be an expert on both apocalyptic imagery and rabbinic law, someone who could find a way to continue studying the Law after the catastrophe of national destruction in 70 C.E., and therefore someone who could help the Jewish people face the challenges of the post-Temple era."[26] Baruch, more insistently than the other apocalypticians, envisions the future not just as a time of great difficulties to be overcome before an ideal age, but also as one with qualities that will define the Jews who enter into it as the "true Israel." The Temple and its restoration is of secondary importance to the revitalization of the law in people's lives and the establishing of moral fortitude among his followers to survive the transition between the ages.[27]

2 Baruch 43–44 addresses the consolation of both Baruch the seer and of Zion in idealized or eschatological contexts. Baruch will understand his revelations as a result of many "consolations which will last forever" (43:1–2), while in the future, "the time again will take a turn for the better" for those who persevere in the law, and they will participate in the consolation of Zion (44:7).[28] "For that which is now is nothing. But that which is in the future will be very great. For everything will pass away which is corruptible, and everything that dies will go away" (*2 Bar* 44:9). As with Daniel 12:2–3 and Ezekiel 37, part of the culmination of these utopian fantasies of the future includes a highly idealized notion of the recovery of the body from death. Three verses in particular address the disposition of the resurrected and the heights that their new lives will endow to them:

> *2 Baruch* 50:2: For the earth will surely give back the dead at that time; it receives them now in order to keep them, not changing anything in their form.
>
> *2 Baruch* 51:3: Also, as for the glory of those who proved to be righteous on account of my law, those who possessed intelligence in their life, and those who planted the root of wisdom in their heart—their splendor will then be glorified by transformations and the shape of their face will be changed into the light of their beauty so that they may acquire and receive the undying world which is promised to them.
>
> *2 Baruch* 51:10: For they will live in the heights of that world and they will be like the angels and be equal to the stars.[29]

This is to say, in death the earth will preserve the righteous as they were, but they will be transformed in *olam ha-ba*, first into a radiantly beautiful countenance and ultimately into beings equal to the angels and the stars—"while those who were evil will be changed into 'startling visions and horrible shapes.'"[30] Finally, as with so many apocalyptic visions, the ultimate hope of *olam ha-ba* pictures an end to illness and death. *2 Baruch* 73:2–3 thus fuses the perfection of personal eschatology with its cosmic counterpart: "And then health will descend in dew, and illness will vanish, and fear and tribulation and lamentation will pass away from among men, and joy will encompass the earth. And nobody will again die untimely, nor will any adversity take place suddenly."

THE JEWISH END-TIME IN CHRISTIANITY

This exact theme of the end of bodily frailty and death is evident in another apocalyptic text, the Christian book of Revelation, which in many ways is a quintessentially Jewish apocalypse, being informed by several of the traditions described thus far. But besides the statement in Revelation 21:4 about the end of death and mourning, it is relatively curt on the picture of the world after the judgment. Of the New Jerusalem, it states, "And the city has no need of sun or moon to shine on it, for the glory of God is its light, and its lamp is the Lamb. The nations will walk by its light, and the kings of the earth will bring their glory into it" (Rev 22:23–24 NRSV). But these are about the only clues it offers concerning life on the new earth.

The development of the Christian notion of the world to come would be the subject of an entirely different study. Still, one particularly apocalyptic strand of Christianity is worth examining for the centrality of the Jewish view of *olam ha-ba* to its extremely rich and detailed rendering of the messianic age: the Jehovah's Witnesses.

The Jehovah's Witnesses are the product of Charles Taze Russell's struggles with the legitimacy of religious and governmental institutions in the latter half of the nineteenth century. As a result, he sought a form of Christianity that reflected "true" and original biblical traditions and authority. By necessity, then, much of his theology reflected the original Jewish sources as articulated by the prophets of the Christian Old Testament. What Russell was most concerned with was alerting the world to the coming judgment by Jesus Christ and the subsequent supplanting of the current order with God's Kingdom. He predicted this event first for 1914, then 1918. His successors later set the date at 1925, and lastly at 1975, before abandoning date-setting in favor of a generalized, but diffused, anticipation of the coming of the "New World Society."[31]

If we look at how the Witnesses actually represent this New World Society, we see all of the themes that had been developed in the biblical prophets, which they quote (that is, "proof-text") extensively. But we also find much of the same subsequent elaboration and refinement as on display in the Jewish apocalypses examined in the present study. For example, the tract titled "A Peaceful New World—Will It Come?" features an idyllic scene that depicts people and animals—predators and prey—joyously comingling in an abundant, green landscape.[32] The tract asks:

> When you look at the scene in this tract, what feelings do you have? Does not your heart yearn for the peace, happiness, and prosperity seen here? Surely it does. But is it just a dream, or fantasy, to believe these conditions will ever exist on Earth?
>
> Most people probably think so. Today's realities are war, crime, hunger, sickness, aging—to mention just a few. Yet there is reason for hope. The Hebrew Scriptures foretell that God will create a "new heavens and a new earth" and that "the former things will not be called to mind, neither will they come up into the heart."
> —Isaiah 65:17

It then proceeds to check off the essential promises of the Jewish messianic age: a "righteous society of people living on earth," a "perfect heavenly kingdom, or government, that will rule over this earthly society of people," "earthly benefits beyond compare," "[h]atreds and prejudices will cease to exist, and eventually everyone on earth will be a true friend of everyone else." The renewal of the earth, as in the time of Eden, is referenced, and never again "will people feel hunger because the 'earth itself will certainly give its produce.'" Even sickness and death will end. The tract cites Psalms, Isaiah, and Hosea as evidence, putting into practice Russell's principle that an authentic form of Christianity must adhere as closely as possible to its original Jewish roots in Scripture. Perhaps because the traditional Jewish resistance to producing divine imagery is absent, this Christian sect has been able to imagine and illustrate this Jewish view in a lush and vibrant way.

CONCLUSION: THE END OF THE WORLD AS WE KNOW IT

This overview of the Jewish expectations regarding what the world will look like after its end and divine judgment reveals, if nothing else, that while there was no shortage of ideas and beliefs on this matter in circulation in the centuries prior to the era of the talmudic sages, nothing resembling a cohesive, systematic, or consensus doctrine ever existed. In fairness, expressing anything concrete about what will replace everything that currently exists is understandably a tricky affair. It is a paradox, the ultimate end that is not the ultimate end, and paradoxes are notoriously hard to reduce to direct language. At best, these texts articulate deeply held hopes that somehow the next world will compensate for the flaws and failures of this world. But as always, the devil is in the details, and who is rewarded and punished, why, and in what ways, are worked out differently in different texts under different cultural and historical circumstances.

With the decline of apocalyptic speculation in the centuries following the destruction of the second Temple and the emergence of rabbinic Judaism in the Diaspora, Jews more or less definitively put to rest the cosmic, world-historical speculation of apocalypticism. The term *olam ha-ba*, in this new context, shed its original roots in cosmic eschatology and brought to the fore the other half of the tradition that emphasized morality and one's personal postmortem state, the signification it has more or less retained through the millennia to this day.

Still, the former meaning is never that far removed. Death is always the end of the world for somebody.

NOTES

1. Simcha Paull Raphael, *Jewish Views of the Afterlife* (2nd ed.; Lanham: Roman & Littlefield, 2009), 68–69, 125–28. The Enochic provenance of the phrase from the equivalent construction in Ethiopic Ge'ez was first suggested by R. H. Charles, *The Ethiopic Version of the Book of Enoch: Edited from Twenty-Three MSS. together with the Fragmentary Greek and Latin Versions* (Anecdota Oxoniensia, Semitic Series 11; Oxford: Clarendon, 1906), 145; see also George W. E. Nickelsburg and James C. Vandercam, *1 Enoch 2: A Commentary on the Book of 1 Enoch Chapters 37–82* (Hermeneia; Minneapolis: Fortress, 2012), 329 n24. While scholarly consensus supports this origin, Leila Leah Bronner cautions that the actual connection to the Enoch literature may be far more complicated and less clear: "Olam ha-ba, 'the World to Come,' was a favorite expression of the rabbis, but it is unclear where the term comes from. Although there is a similar expression in *1 Enoch* 71:15 ('He will proclaim peace to you in the name of the world that is to become'), the rabbis . . . apparently did not approve of the Apocrypha and the Pseudepigrapha, so they may not have found the term in Enoch. It may never be known for certain whether the term was borrowed and, if so, by whom." Leila Leah Browner, *Journey to Heaven: Exploring Jewish Views of the Afterlife* (Brooklyn: Urim, 2011), 70–71.

2. Namely, the prophecies of Second and Third Isaiah as well as aspects of Zechariah and Ezekiel, among others. Paul Hanson, *The Dawn of Apocalyptic* (Philadelphia: Fortress, 1979), 27, 62.

3. It is in the book of the prophet Amos that this phrase most clearly takes on its signification as a harbinger of doom for the Jewish people. Oracles against other nations were certainly a standard component of many prophets, including Jeremiah and Isaiah, but the complacency of the Israelites is directly skewered in Amos 5:18–20, for they of all people should know what consequences await those who neglect God.

4. All English citations of the Hebrew Scriptures are from JPS85.

5. Bronner, *Journey to Heaven*, 166.

6. J. J. M. Roberts, "The Old Testament's Contribution to Messianic Expectations," in *The Messiah: Developments in Earliest Judaism and Christianity* (ed. James H. Charlesworth; Minneapolis: Fortress, 1992), 44–45.

7. It is important to note Roberts's conclusion that "[n]owhere in the Old Testament has the term [messiah] acquired its later technical sense as an eschatological title. . . . [E]xpectations of a new David are probably to be understood in terms of a continuing Davidic line. There is little indication that any of these prophets envisioned a final Davidic ruler who would actually rule for all time to come" (Roberts, "Messianic Expectations," 51).

8. Joseph Blenkinsopp, *Isaiah 1–39* (The Anchor Bible; New Haven: Yale, 2000), 191.

9. Some may take this verse to imagine an "eschatological state of sinlessness," but Johannes Vlaardingerbroek argues that it is consistent with the calls in Isaiah, Hosea, Jeremiah, and Ezekiel to repent of specific sins and thus lead an "irreproachable life" within a sinful existence. See his *Zephaniah* (Historical Commentary on the Old Testament; Leuven: Peeters, 1999), 205.

10. Raphael, *Jewish Views*, 66–67.

11. Ibid., 67.

12. With the development of the concept of resurrection in Daniel 12, for the first time a biblical text asserts that both the righteous and the wicked will be resurrected from Sheol in order to face separate judgments according to the reward or punishment they have merited. "Thus, within the Book of Daniel, Jewish postmortem teachings become apocalyptic and dualistic in nature [and] is a seed for the notion of heaven and hell that characterizes later Jewish and Christian afterlife teachings." Raphael, *Jewish Views*, 72–73.

13. John Collins, *Daniel* (Hermeneia; Minneapolis: Fortress, 1993), 392. He also notes, "'Everyone who is found written in the book' includes the righteous who have not died and so are not resurrected in 12:2, but they too are surely destined for eternal life." (391).

14. Neil Gillman, *The Death of Death: Resurrection and Immortality in Jewish Thought* (Woodstock: Jewish Lights, 1997), 89.

15. Ibid., 115–27.

16. John Collins, *The Apocalyptic Imagination: An Introduction to Jewish Apocalyptic Literature* (2nd ed; Grand Rapids: Eerdmans, 1998), 29–33; Gillman, *Death of Death*, 96.

17. Bronner, *Journey to Heaven*, 49.

18. R. H. Charles, *The Apocrypha and Pseudepigrapha of the Old Testament in English Volume 2: Pseudepigrapha* (Oxford: Clarendon, 1913), 164.

19. All English citations of *1 Enoch* are from E. Isaac, tr., "1 (Ethiopic Apocalypse of) Enoch," in *The Old Testament Pseudepigrapha Volume 1: Apocalyptic Literature and Testaments* (ed. James H. Charlesworth; New York: Doubleday, 1983), 19–89.

20. Bronner, *Journey to Heaven*, 52.

21. Ibid., 167.

22. George Nickelsburg notes that this verse references both a local/spatial and a temporal shift in the sequence of judgment, making the picture all the more complex and difficult to pin down definitively. See his *1 Enoch 1: A Commentary on the Book of 1 Enoch, Chapters 1–36, 81–108* (Hermeneia; Minneapolis: Fortress: 2001), 308.

23. Bronner, *Journey to Heaven*, 51.

24. Referring specifically to Daniel's four kingdom structure, *4 Ezra* 12:11 states categorically, "The eagle that you saw coming up from the sea is the fourth kingdom that appeared in a vision to your brother Daniel." The twelve kings of the interpretation are invariably understood to be Roman emperors, and the three heads, it is generally agreed, are the Flavians (69–96 C.E.). *4 Ezra* was likely composed under the reign of the last, Domitian, in the early 90s C.E. See Michael Stone, *Fourth Ezra* (Hermeneia; Minneapolis: Fortress, 1990), 365. All English citations of *4 Ezra* are from B. M. Metzger, tr., "The Fourth Book of Ezra," in *The Old Testament Pseudepigrapha Volume 1: Apocalyptic Literature and Testaments* (ed. James H. Charlesworth; New York: Doubleday, 1983), 525–79.

25. Stone, *Fourth Ezra*, 172.

26. Bronner, *Journey to Heaven*, 41.

27. Dereck Daschke, *City of Ruins: Mourning Jerusalem through Jewish Apocalypse* (Leiden: Brill, 2010), 144–46. See also F. J. Murphy, *The Structure and Meaning of Second Baruch* (SBLDS 78; Atlanta: Scholars, 1985), 37–70; 106–7, on the central role of the theology of the two ages in all aspects of *2 Baruch*'s message.

28. All English citations of *2 Baruch* are from A. F. J. Klijn, tr., "2 (Syriac Apocalypse of) Baruch," in *The Old Testament Pseudepigrapha Volume 1: Apocalyptic Literature and Testaments* (ed. James A. Charlesworth; New York: Doubleday, 1983), 621–52.

29. Daschke, *City of Ruins*, 170.

30. Bronner, *Journey to Heaven*, 41.

31. Dereck Daschke and W. Michael Ashcraft, *New Religious Movements: A Documentary Reader* (New York: New York University Press, 2005), 279–83.

32. "A Peaceful New World—Will It Come?" *Jehovah's Witnesses* (Watch Tower Bible and Tract Society of Pennsylvania, 2016); https://www.jw.org/en/publications/books/a-peaceful-new-world-will-it-come/1101991230, accessed July 26, 2016. Here, Bible quotations are from the New World Translation of the Holy Scriptures, a translation by and for Jehovah's Witnesses.

Warriors, Wives, and Wisdom: This World and the World to Come in the (So-Called) Apocrypha

Nicolae Roddy

The vast assembly of late Second Temple period religious texts written under the pressures of imperial domination and Hasmonean self-rule offer the modern scholar a window open toward the tumultuous world of Judea of the Second Temple period, testifying to various responses to the political and cultural challenges of the times. To be sure, the real and perceived hostilities of the Hellenistic world could not help but provoke real concerns for the inhabitants of Judea, raising existential questions about what it might mean ultimately to be a Jew.

Most of these writings witness to courses of thought and action arising within a range of accommodation in the faces of structures of power, suspended between extremes of resistance on the one hand and complete assimilation on the other. Taken together, the literature witnesses to the complete absence of any dogmatic orthodoxy among Jews living in the four centuries following Alexander the Great (333 B.C.E.) and culminating in the destruction of the Temple (70 C.E.). Their scenarios often testify to distressing, even precarious social contexts, which is why one finds among these writings a variety of perspectives regarding the world at hand [*olam ha-zeh*] and the world to come [*olam ha-ba*], sometimes vying together within a single book. These perspectives challenge biblical scholars to bring these ancient texts into dialogue with their troubled worlds, while offering theologians an opportunity to explore the processes involved in the production and development of theodicies. Speculation about the relationship between this world and the world to come is more than a passing fancy for these authors. It arises out of dire concerns for making sense of the world in light of threatening challenges to it.

The present study will focus on identifying a few among several distinct present world/coming world scenarios contained within the deuterocanonical corpus, highlighting points of contrast that demonstrate the wide range of speculation entertained by their respective authors. Although the deuterocanonicals are Jewish texts that were officially abandoned by the rabbis shortly after the destruction of the Second Temple, they remain authoritative for the Roman Catholic, Eastern Orthodox, and Oriental Orthodox biblical and liturgical traditions.[1] Having circulated with the Septuagint (LXX) they are regarded as canonical by the Western Church, however only secondarily so (hence, deutero-). Their canonicity has never been in question among the churches of the East.[2] It is often necessary to remind Christians that, like the Older Testament itself, these texts are inherited from Judaism—that is, written by Jews for Jews living throughout the Greco-Roman world. Eventually marginalized by both rabbinic and Protestant traditions, they have been of modest significance for biblical scholars until recent times.

Given the number of texts at hand, only a representative sampling of models of Jewish speculation about present and future worlds can be presented here—models ranging from a traditional biblical worldview maintained by the privileged conservative elite (most notably the ruling Sadducee party), to the radically apocalyptic scenarios of the resistance, as well as other groups perceiving themselves to be under siege. Christians, who frequently hear excerpts of these texts read aloud in liturgical contexts, might gain a deeper understanding of the beginnings of their own tradition, rooted as it is in the seedbed of Second Temple period Judaism. Although no longer part of the Jewish canon, their value derives from the insight they provide into the diversity of Jewish speculation about the world in which they lived, as well as any world to come. Because many of these texts contain theological elements that were attractive to Christians, they also serve to reacquaint Christianity with its own (Jewish) roots.

CORPORATE (NATIONAL) PRESENT WORLD RESOLUTION

The first category includes present world scenarios that posit divine deliverance through the agency of righteous human warriors, whose personal bravery and zeal for Israel and for the Torah overcome the nation's enemies. Standing in the tradition of Ezekiel 37's vision of the dry bones, which speaks to a future revitalization of the nation and the rebuilding of Solomon's temple, and Isaiah's famous "swords to plowshares/spears to pruning hooks" oracle (Isa 2:1–5), some deuterocanonical texts affirm the restoration of justice in this world in a collective, nonindividualized way. As in the prophetic books [*Nevi'im*], divine justice is meted out in the fearsome age of empires, looking forward toward full resolution in the near future of a present world characterized by peace and well-being [*shalom*].

In the deuterocanonical texts in this category, powerful earthly forces threaten Israel's security and national well-being, bringing about the need for an agent of divine deliverance to arise and set the world aright. Resolution (salvation) is corporate and national, not personal. For example, in 1 Maccabees, the deaths of Judah, Jonathan, and Simon are presented in a matter-of-fact way as necessary sacrifices for the greater cause, rather than as martyrdoms or personal tragedies. For this reason, the theodicy of this worldview remains traditionally biblical. There are no references to an afterlife, including any sort of individualized resurrection, bodily or otherwise, which despite its centrality to the Christian tradition is a notion that appeared relatively late in the Second Temple period.[3]

1 MACCABEES

The book of 1 Maccabees is a late second century text that recounts the events from the death of Alexander the Great to the installation of John Hyrcanus, self-proclaimed king and high priest of Judea, almost exactly two centuries later. Its author interprets current events in a way that supports the legitimacy of the early Hasmonean high priestly dynasty, whose founders, the heroic Maccabees, brought Antiochene persecutions to an eventual end, established national independence, and reinstituted the rule of the Torah. In contrast to the many texts that arose out of the crucible of suffering and persecution, here the righteous celebrate victory through the Maccabean triumph, most notably on the part of Judah, warrior par excellence, whose brave deeds are heralded as too numerous to record (9:22).

It is noteworthy that the author of this celebratory text does not record the violence and self-serving corruption that would ensue under the leadership of the Hasmoneans. Although the text witnesses to what was for many a troubled time, it appears the author was not adversely affected by these events and was likely a supporter of the ruling family.[4] In any event, the theodicy remains earthbound and rooted in the present, consonant with the worldview of the Hebrew Bible, in which human action plays out on the face of the earth, with God and his heavenly hosts in the heavens and the shadowy realm of the dead below (Sheol).[5]

JUDITH

The book of Judith tells the story of a pious and beautiful widow who delivers her village from an Assyrian siege. Although the characters, time, and plot lines are radically different and influenced by Hellenistic gender-specific roles and language, some scholars suggest that Judith's character may have been inspired by the warrior exploits of Judah the Maccabee; thus one might expect similar themes and outlooks.[6] Still others have suggested that the book of Judith was composed by a member of the Pharisee party and that the book, full of rich irony, is cryptically anti-Hasmonean. If these scholars are correct, then—as I have suggested elsewhere[7]—the whole point of this ironic tale almost certainly rests upon its implication that Judah and his brothers should have emulated Judith by returning to private life following the liberation of their people, instead of wresting power for themselves and eventually becoming corrupt. Thus, the book of Judith projects an alternative history in which the cruel tyranny of Hasmonean rule would never have come about.

Judith's story of seduction, deception, and assassination unfolds in a cleverly reconfigured, conflated historical past, one in which the Assyrian conquest is led by the Babylonian king Nebuchadnezzar who conquered Judah in the early sixth century B.C.E. Such seeming historical inaccuracies are not mistakes, for they signal the reader to pay attention to the details, which hearken to a present world situation in which things are set aright by a mortal agent of divine deliverance. Although there is no indication that the residents of Bethulia are particularly righteous folk, they are nevertheless delivered by the God-fearing Judith's formidable beauty and warrior fierceness: she actively embodies God's justice on the earth. Thus again, deliverance comes at the hands of a warrior-type human agent who brings corporate deliverance to the nation.[8]

PERSONAL PRESENT WORLD RESOLUTION

Like the previous texts, these narratives reflect a worldview consonant with that of the Tanach generally, namely, one in which human activity from birth to death takes place in an arena sandwiched between the heavens [*ha-shammaim*] and the grave (Sheol). Whatever plays out on the face of the earth, the Most High watches and resolves upon the earth before the eyes of everyone involved—especially the righteous—but also for their sake, sometimes also the punishment-deserving wicked. This perspective is rooted in the traditional deuteronomistic worldview, explicitly laid out in Deuteronomy 28, which asserts that God's justice in relation to covenantal fidelity is meted out in the present life.

Although this worldview is rooted in a corporate view of deliverance, one cannot help but notice the implications for personal life as well. Living one's life according to the Torah brings personal health, wealth, and abundant life, while forsaking the Torah results in disease, misfortune, and death. Thus for some deuterocanonical texts, the righteous enjoy divine favor in the present world even though they experience great distress. Such favor includes being able to behold the ruin of their oppressors, who in turn see the reestablishment of justice in the vindication of the righteous. These texts rest on the underlying conviction that the divine will for human existence is the default mode for ultimate reality, seen only by the wise righteous ones. Given that biblical wisdom is defined as "fear of the LORD," such stories are rightly called wisdom tales.[9]

SUSANNAH

The story of Susannah came to circulate with the book of Daniel. Read during the fifth week of Lent in the Latin tradition, it concerns a pious woman who is sexually compromised by two elders of her own community. The elders spy on the God-fearing Susannah as she bathes and then threaten to publically accuse her of adultery with a stranger—an action punishable by death—should she refuse to acquiesce to their salacious advances. The righteous Susannah has no choice but to call upon God for deliverance, who immediately stirs up the spirit of the young prophet Daniel. In what some have called the world's first courtroom drama, Daniel interrogates the elders; but this is not the usual cross-examination, for Daniel as prophet (and master of wordplay, one should add) is able to convict first one elder and then the other on the basis of their individual testimonies alone.

The story of Susannah's persecution and vindication calls to mind stories about Daniel standing before the Babylonian king in chapters 3 and 6, but here Susannah is simply an ordinary God-fearing person. Furthermore, her enemy is not some wicked emperor, but putatively respected leaders of her own community. Unlike other deuteroncanonical tales, the narrative is set in a village that does not appear to be troubled by outsiders; however, one could argue that the actions of these devious elders, antithetical to the life of the Torah, pose a threat to the interior life of the community equal to or greater than that of any foreign despot. In any event, swift to deliver the righteous, the Most High rescues Susannah from certain death and vindicates her in the present world.

TOBIT

The book of Tobit, from which large portions are read in the church's lectionary, offers another present world, present life resolution, only here the agent of divine justice is not a human agent like the prophet Daniel, but an angelic being named Raphael. Set in the Assyrian exile in the late eighth century B.C.E., the book of Tobit is a wisdom novella focusing on the struggles of the righteous in the face of powerful human and supernatural forces. Full of rich irony and humor, the story resolves all its righteous characters' struggles in a happy ending in the present world.

Tobit, the eponymous protagonist, is persecuted by the Assyrian king Sennacherib for burying the exposed corpses of fellow Israelites—a death mitzvah [*met mitzvah*] that brings him into repeated contact with what rabbinic sources call the "mother of all impurities," raising the need for repeated repurification rituals. At one point, Tobit's sufferings are compounded when he sleeps outside the house during the repurification process. While he is asleep, sparrows defecate upon his eyes and render him blind. Meanwhile, in faraway Ecbatana, a distant cousin named Sarah is suffering at the hands of the demon Asmodeus, whose jealous desire for her leads him to kill seven husbands in succession before any of her marriages could be consummated.

Both Tobit and Sarah are righteous Israelites who suffer hardship at the hands of malevolent powers, human and superhuman; both suffer reproach from the people around them, and both resort to prayer in the midst of their despair. Their parallel plights are brought together and resolved in a third cycle, in which God sends the angel Raphael—disguised as a distant kinsman—to accompany Tobias, Tobit's son, on a journey to reclaim some money held in trust. During the journey they stop at the Tigris River to refresh themselves, when suddenly a large fish jumps out. The angel instructs Tobias to take hold of the fish and secure its gall, heart, and liver, organs that will later become the means by which the demon is driven off and Tobit's eyes healed (6:1–8), bringing about a happy ending.

The narrative world of the book of Tobit is full of hardships, and the righteous seem to suffer by dint of their righteousness. However, the righteous are never out of sight of the Most High, who bestows upon them the rewards of their faithful perseverance in the present life. Tobit becomes highly respected in his community. He dies peacefully at the age of 112 and is buried in Nineveh with great honor (14:2). Tobit's son Tobias enjoys even greater wealth and honor and lives to the ripe old age of 117, three years short of the divinely appointed limit for mortals (Gen 6:3). Shortly before his death, Tobias receives news of Nineveh's destruction, for which he rejoices. Praising God for the restoration of justice for which his father had prayed, Tobias now goes to his grave in peace, a blessed ending to righteous life.

THE INSTRUCTION OF BEN SIRA

Moving now from wisdom tale to wisdom discourse, "The Instruction of [Joshua] ben Sira" (known to Christians as Ecclesiasticus or the Book of Jesus, son of Sirach) affirms that a life devoted to wisdom is a reward in itself. Such a life is characterized by prudent speech, unwavering uprightness, and an honorable reputation. At the end of life, both sage and sinner inescapably meet up with maggots, worms, and decay (10:11, 38:21); however, the former, whose life is lived in the fear of God (i.e., awesome reverence), enjoys a happy and prosperous end (1:13, 2:3), while his or her virtue and acts of righteousness live on. In contrast to the books of Susannah and Tobit, ben Sira asserts that even a happy, prosperous end is not necessarily without pain and suffering; but even in the midst of persecution leading to death, the life of wisdom brings reward and satisfaction to dimming eyes: "The prayer of the humble pierces the clouds, and will not rest until it reaches the goal; it will not desist until the Most High responds and does justice for the righteous, and executes judgment. Indeed, the Lord will not delay" (35:21–22).

PERSONAL OTHER WORLD RESOLUTIONS

Some deuterocanonical texts imagine a world that is irredeemably broken and wholly unsalvageable, necessitating some kind of cosmic reset. For some writers, Trito-Isaiah's vision of a new heaven and a new earth (Isa 65:17) inspired an apocalyptic hope among groups that perceived the world in this way. Likely influenced by Orphic pessimism, this view inspires the hope for a new creation—a new heaven and earth—set apart from a world no longer worth saving. Augmented by Daniel 12:2, the persecuted righteous ones find hope for transformed existence delivering them from the time and place of present anguish:

> Your people shall be delivered, everyone who is found written in the book. Many of those who sleep in the dust of the earth shall awake, some to everlasting life, and some to shame and everlasting contempt. Those who are wise shall shine like the brightness of the sky, and those who lead many to righteousness, like the stars forever and ever (Dan 12: 1–3).[10]

Other raw materials for the belief in a resurrection from the dead [*těḥîyat hamētîm*][11] were drawn from Ezekiel 37:1–14 and Isaiah 26:19. Thus, one sees that apocalyptic beliefs emerge from a radical intensification of convictions voiced in prophetic literature.[12] What is new is that the belief in a resurrection of the dead, once a hope for the rebirth of the nation, now becomes personal.

2 MACCABEES 7

The deuterocanonical texts offer a variety of present and future world theodicies; however, 2 Maccabees manages to offer several aspects of divine deliverance within a single text. The narrative is set in a world dominated by the wicked Seleucid king Antiochus IV, who in chapter 7 presides over the gruesome torture of a family of Torah-abiding Jews. The story calls to mind the story of Taxo and his seven sons in *Testament of Moses* 9, both of which stand in the tradition of persecution and vindication in Daniel 3 and 6. But for the mother and her sons—quite unlike the stories of Susannah and Tobit—deliverance follows an agonizing, torturous death. In one sense, the imagery calls to mind Isaiah 65:17–25, in which the righteous are promised a long life in a new heaven and earth, while God judges and kills the wicked, leaving their corpses exposed (66:15–17); however, here it is the corpses of the suffering righteous that remain exposed. Nevertheless, vindication occurs in the form of resurrection to new life.

This martyrology of the pious woman and her seven sons presents a situation in which imminent and inescapable death arises from living a life according to the Torah, for it is the family's faithfulness to the Torah that incurs the anger of the king and fuels his primary motivation for ordering their torture and death. Their choice is clear, but antithetical to any previous understanding of how the world is supposed to operate. Despite their horrendous agony, several hopeful convictions are voiced:

- God sees their plight and has compassion upon them. (v. 6)
- God will raise up the righteous to an everlasting life. (v. 9)
- Severed body parts will be restored. (v. 11; see also Razis, 14:30 ff)
- There will be no resurrection for the wicked king. (v. 14)
- God will torture the wicked king and his descendants. (vv. 16–17)
- The calamity ultimately is not in the king's power to carry out, but is the result of Israel's sins against God. (v. 18)

Their situation sets up a kind of cognitive dissonance in which the inherent conviction that fidelity to the Torah brings life comes to be challenged by the reality that clinging to the Torah now brings certain torture and death. Underscored by the conviction that the Most High is omnipotent, omniscient, compassionate, and just, suddenly all evidence has shifted to the contrary. Something has to give. The displacement activity forced by the cognitive dissonance in this clash of realities reaffirms that God's justice is certain; therefore, if justice is not being realized in the present world, then it must be taking place somewhere else. Thus traditional notions concerning the finality of death are rewritten to accommodate the conviction that the end is not the end.

WISDOM OF SOLOMON

A somewhat similar situation obtains in the Wisdom of Solomon, namely, that fidelity to the Torah leads to persecution and death; only here the classic distinction between immortality and bodily resurrection seems confused. In words that clearly affirm the preexistence of souls, the author writes, "As a child I was naturally gifted, and a good soul fell to my lot; or rather, being good, I entered an undefiled body" (8:20); however, vindication of the righteous protagonist clearly involves resurrection [*anastasis*] from the dead.

Like ben Sira, the author of Wisdom of Solomon acknowledges the reality of death and asserts that righteousness is immortal. He insists that God did not make death (1:13), but that death is brought into being through the actions of the wicked (v. 16). The speech attributed to the wicked reflects an Epicurean worldview that denies the existence of any personal afterlife. The wicked lie in wait to murder the righteous ones, but when they do, the righteous ones only appear to have died. Their souls are in the hand of God, he asserts, where torments of the present world will never touch them (3:1–2).

In contrast to the deuteronomistic notion that righteousness brings long life and prosperity, the author of the Wisdom of Solomon accounts for the untimely deaths of the righteous by asserting that their perfected souls were pleasing to God, thus he snatched them from the midst of earthly wickedness (4:14). By contrast, the wicked may enjoy a long and profitable life, which is contrary to the deuteronomic view, but after death they will be raised just long enough to see the error of their ways and be judged by the righteous ones they had condemned. Ironically, the distorted worldview they held in the present world becomes a self-fulfilling prophecy, for the paradoxical reversal of fortunes on the Day of Judgment forces them to behold the righteous ones whom they killed standing at the right hand of God to convict them. As a result, the wicked endure acute pangs of fear and anguish before fading into oblivion, unremembered as though they were never born.[13]

CONCLUSION

Despite a wide range of outlooks and outcomes, the deuterocanonical texts all share one fundamental conviction: that the Most High is unique (Deut 6:4), omnipotent, omniscient, and providentially just—a unique and powerful God of steadfast lovingkindness [*hesed*] willing and able to act in establishing and maintaining justice and righteousness [*mishpat ve-zedekah*] in ruling the universe. Even a cursory reading of these texts shows a broad spectrum of speculation concerning how the Deity might act in vindicating righteous ones and righting earthly wrongs. Particular convictions about the world to come are predicated on the situation of the present world, as the oppressed look desperately to the divine for help.[14]

They arise out of particular social contexts and at no point do they presume to be dogmatic or universal in scope. As such, one cannot expect these texts to have the clarity and resolution of systematic theology, so they often remain ambiguously raw and undeveloped and distinct from the corpus as a whole. Nevertheless a thorough comparison of these texts brings great appreciation for the colorfully rich spectrum of light refracted through the prism of a shared conviction about divine steadfast lovingkindness [*hesed*] manifested through the cosmic administration of justice and righteousness [*mishpat vezedekah*].

NOTES

1. The expanded canon of inspired books in the western half of the Roman Empire was promulgated by Pope Damasus at the Synod of Rome (382) and reaffirmed by subsequent regional councils at Hippo (393) and Carthage (397, 419). The Council of Trent (1545–1563) affirmed the infallibility of these books as Scripture. The canonicity of these texts was never officially in question among churches of the East.

2. See Eugen Pentiuc, *The Old Testament in Eastern Orthodox Tradition* (Oxford: Oxford University Press, 2014), 101–35.

3. James Charlesworth, et al., eds., *Resurrection: The Origin and Future of a Biblical Doctrine* (New York: T & T Clark, 2006), 223.

4. For more information, see George W. E. Nickelsburg, *Jewish Literature Between the Bible and the Mishnah* (Philadelphia: Fortress Press, 1981, 2005), 102–6.

5. The worldview stands in marked contrast to that of 2 Maccabees, where Judas and his companions pray on behalf of the souls of their fallen comrades, that they may be absolved of their sins (2 Macc 12:43–46). It does agree with the view of the Saducee party, who disparaged any belief in resurrection (see Matt 22:23; Mk 12:18; Lk 20:27; Acts 23:6–10; also, Josephus, *J.W.* 2.165 and *Ant.* 18.16).

6. Judith can be seen as having been modeled on a number of Jewish female heroes, especially Deborah and Jael, but also Miriam and the woman of Abel-beth-maacha (2 Sam 20:14–22); see Nickelsburg, *Jewish Literature*, 100.

7. Nicolae Roddy, "The Way It Wasn't: The Book of Judith as Anti-Hasmonean Propaganda," *Studia Hebraica* 8 (2008): 269–77.

8. For more information, see Nickelsburg, *Jewish Literature*, 97–102.

9. It is almost certain that the Deuteronomist did not actually hold such a naïve view of the world; however, the idea that sin brings ruin (and its converse, that ruin is the result of sin) offered itself as a plausible explanation for what had gone so terribly wrong in that God had permitted Jerusalem and its temple to be destroyed.

10. The belief in bodily transformation, in this case shining like stars, may refer to some sort of angelic state of being. Compare *1 Enoch* 39:7, 58:1–4; *Psalms of Solomon* 3:15; *2 Esdras* 7.55; and *2 (Syriac Apocalypse of) Baruch* 50:10; see also Matthew 13:43.

11. The earliest datable postbiblical reference is the Enochic *Book of the Watchers* (*1 En* 1–36). See George Nickelsburg, *Resurrection, Immortality, and Eternal Life in Intertestamental Judaism and Early Christianity* (Expanded edition; Cambridge: Harvard University Press, 2006), 5. Nickelsburg's 1972 dissertation cited Daniel 12:2 as the "earliest datable intertestamental reference to a resurrection from the dead," but later ascribed it to the Enochic Book of the Watchers (1 En 1–36), which antedates the book of Daniel. He later concluded that Daniel 12:2 likely reflects the interpretation of Isaiah 65–66 in *1 Enoch* 24:2–27:5. See George Nickelsburg, *1 Enoch 1: A Commentary on the Book of Enoch, Chapters 1–36; 81–108* (Minneapolis: Fortress Press, 2001), 315–16. For a thorough general study of resurrection, see Charlesworth, *The Origin and Future*.

12. Paul D. Hanson, *The Dawn of Apocalyptic: The Historical and Sociological Roots of Jewish Apocalyptic Eschatology* (Philadelphia: Fortress Press, 1979), 35–36.

13. Note that the fate of the wicked stands in contrast to the classical conception of eternal hellfire rooted in the book of Enoch and implied in the Gospels.

14. Such desperate situations could not help but bring several psalms to mind, e.g., Psalms 18, 22, and 28, in which the Lord is said to be a personal rock, strength, shepherd, shield, salvation, and so on.

The Afterlife in the Septuagint

Leonard Greenspoon

INTRODUCTORY OBSERVATIONS

It may seem odd or perhaps even off-putting to begin an analysis of the Septuagint and eschatology with a series of caveats. Nonetheless, as we shall see, these "warnings" form the necessary prelude to any responsible discussion of this topic. If, as turns out to be the case, there is no single perspective on this fascinating topic, then it is far better for readers to recognize this earlier, rather than later, in the process.[1]

First, it is necessary to remind readers that the Septuagint is for the most part a translation, in fact the first translation of the Bible, in this case the Old Testament or Hebrew Bible. There is little reason to doubt that the process that resulted in this Greek text, which can be abbreviated as LXX, began in Alexandria, Egypt, sometime in the first third of the third century B.C.E. It is probable that the translation resulted both from the Alexandrian Jewish community's rapid loss of fluency in Hebrew and from the reigning monarch's (Ptolemy II) desire to have a copy of the Jewish law in his ever-expanding Library.[2]

Thus it makes eminently good sense, historically and theologically, that the Five Books of Moses or Pentateuch were the first books tackled by the translators (numbering 72 or 70 according to ancient sources) assembled at Alexandria. There are sufficient similarities between the translations of the first five books of the Hebrew Bible to posit some connection between their translators. On the other hand, there are enough demonstrable differences in translation technique to insist on the relative independence of those responsible for each of the books of the Pentateuch.

As we move to the books beyond the Pentateuch, there are no sure signs of the relative (to say nothing of the absolute) chronology in which they were translated, nor are we even close to certainty about the location(s) in which later translators worked. Thus, it is not entirely surprising that many LXX books appear to be rather literal renderings of the Hebrew being translated [also called *Vorlage*], while other books almost certainly reflect a far freer, even periphrastic, approach to the Hebrew text. And then there are a considerable number of books that occupy more moderate (or median) places in the continuum that separates (but also joins) literal and free.

It must be immediately acknowledged that our judgment on a given LXX translator's handling of his *Vorlage* remains somewhat speculative, inasmuch as we do not know precisely what consonantal Hebrew text (vocalization was a much later development) lay before those rendering the Bible into Greek. Undoubtedly, a consonantal text very much like (in fact, sometimes identical to) the traditional Hebrew or Masoretic Text (MT) underlies much of the LXX. LXX translators, we can readily imagine, typically followed that Hebrew text, but may have consciously changed it for any number of reasons. A consonantal Hebrew text at variance, to a lesser or greater degree, with the MT lay before other LXX translators. Again, there is good reason to posit that they often followed this Hebrew text, while parting company with it on occasion.

Thus, we have to imagine that the collection of individual or group efforts that we designate by the term "Septuagint" was always somewhat uneven in the approach of its translators toward their Hebrew *Vorlage*. In the absence of any overall effort at editorial standardization or redaction, it would be difficult to imagine that there are a large number of grammatical, lexicographical, or ideological elements that are found throughout the Septuagint or even in most of its books.

What I have been speaking of in the previous paragraphs could more properly be called the Old Greek, that is, the form of the text as it appeared when the translators completed their task. Unfortunately, no autographs (that is, originals) or any book or block of books of the LXX are extent. In the absence of such autographs, it might be hoped that textual criticism would allow for the reconstruction of the original formulations of the LXX translators. Although such a procedure might well work on a limited amount of text, we are far from being able to determine the Old Greek for an extended amount of LXX text.

Even under the best of circumstances, when scribes carefully copied the Old Greek over several centuries, we could expect a plethora of new readings to be introduced by chance or by design. This is simply the result of the fact that scribes, even the most careful scribes, were after all fallible humans.

But more than a few years passed between the creation of the Septuagint and extant manuscripts that contain all (or most) of the books that came to constitute the LXX canon. The Septuagint was probably completed in the late second century B.C.E.; the great uncial codices (Alexandrinus, Sinaiticus, and Vaticanus) that constitute our earliest extant evidence for the LXX as a collection of books date to the third and fourth centuries C.E. During the extended intervening period that separates these two events, the Old Greek of some books was completely or partially lost, and later revisions were substituted. In other instances, there is good reason to think that conscious efforts on the part of scribes or tradents introduced extensive changes that were perhaps originally intended as commentary on a passage of the LXX, but ultimately took the place of the older Greek.

All of these factors introduce even more heterogeneity to the Septuagint as a collection of varied texts stemming from different time periods and locales. Further, these factors serve to reinforce the observation made above about the difficulty of locating and defining LXX characteristics on what we might call a global basis. It may be possible, for example, to discern a marked interest in eschatology on the part of the translator responsible for LXX Psalms or LXX Isaiah, but it would be sloppy methodology to seek to apply such interest to other books or blocks of material without careful, one might say painstaking, analysis of the work of each translator.

The cautionary flags thrown down above are admittedly formidable, but they do point in the direction that any serious study of the LXX and eschatology must take. But they are not the only cautionary flags. Recognition that any statement beginning "The LXX says . . ." must be heavily nuanced, if not abandoned outright, is necessary. But how are we to deal with assertions that are limited to a given book or group of books in the Septuagint? In short, what are we looking for?

Typically, in searches such as this (that is, how is eschatology handled by specific LXX translators) greatest importance is attached to readings that veer from the supposed Hebrew *Vorlage* with which the translator worked. Sometimes, as with quantitative changes (that is, those that involve differences in length between the Hebrew and Greek texts), it is fairly easy to detect differences and perhaps even to explain or account for them. However, in general, qualitative differences (where the number of words is about the same, but the meanings appear to be distinct) are more difficult to determine.

Nonetheless, it would not be appropriate to discount the value of the Greek text where it essentially follows the Hebrew that underlies it. In such instances, we may well envision that the translator's viewpoint is identical (or nearly so) to the stance presented in his Hebrew *Vorlage*.

Upon further reflection, almost each of the statements in the two paragraphs just above require further analysis. For example, even if we posit that the LXX translator made use of a Hebrew text that was identical to the consonants of the MT, we have no way of knowing whether he vocalized it in exactly the same way that the Masoretes did. Although differences in vocalization are often minor and make little or no difference in meaning, that is certainly not always the case.

At some point, we will need to ascertain whether, in our best judgment (and in the judgment of others who have studied the material) a given LXX translator generally followed closely his Hebrew *Vorlage* or whether he was given to frequent insertions and omissions, such that we cannot know whether a possibly significant passage was due to a Hebrew text different from the MT or is the result of the translator's own conscious intervention.

Beyond these considerations are two others. First, the LXX is after all a translation and thus not necessarily the optimal medium to express views even (especially?) on topics of current interest. It is clear that those responsible for the LXX had differing views on the best way to render the Hebrew wording into intelligible Greek. Nonetheless, it does seem methodologically sound to assume that the translator followed his text, unless there is some reason to think otherwise. And this would be true, at least in general, whether or not the translator agreed with the text. Therefore, unless we have evidence to the contrary, we cannot make too much of any instance where the Greek translation agrees with its reputed Hebrew *Vorlage*. Emphatically stated, agreement between texts does not necessarily indicate that the translator agreed with a given sentiment expressed in that text.

The second consideration is especially apt when considering eschatology and related issues. As is well known, the Septuagint, in origin a Jewish document for a Jewish audience, became the Bible (specifically the Old Testament) for Christians. In this guise, Christian theologians routinely mined the text for support of what were to become characteristic beliefs. An eschatological focus was one area that saw particularly rich development in early Christianity. Thus, many LXX passages came to be understood as bearing an eschatological meaning, whether or not such was the intention (or likely to have been the intention) of the Old Greek translators themselves. In short, we must be ever cautious not to read back into the Septuagint meanings that pertain to a chronologically later and religiously different culture.

The afterlife, as a means to reward and punish individuals (or perhaps groups of individuals), is clearly a part, but only a part, of the constellation of beliefs centered on the term "eschatology." With its focus on the end of time (at least, time as we know and experience it), eschatology has both global, even universal, significance as well as importance in terms of the fate of individuals. Often, but not always related to the end of times is the figure of the Messiah (or, for some Second Temple Jews, messiahs). That is, biblical passages that highlight the role of the Messiah may be directly relevant to a larger eschatological vision, or they may not be. Much, but not all eschatology envisions a fiery end to our world, brought about by God and his angelic host, often aided by those humans allied with him against the forces of cosmic evil. This is apocalypticism, which, as I see it, adds a sense of urgency to eschatological speculation that might otherwise seem to pertain only to the distant future.

On the one hand, careful delineation of different strands of eschatological and messianic thought is essential in order to plot what can be conceived of as parallel, but nonetheless divers developments. On the other hand, it is not likely that any individual or likeminded group of individuals delved very deeply into differences of definition or emphasis in their eschatological considerations. That is to say, for the sake of analysis we as observers of an earlier period might well wish to differentiate beliefs that those who maintained them would have held in common. With this in mind, I will discuss below a number of passages that might have been understood as eschatological, whether or not a claim could be made that they relate specifically to the afterlife.

THE PSALTER

We will start with the book of Psalms (or the Psalter) since this has been the starting point for much of the most spirited discussion and analysis in past discussions. Psalm 1, the initial and in many ways introductory composition to the entire collection, begins by contrasting the fate of the righteous with that of the wicked. A fairly literal translation of Psalm 1:5 in the Hebrew text is provided by the New American Standard Bible (NASB): "Therefore the wicked will not stand in the judgment, Nor sinners in the assembly of the righteous." Within the context of the Hebrew of this Psalm, this clearly refers to God's actions, within this world, to separate and reward those who are faithful to him, while punishing those who turn from him. This is a common theme of Wisdom Literature, of which Psalm 1 is an exemplar.

According to Joachim Schaper, "the Greek, on the other hand, has altered the psalm's nature as a whole by reinterpreting a single word. The use of *anisthmi* as an intransitive verb referring to the future state of a group of individuals clearly confers the idea of 'rising from the dead,' 'be resurrected'. . . . The idea of a last judgment is implied in the Greek of Ps 1:5," which Schaper translates: "Therefore unbelievers will not rise [from death] in judgment nor will sinners [rise] in the counsel of righteous men." Schaper supports this interpretation with reference to other Jewish literature (e.g., 2 Maccabees) that also dates to the second century B.C.E., when, he believes, the Greek Psalter was produced.[3]

It is noteworthy, especially in the view of those who oppose Schaper's interpretation (here and, as we shall see, in other passages) that he does not cite any other uses of this Greek verb in the Psalter. Focusing on this point, Karen Jobes and Moises Silva observe: "Although Schaper's interpretation may seem at first attractive, there is evidence to diminish its force. For example, the material in Hatch-Redpath shows the same Greek root translating the same Hebrew root even in contexts where the sense of resurrection is impossible. One such instance is in the Psalter itself at Psalm 93:16. With this in mind, we can characterize Schaper's interpretation at best as 'ambiguous.'"[4] Given our introductory remarks above, it does not seem that Jobes and Silva have set too high an interpretive bar for efforts such as Schaper's.

We will now look at a selection of Schaper's other examples from the first third of the Psalter. The first passage adduced by Schaper is Psalm 16 (15 in the LXX):9–10. In the Hebrew the text reads (so NASB): "Therefore my heart is glad, and my glory rejoices; My flesh also will dwell securely. For Thou wilt not abandon my soul to Sheol; Neither wilt Thou allow Thy Holy One to undergo decay." Schaper, along with others, suggests that the word translated "my glory" should instead be read "my liver." This does not entail any change in consonants. Schaper renders the Septuagint for these two verses as: "There my heart was glad//and my tongue gave praise;//also, my flesh will rest upon hope//because you will not abandon my soul to Hades//nor let your righteous see corruption."

For Schaper, the eschatologically significant differences between the Hebrew and the Greek are two in number: the change from "securely" to "upon hope" and from "pit" (NASB "decay") to "destruction," "physical corruption." As Schaper argues: "These changes indicate the introduction of the notion of physical resurrection (again only of the righteous) into the sacred text. . . . The Hebrew text does not confer this idea. It just stresses that God will not let the righteous die an untimely death."[5]

In this instance, Schaper's second point is obscured by the NASB rendering, which here is not literal. For its "Neither wilt Thou allow Thy Holy One to undergo decay," the New Revised Standard Version (NRSV) has: "or let your faithful one see the Pit." It is as if the translators of the NASB introduced their later, Christian interpretation of the Hebrew into their translation—never, in my view, a wise decision. But, can we say, with Schaper, that "the Greek version puts forward the promise of personal, physical resurrection.

We have here one of the first, if not *the* first, instance of this hope"?[6] On the basis of the further evidence Schaper uses for support; namely, a midrash on Psalm 16, I cannot follow his argumentation, especially in the absence of any collaborating evidence from elsewhere in Greek Psalms, to say nothing of the corpus of the full Septuagint.

It is Schaper's judgment that the last three verses of Psalm 22 (21 in the LXX), that is, verses 30–32, provide "an illustration of the traditional Hebrew concept of divine justice with regard to human life and death." This is an especially difficult passage in the Hebrew, especially in its first verse. NASB (where the verses are numbered 29–31) renders this passage as follows: "All the prosperous of the earth will eat and worship, All those who go down to the dust will bow before Him, Even he who cannot keep his soul alive. Posterity will serve Him; It will be told of the LORD to the coming generation. They will come and will declare His righteousness To a people who will be born, that He has performed it." Whatever ambiguities reside in the Hebrew, the Greek is, in Schaper's view, unambiguous. In his translation, it reads: "And the rich ('fat ones') of the earth ate and bowed low,//all those going down to earth will fall down before him.// But my soul lives for him//and my seed will serve him://the coming generation will be proclaimed to the Lord,//and they will proclaim his righteousness//to the people which will be born, [all the things] which the Lord did."

Of the three differences Schaper discerns between the Hebrew and the Greek, only one is of interest in matters eschatological. For the Hebrew NRSV rendered "Even he who cannot keep his soul alive," LXX has "But my soul lives for him." In Schaper's analysis, the Greek reading could be an interpretation of the same Hebrew or one that varied, but only slightly, from this Hebrew. The significance of this is, for Schaper, clear: "my soul lives for him" means "lives for him in eternity," as is suggested by the use of the future tense in the immediate context.[7] For those who follow Schaper's eschatologically oriented interpretation of other psalms, this understanding of Psalm 21 (LXX enumeration) surely carries considerably more weight than it does for those who remain skeptical of Schaper's overall approach to the Psalter.

Psalm 46 (45 in the LXX) provides the next example within Schaper's listing of psalms with a noticeable eschatological reworking on the part of the Greek translator. In the Hebrew text of this psalm, v. 9 reads (again, as rendered in the NASB, where it is v. 8): "Come, behold the works of the LORD, Who has wrought desolations in the earth." At this point, the LXX has (in Schaper's translation): "Come, see the works of the Lord//which he has set upon the earth as portents." As understood by Schaper, "the change from 'devastation' [NASB: 'desolations'] to 'portents' obviously expresses the need to adjust the text to reflect a modified concept of the inception of the messianic age.... The shift probably also served to alter the idea itself, to make it more 'humane.' The stress was no longer laid on the destruction wrought by God but rather on the hope (for the coming of the Messiah?) itself." There is certainly reason for even an impartial observer to doubt whether this LXX reading is in fact "an interpretative translation" of the sort Schaper extrapolates. Even if it is, there is no clear connection between this reading and the others Schaper develops in his section on eschatology.[8]

The situation in Psalm 48 (LXX 47) is quite interesting. The last verse of this Psalm, as rendered in NASB, (where it is verse 14) reads: "For such is God, Our God forever and ever; He will guide us until death." For the Septuagint, Schaper translates: "Because this is God, *our* God,//in all eternity and forever and ever,//he himself will shepherd us forever." As Schaper sees it, the Greek equivalent for Hebrew "guide" is exact. However, the Hebrew expression "until death" has led in the Septuagint to "a theologically tendentious interpretation.... The Hebrew text ... simply alludes to an inner-wordly guidance given to the righteous.... The Hebrew of Ps 48 does not confer any ideas about personal eschatology." The Greek expression *eis tous aiwnon* (variants of this are found three times in the preceding line), which Schaper renders "forever," is in his analysis a term that has been "democratized," such that "it could be employed to lay out the prospects of personal salvation. The flock tended by the eternal shepherd could now hope to *participate* in his eternity." This is, at first glance, a more impressive example than some of the others Schaper adduced. However, given the fact that a similar form shows up three (other) times in this verse, we cannot overlook the seemingly simpler explanation of textual corruption at the stage of translation and/or transmission.[9]

The very next composition, Psalm 49 (LXX 48), is more complex and provides Schaper with the context for one of his more lengthy analyses.[10] Verse 12 (v. 11 in the NASB) reads as following: "Their inner thought is, that their houses are forever, And their dwelling places to all generations; They have called their lands after their own names." This difficult text is often emended at its beginning, such that the Hebrew word for "grave" or "graves" appears rather than "inner thought." Such a change, which would involve the rearrangement of two of the consonants, is by no means impossible, but it is sharply rejected by Schaper. Thus, he argues, the LXX of this verse is another "theological innovation" on the part of the translators: "And their graves are their houses forever,//their dwellings for many generations [=forever]." This "theological exegesis," in Schaper's words, "serves to stress the eternal death of the wicked . . . over against the eternal salvation of the righteous. . . . [In other words,] there will be neither judgment nor resurrection for the wicked."

From Schaper's perspective this interpretation is strengthened by the LXX rendering at v. 15 (v. 16 in the LXX), where a notoriously difficult Hebrew text is rendered in Greek as: "They put [them] into Hades like sheep, Death tends them://and the righteous will rule over them in the morning,// and their help will wither away from their glory [once they are] in Hades." This Greek is similar, in Schaper's view, to what is implied in the Hebrew text, "but it further stresses an already prominent feature, i.e. the existence of the wicked in Hades. Whereas the Hebrew text tells us that their 'form will vanish,' the Greek claims that there will be no 'help' for them in the nether world." As is so often the case with the passages Schaper chooses to highlight, there are both textual and interpretative difficulties in this psalm. This makes it difficult to offer complete support for the positions in favor of which Schaper makes his definitive claims.

Another "striking instance of reinterpretation" occurs in Psalm 56 (LXX 55), according to Schaper. The NASB renders this difficult verse (v. 8 in the NASB; v. 9 in the LXX) as: "Thou hast taken account of my wanderings; Put my tears in Thy bottle; Are they not in Thy book?" Schaper would exclude the last line of this verse ("Are they not in Thy book?") as a likely gloss. How then are we to deal with what is apparently the Greek rendering of the first two lines of this verse: "I have told you my life,//[and] you have put my tears before yourself, just like in your promise"?

Most important, for Schaper, is the question of which "promise" is being alluded to in this interpretative Greek rendering. For Schaper, as for some other researchers, it is to Isaiah 25:8 that this allusion draws us. Within "the description of the great eschatological banquet drawing together the nations in Jerusalem it is announced that God 'has wiped away the tears from every cheek'" (so the New Jerusalem Bible). Schaper also constructs the argument that the Greek word for "promise" used here, *epaggelia*, was intended "to mean the holy scriptures of Judaism *qua* embodiment of God's promise to Israel." The use of such technical terminology serves, to use a colloquial expression, to seal the deal. Here, as elsewhere, I would prefer a far more cautious evaluation of LXX Psalms that stresses possibility, rather than likelihood or even certainty.[11]

Psalm 59 (LXX 58) provides the next example for Schaper. The key verses, 12–13 in the Hebrew and 13–14 in the LXX, are translated in this way by NASB: "On account of the sin of their mouth and the words of their lips, Let them even be caught in their pride, And on account of curses and lies which they utter. Destroy them in wrath, destroy them, that they may be no more; That men may know that God rules in Jacob, To the ends of the earth." For this, LXX has, in Schaper's rendering: "With regard to the sin of their mouth, to the word of their lips,//let them be taken in their pride.//And because of their curses and their lies, acts of judgement will be pronounced// on the day of consummation, and they will be no more.//And they will know that God rules over Jacob, until the ends of the earth."

The key lexical item here is the Greek term *sunteleiai*. In general, this term refers to "destruction" in any number of possible contexts. In this instance, so Schaper submits, it is to be understood specifically as "an apocalyptical *terminus technicus.*" Schaper cites passages from LXX Daniel in support of his rendering "consummation" or "final judgement." Schaper also references the New Testament's frequent resort to "this particular usage ... in many of its copious references to the last judgment." We cannot but wonder if this later, Christian understanding of the term has influenced Schaper's analysis of its signification in this LXX passage.[12]

The last of Schaper's eschatologically significant passages from LXX Psalms derives from Psalm 73 (LXX 72). In his view, this psalm is a counterpart to Psalm 1: "Whereas in the former we find the idea that only the righteous will rise from the dead, the latter demonstrates another aspect of this fundamental belief, i.e. the concept that the wicked will forever be confined to the nether world." The key verse here is v. 4 in the Hebrew (v. 5 in the LXX), rendered in NASB as: "For there are no pains in their death; And their body is fat." For this verse in the Hebrew, Schaper prefers a different interpretation, as embodied in the RSV: "For they have no pangs; their bodies are sound and sleek."

In any case, so Schaper, the LXX translator understood the Hebrew in a way that comes closer to the literal translation of the NASB. So, "they [i.e., the sinners] will see no return from death//nor find steadfastness in their affliction." Schaper also offers an alternative rendering for the decidedly difficult second part of this verse in the Septuagint, "and there is steadfastness in their scourge (i.e. their punishment is perpetual)."[13] Whichever approach of Schaper finds favor, it definitely supports his overall picture, pieced together from the LXX Psalms passages he discusses, of eternal damnation, ceaseless punishment, and misery as the postmortem fate of the wicked. For them, there will be no resurrection and no reward.

I hope this presentation of Schaper's analysis of eschatologically significant LXX renderings in Psalms has been both fair to him and clear to readers.

It is possible to make a similar presentation of his discussion of passages where an enhanced sense of messianism has reputedly been introduced by the translator of LXX Psalms. However, it seems as if it would be more productive at this point to look at some of the reviews that Schaper's book garnered. In this instance, we are especially interested in reviewers' judgments as to the soundness (or lack thereof) in Schaper's methodology, for it is appropriate, as I see it, to be doubtful that unsound methodology will produce sound results.

Melvin K. H. Peters is critical of Schaper's lack of concern with "the history of the transmission of the Greek text on the one hand . . . [and] of the immediate context of a passage in question on the other. . . . Rather, he is more interested in tracing connections (echoes) in other parts of the Greek Bible, the Talmud, the Apocrypha, or Pseudepigrapha. For those enamored by that sort of midrash-like 'eclecticism,' this monograph will prove quite engaging; for those accustomed to more thoroughgoing, context-sensitive interpretive techniques, it will be disappointing." His summary judgment, to which I am sympathetic if not entirely in agreement with, is as follows: "Some may be convinced that a collection of weak examples makes a strong case, or that similarity indicates dependence, but such views are not everywhere held and certainly not in this quarter."[14]

In an article centering on LXX 49:15 (see above for Schaper's interpretation), but ranging far beyond this particular passage, Staffan Olofsson makes numerous observations about Schaper's methodology, not many of them positive in tone. While acknowledging that an LXX "translator [was] influenced by the interpretation prevalent in his lifetime and by his cultural and religious environment," Olofsson rejects the idea that this entitles a modern scholar "to suggest from differences between the meaning of the MT and the Greek translation and the use of certain Greek terms in Jewish interpretations of the Hebrew Bible that the translator is engaged in theological exegesis."[15] He quotes with approval Albert Pietersma's observation, in a review of Schaper, that it is "not acceptable methodologically, that one (or several) instances be given special treatment and be elevated to a higher level of interpretation . . . in distinction from the more mundane text-criticism."[16]

In outlining his own approach, Oloffson forthrightly states: "My methodological proposals do not presuppose that the theological convictions of the Septuagint translator . . . have not affected his translation in any way. They only suggest that in order to make that proposition probable one has first to take a look at more obvious possibilities of interpretation, since theological exegesis is not the primary aim of [the] translator [of LXX Psalms]."[17] Put succinctly, "the burden of proof is thus on the scholar who suggests that an interpretation of the [Greek] translator of the Hebrew text is at variance with the translation of the same or a similar Hebrew text in a modern translation is based on the theological *Tendenz* of the [Greek] translator."[18] The upshot of this criticism is, if I may put it this way, that Schaper has put the cart before the horse, the presupposition before the evidence, the conclusion before the hard work of textual criticism. Overall, if not at each particular point, I am in agreement with this assessment.

In one of his numerous articles on the LXX, Pietersma invites us to consider this issue from a larger perspective, even as we remain focused on the Greek Psalter. Here Pietersma constructs "a continuum for the field of Septuagint hermeneutics with minimalism at the one extreme and maximalism at the other." At the farthest reaches of the realm of the "minimalist," "the translator [is seen and understands himself or herself] as a mere medium (a conduit) of the source text. Such a translator, prototypically, does not add to nor subtract from the text being transmitted, nor are alterations made to it."[19] A "maximalist" understanding, with which Pietersma identifies Schaper, effectively elevates the Greek translator "to the status of an author, whose work becomes a substitute or replacement for the source text."[20] And, Pietersma adds, "Schaper is evidently not speaking of exegetical *potential* inadvertently created by the Greek translator, but about *actual* exegesis, consciously breathed into his text in the process of translating his source."[21]

This distinction, between actual and potential, is of utmost importance, as Pietersma effectively displays later in this same article through his analysis of several examples, also from LXX Psalms, on the part of Martin Rösel. After carefully examining these examples, he concludes: "All of [this] is not to say that the phrase in question cannot possibly be read in the way that Rösel seeks to read it. That the church Fathers often read [the Greek terms under investigation] as having to do with eschatological revelation is certainly true. . . . What I would suggest, however, is that here we are no longer in the domain of the original Septuagint, but at a certain stage in its reception history."[22] I yield to none in my almost unquenchable interest in the reception history of the Bible; however, I hope that I keep that interest separate from a focused concern on the meaning that a given word or passage held in its initial context. As I have observed at several points earlier in this article, it is not so clear that Schaper has consciously acknowledged these different stages and maintained the requisite distance between them.

The Afterlife in the Septuagint

This is not quite, however, the last word on eschatology in the LXX Psalter. In his monograph on the "translational technique" in LXX Psalter 3–41 for Hebrew verbs and participles, John Sailhamer subjects Psalm 37 to an extended study.[23] He determines that "the LXX translator was guided in his choice of equivalences by a social and religious interpretation of the psalm. The interest . . . is eschatological. This interest, the expectation of the coming age, had a significant impact on the choice of tenses in the LXX psalm. . . . In this area there was a measure of freedom to translate according to the understanding of the psalm by the translator, and thus the religious concerns of the translator show through."[24] Thus, it would be inappropriate to discount a heightened emphasis in eschatology in LXX Psalms simply by raising red flags at possible methodological shortcomings on the part of an individual scholar, in this case Schaper. The Greek Psalter undoubtedly merits further research.

THE BOOK OF JOB

Given the extensive length of the Psalter and its varied subject matter, we are not surprised that it has been the focus of numerous hypotheses, such as those related to eschatology and messianism. Another biblical book to which we might imagine researchers would turn is Job. It is an extraordinarily difficult book in almost all respects: its language, its structure, its probable (or possible) meanings. The Greek version of the book of Job is shorter than the traditional Hebrew or Masoretic text and exhibits a number of renderings that are demonstrably not literal.

In an article in the mid-1950s, Donald Gard discussed what he viewed as major components of the concept of the future life as constructed by the LXX translator of this book. He listed his examples in three categories: "one in which the future life is stated as a fact in G, one in which an afterlife is implied in G, and one in which the Greek translator describes conditions in the future life."[25]

For Gard, the prime example for category 1 (the future life is stated as a fact) is found in the Greek rendering of Job 14:14 (according to the verse numbering in the Hebrew). In Gard's translation, the Hebrew reads, "If a man die, will he live (again)?//All the days of my service I wait,//Until my relief should come." For this, the LXX has (again, in the rendering of Gard): "For if a man dies, he will live,//Having completed the days of his life;//I will abide until I be born again." "In other words," concludes Gard, "the Hebrew text merely raises the question concerning life after death, while G states it as a fact with the further assertion of a new existence for Job."[26]

In introducing examples from category 2, Gard writes: "It is the Greek translator's theology of the future life which governs his treatment of passages in the Hebrew in such a way as to *imply* a future life."[27] As his first example in this category, he cites Job 4:20b in the MT, where "Eliphaz stresses the ephemeral existence of human kings" with these words (as translated by Gard): "Without anyone's heeding they perish forever." By not providing a translation for the Hebrew word for "forever," "the rendering by the [Greek] translator does not exclude future life": "Because they were not able to help themselves, they perished" (in Gard's translation).[28]

Gard begins his discussion of examples in category 3 by asserting: "Since the translator does accept a life after death, it should not be surprising to note that he also indicates *conditions* in the afterlife."[29] The Greek rendering of the difficult Hebrew at 6:10, especially in its third line, "suggests a reason for Job's joy at the prospect of death—he has a claim to vindication in afterlife." Thus, the LXX reads (in Gard's translation): "So may my city be a grave,//Upon which, upon whose walls I used to leap, I will//not spare (i.e., refrain from, forbear);//For I have not falsified the holy words of my God."[30] "The kind of punishment which the Greek translator sees for the wicked in the future life is seen," for example, in his rendering of MT 40:13: "Hide (them) in the earth outside together;//But fill their faces with dishonor."[31]

Gard clearly set out his overall conclusions: "For the book of Job, the writer [Gard] concludes that differences between [the MT] and [LXX] in passages relating the afterlife are not due to a completely different *Vorlage*. The differences are due rather to a tendency on the part of the Greek translator to introduce a theological point of view."[32] Not surprisingly, Gard's methodology and conclusions have not stood unchallenged. In his criticism of a different but similarly situated book, Harry M. Orlinsky states forthrightly: the true nature of both the Hebrew and the Greek texts of Job "would be clear to anyone who would allow the Jewish translator and the author of the Hebrew text to speak for themselves where their texts are not obscure."[33] Orlinsky is surely not alone in judging that Gard is among those who have carried on a one-sided dialogue rather than an interactive discussion with the texts of Job. Nonetheless, we cannot exclude the possibility or even the probability that an enhanced interest in the afterlife does show up, if only very rarely, in LXX Job.

THE BOOK OF ISAIAH

The next examples are taken from the book of Isaiah. As is well known, it is this book that provided New Testament authors with their richest source of "scriptural" quotations and citations. Many factors led to this frequent use on their part, among them a number of passages that they read as predictive of the coming of Jesus and of the life, including the afterlife, that this momentous event (or, better, series of events) brought forth. However, as we saw earlier, especially in connection with the Psalter, we must try, even if we cannot always succeed, to distinguish the initial meaning of a Greek text from the way(s) it was later received.

Rodrigo de Sousa published an important monograph on eschatology and messianism in the Greek Isaiah chapters 1–12.[34] The first passage that he subjects to extended analysis is LXX Isaiah 2:2–4. This well-known passage, which in the Hebrew begins with "in the days to come" and concludes with the nations "never again know war," is obviously set in an eschatological context. Does the LXX rendering add to, subtract from, or simply maintain the contours of this context? The same question arises with reference to Isaiah 4:2–6, which in the Hebrew commences with a significant phrase, "in that day."

De Sousa concludes:

> A measure of contextual awareness would inform translational decisions in these sections. . . . It was noted that several of the eschatological ideas identifiable in the rendering are in common with other LXX texts, in both Isaiah and the larger LXX corpus. . . . It was also observed that . . . linguistic and co-textual considerations often impeded the identification of a particular "eschatological" rendering of a passage. . . . In this regard, I point to the fact that all the echoes of eschatological traditions supposedly identifiable can find some explanation in the translator's rendering of the *Vorlage*.[35]

In other words, the translator of Greek Isaiah was not engaged in the rewriting of some admittedly difficult Hebrew phrases, but instead sought to understand the text as best he could and to convey this understanding to his audience. Such nuanced conclusions lack the pyrotechnics of some others' pronouncements, but at the same time they inspire more confidence on the part of those seeking to determine the stance of a given LXX translator.

Let us conclude this section by looking at LXX 7:14–16, a passage that often forms a centerpiece in discussions of eschatology and messianism.

In de Sousa's rendering of the Greek, the LXX reads: "Therefore the Lord himself will give you a sign://See, the virgin will be pregnant and bear a son,// and you will call his name Immanuel.//He will eat butter and honey,// Before his either knowing or preferring evil// he will choose the good. For before the boy knows good or evil,//he refuses evil in order to choose the good;//and the land will be deserted//that you fear//because of its two kings."[36]

In spite of its later use, de Sousa maintains "that the rendering of LXX Isa 7:14–16 does not give sufficiently strong evidence of a conscious, systematic messianic reading of the passage. . . . The choice of *parthenon* does not seem to have any special significance. . . . The important points to note are that the translator of LXX Isa 7:16 understood the promised child of Isa 7 as having a proper name . . . and that he sought to safeguard his extraordinary moral character. In so doing, he inserted elements that belonged to wider streams of Jewish thought."[37] In reaching these conclusions, de Sousa is in basic agreement with Johan Lust, who writes: "Our reading . . . does not deny that the LXX facilitates a Christological-Messianic interpretation, especially with respect to its choice of words, in particular the use of the term *parthenon* 'virgin' and the future tense of the verbal expression 'she shall become pregnant.' On the other hand, it would seem that such a messianic accentuation was not intended by the translator."[38]

CONCLUDING OBSERVATIONS

It would be possible to draw further examples from passages here or there in other books of the Greek Bible. However, at this point such an approach, which would necessarily ignore larger contextual issues within the book or books selected, does not exemplify the careful methodology that was presented at the beginning of this paper and promoted in the following sections.

For some readers, the results of my analysis will be disappointing and largely negative. We cannot, for example, make any general statement about the Septuagint's stance toward major eschatological issues. Or, put another way, we simply cannot assert that the LXX translators consciously and deliberately changed their Hebrew *Vorlage* to reflect a heightened interest in the afterlife, even if that heightened interest was a growing influence within their Jewish community.

These "negative" judgments result from the make-up of the Septuagint as we now have it; namely, it is a heterogeneous collection of texts from different centuries, different cultural and religious milieus, different translators making use of diverse techniques to present the Hebrew to their Greek-speaking audience. While at the lexical level, there were some efforts to standardize the Greek representation of key Hebrew terms across the Septuagint, we can detect no such efforts in the realm of theology or ideology.

In the face of claims to the contrary, that is, claims that certain books of the LXX Bible do indeed reflect efforts by their translators to introduce eschatological concepts that go beyond the Hebrew *Vorlage*, only careful analysis, often word-by-word analysis, can determine the validity (or lack of validity) of such viewpoints. Most important with respect to methodology, the hard work of textual criticism must precede any claim of theological exegesis on the part of any translator of the Septuagint. It is, then, the responsibility of those who claim to detect such theological exegesis to prove their point. Setting the bar this high, which is an impediment to facile reasoning, is essential if we indeed seek to determine, to the best of our ability, what the translators themselves intended. And, as noted above, this is decidedly not the same thing as how these texts were interpreted later in very different religious and cultural contexts.

Beyond these considerations, we should remember this important observation: "In fact, it is not clear that the LXX translators would have viewed their task as compatible with giving expression to their (own) views of the afterlife. Other types of works, including (speculatively) commentaries and midrashim on the LXX, would have provided more likely vehicles for the presentation and reflection of their authors' views on eschatology."[39] We don't have ancient commentaries on the LXX composed by the translators themselves. But we do have many documents from the Jewish communities of the last centuries B.C.E. and first centuries C.E. It is to these that scholars turn to determine what Jews of this period were thinking about the afterlife and the postmortem vindication of the righteous and punishment of the evil. And that is as it should be.

ACKNOWLEDGMENT

This article first appeared as "The Afterlife in the Septuagint," in *Heaven, Hell, and the Afterlife: Eternity in Judaism, Christianity, and Islam*, volume 1 (ed. J. Harold Ellens; Santa Barbara: ABC-CLIO, 2013), 43–59. It is reprinted here, with slight revision, with permission of the publisher.

NOTES

1. See also, for example, the preliminary remarks in Alison Salvesen, "Messianism in Ancient Bible Translations in Greek and Latin," in *Redemption and Resistance: Festschrift*

for William Horbury (ed. M. Bockmuehl and J. N. Carlton Paget; Edinburgh, 2007), 245–48.

2. For details on the topics mentioned in this and the following paragraphs, see Leonard Greenspoon, "The Septuagint," in *The New Interpreter's Dictionary of the Bible* (Nashville: Abingdon, 2009), 5.170–77.

3. Joachim Schaper, *Eschatology in the Greek Psalter* (Wissenschaftliche Untersuchungen zum Neuen Testament—2. Reihe 76; Tübingen: J. C. B. Mohr [Paul Siebeck]), 46–48.

4. Karen H. Jobes and Moisés Silva, *Invitation to the Septuagint* (Grand Rapids: Baker, 2000).

5. Schaper, *Eschatology*, 49.

6. Ibid., 50.

7. Ibid., 50–52.

8. Ibid., 52–53.

9. Ibid., 53–57.

10. Ibid., 57–62.

11. Ibid., 62–65.

12. Ibid., 65–68.

13. Ibid., 68–72.

14. Melvin K. H. Peters, "Review of *Eschatology in the Greek Psalter*, by Joachim Schaper," *Journal of Biblical Literature* 116 (1997): 350–52.

15. Staffan Olofsson, "Death Shall Be Their Shepherd: An Interpretation of Ps 49:15 in LXX," in *Helsinki Perspectives on the Translation Technique of the Septuagint: Proceedings of the IOSCS Congress in Helsinki 1999* (ed. Raija Sollamo and Seppo Sipilä; Publications of the Finnish Exegetical Society 82; Helsinki: Finnish Exegetical Society, 2001), 143–44.

16. Ibid., 144.

17. Ibid., 144–45.

18. Ibid., 145.

19. Albert Pietersma, "Exegesis in the Septuagint: Possibilities and Limits (The Psalter as a Case in Point)," in *Septuagint Research: Issues and Challenges in the Study of the Greek Jewish Scriptures* (ed. Wolfgang Kraus and R. Glenn Wooden; SBL Septuagint and Cognate Studies 53; Atlanta: Society of Biblical Literature, 2006), 35.

20. Ibid., 36.

21. Ibid.

22. Ibid., 41–42.

23. John H. Sailhamer, *Translational Technique of the Greek Septuagint (Pss. 3–41)* (New York: Peter Lang, 1991), 149–73.

24. Ibid., 149–50, 173.

25. H. Gard, "The Concept of the Future Life According to the Greek Translator of the Book of Job," *Journal of Biblical Literature* 7 (1954): 137.

26. Ibid., 137–38, followed by other examples from category 1.

27. Ibid., 139.

28. Ibid., 139–40.

29. Ibid., 140.

30. Ibid., 141–42.

31. Ibid., 142–43.

32. Ibid., 143.

33. Harry M. Orlinsky, "Review of *Studies in the Septuagint: I. Book of Job; II. Chronicles* by Gillis Gerleman," *Journal of Biblical Literature* 67 (1948): 386.

34. Rodrigo F. de Sousa, *Eschatology and Messianism in LXX Isaiah 1–12* (The Library of Hebrew Bible/Old Testament Studies 516; New York: T & T Clark, 2010).

35. Ibid., 68.

36. Ibid., 70–71.

37. Ibid., 101–2.

38. Johan Lust, *Messianism and Septuagint: Collected Essays* (Louvain: Peeters, 2004), 175.

39. Jobes and Silva, *Invitation*, 302.

Rabbi Akiva, Other Martyrs, and Socrates: On Life, Death, and Life After Life

Naftali Rothenberg

The passing of sages in general and the execution of the Ten Martyrs in particular feature prominently in talmudic and midrashic legend. Rabbi Akiva's death, however, would seem to have left a greater impression in rabbinic literature than the deaths of all of the other *Tannaim* and *Amoraim*. The legends about Rabbi Akiva's death contend with two main dilemmas. First, horror at his cruel end and the manner in which this very old man (120 years old, according to legend) was executed. The dilemma here pertains to the issue of theodicy, in the case of one who lived a long and full life and came to such a terrible end. The second dilemma concerns the meaning of the death of someone who strove so hard to give meaning to his life, and especially to the suffering and misfortune that befell him throughout it. Life is the ground upon which meaning is built, and when it comes to a close, is death meaningless?

IS THIS THE TORAH AND THIS ITS REWARD?!

The talmudic and midrashic legends tell how Rabbi Akiva captured the attention of figures such as Adam and Moses. These legends further enhanced the status of Rabbi Akiva in cultural consciousness—by comparing him to the fathers of the world and the nation and placing him on a par with them. As recounted in the Talmud, the first to be struck by the unreasonableness of Rabbi Akiva's death was Adam, who, "when he reached the generation of Rabbi Akiva, rejoiced in his Torah and was saddened by his death."[1] Another well-known legend, which tells of Moses's discovery of Rabbi Akiva, heightens the dilemma associated with the latter's death:

> Rabbi Yehudah said in the name of Rav: When Moses ascended to heaven, he found God sitting and tying crowns to the letters. He said to Him: "Master of the Universe, who requires this of you?" He said to him: "There is a man who will live in a few generations and Akiva ben Joseph is his name, who will learn mounds and mounds of laws from each cusp. . . ." He [Moses] said to Him: "Master of the Universe, You have shown me the Torah; show me its reward!" He said

to him: "Look behind you.' He looked behind him and saw them weighing his [Rabbi Akiva's] flesh in the market. He said to Him: "Master of the Universe, is this the Torah and this its reward?" He said to him: "Silence! That is how I conceived it." (BT, *Menahot* 29b)

There is no attempt whatsoever, in this text, to justify the fact of Rabbi Akiva's brutal murder, merely arbitrary and unquestioning acceptance of God's decree. The bluntness of God's answer to Moses, as formulated by the author of this legend, heightens the pointlessness of theodicy and strengthens the sense of injustice at the death of Rabbi Akiva. Consequently, it is not God's reply—unequivocal, absolute, and so hard for the human mind to accept—that has remained in the minds of readers and scholars, but rather Moses's resounding cry: "Master of the universe, is this the Torah and this its reward?!"

Although some explain God's answer to mean that one must not question His ways and deeds[2] or "investigate that which is beyond one's understanding,"[3] and although the reply was ultimately intended for ordinary readers and students, we cannot overlook the fact that, in the context of the legend itself, it was not given to just any prophet or sage, but to Moses our teacher, greatest of all the prophets past and future. It would not be the way of readers of the Aggadah to be satisfied with a simple a fortiori deduction ("If even Moses received such an answer, who are we to expect anything more?"). As noted, what has remained most impressed upon the minds of these readers is in fact Moses's anguished cry: "Is this the Torah and this its reward?!"

Indeed this cry has reverberated throughout Jewish history, from the days of the Talmud to the present, and lies at the heart of discussion of injustice in the world, divine providence, reward and punishment, the suffering of the righteous, and the prosperity of the wicked. The cry is echoed in the words of the rabbis concerning the Ten Martyrs,[4] brutally executed by the Romans.

According to the midrash of the Ten Martyrs, the first to be executed was Simeon ben Gamaliel, president [*nasi*] of the Sanhedrin, who was beheaded. Rabbi Ishmael the High Priest is said to have held Rabbi Simeon's head in his hands, bitterly crying, "Where is the Torah and where is its reward! How the tongue that explained the Torah in seventy tongues now licks the dust!"[5] Rabbi Ishmael justifies his outburst, explaining that Simeon ben Gamaliel had been greater than him in Torah and wisdom, and his death was thus a great loss to him personally and to the entire generation. Death itself is meaningless. The consequences of Simeon ben Gamaliel's absence, however, were considerable: for himself, as he was no longer able to engage in in his lifetime pursuit—explaining the Torah in every tongue—for Rabbi Ishmael and for the entire Jewish people.

In a number of midrashim, the cry is attributed to the angels, remonstrating against God. When Rabbi Ishmael was killed, the executioner removed the skin of his face. When he reached the place where the phylacteries are laid, Rabbi Ishmael uttered a terrible cry that shook the divine throne. "The ministering angels [then] said to the Holy One, blessed be He: 'That a righteous man such as he, to whom You revealed all of the mysteries of the upper realms and the secrets of the lower realms, should be killed so horribly by this wicked man. Is this the Torah and this its reward?'"[6] In attributing shock to the upper realms, to the divine throne, and to the angels—whose entire existence is marked by immutable order—the author seeks to ascribe to the deaths of the Martyrs the power to disrupt the very foundations of the universe. At Rabbi Akiva's death, the angels too[7]—not only Moses, as in the source cited above—cry out to God: "Is this the Torah and this its reward?!"

The story of Rabbi Ishmael's death stresses the preferability of observance of the precepts in this world to everlasting life in the world to come. As we will see below, the story of Rabbi Akiva's death highlights the same principle. There is a certain similarity between the modes of execution: Rabbi Akiva's flesh is scored with iron combs, and Rabbi Ishmael's face is skinned. Their behavior is also similar, in the self-restraint they show as they are put to death. Rabbi Akiva fulfils the commandment of reciting the Shema, and Rabbi Ishmael cries out only when the executioner reaches the place where the phylacteries are laid—causing the Roman emperor to ask: "Until now, you neither wept nor cried out, yet now you cry out?" Rabbi Ishmael replied: "I do not cry out for my soul but for the commandment of the phylacteries that has been taken from me." To their dying breaths, Rabbi Ishmael and Rabbi Akiva dedicated every human effort to doing what is right in this world. Their entire interpretive focus, according to the aggadic texts, is on life, not on what happens to the soul after death.

When Rabbi Hanina ben Teradion is burned alive,[8] wrapped in a Torah scroll, his daughter cries: "Is this the Torah and this its reward?!" A dialogue ensues between them, in which Rabbi Hanina rejects her words—perhaps also to comfort her and to give her strength—asserting that such a cry is misplaced: "If it is for me that you cry, I accept my suffering with love, and would rather atone for my sins and be consumed by flames fanned by man in this world than by flames that are not fanned—the flames of Gehenna."[9] He considers the possibility, however, that her shock may be due not to his execution, but to the burning of the Torah scroll, adding: "And if it is for the Torah scroll that you weep, the Torah is fire and cannot be consumed by fire. Its words fly in the air, and the fire merely consumes the parchment."[10] According to this approach, the shock at Hanina ben Teradion's execution by fire and the burning of the Torah scroll was the result of the limited vision of those who, like Hanina's daughter, witnessed the terrible event, but were unable to detach themselves from the horror and interpret it on a deeper level. Extreme suffering was a privilege, purifying him of his sins—perhaps even granted to him as a reward for his devotion, rather than inflicted as a punishment.

One must also transcend the barbaric act of burning a holy book. The holiness of the Torah is not a function of its physical components. The comparison to fire is apt, as fire cannot consume fire. "Its words fly in the air," as the Torah, according to Rabbi Hanina, is its content, not ink on parchment. There is thus no reason to cry out in remonstration or in pain. The human oppressor and the visible horror must be transcended, and the event perceived as one of purification, the significance of which bears no relation to destruction and death, but rather to a fire that cannot be consumed and to words that fly in the air.

Rabbi Akiva's death may also be seen in the context of the eternity of the Torah or the bond to the eternal enjoyed by its students—particularly in light of his exchange with Pappus ben Judah.[11] Although Rabbi Akiva disapproved of some of Pappus's teachings,[12] the following, well-known exchange pertains directly to Torah study at a time when it was prohibited by the authorities and to the punishment incurred by those who violate the interdiction. The exchange takes place on two separate occasions: when Rabbi Akiva teaches Torah in public, in violation of the ban against Torah study, and when the two men find themselves together in a Roman prison:

> The Rabbis taught: Once, the wicked government decreed that the Jews should not engage in Torah study. Pappus ben Judah came upon Rabbi Akiva, who was gathering crowds together and publicly engaging in Torah study. He said to him: "Akiva, are you not afraid of the government?" He replied: "I will give you a parable. It is like a fox who was walking along the river bank, and he saw fish moving together from place to place. He said to them: 'What are you fleeing from?' They replied: 'From the nets that men cast over us.' He said to them: 'Why don't you come up to the land, and you and I will dwell together, as my ancestors dwelled with yours?' They replied: 'Are you the one they call the cleverest of animals? You are not clever,

but a fool! If we are afraid in our vital element, how much more so in an element in which we would die!' So too are we. If this is the way things are now that we sit and engage in the Torah, of which it is written 'for that it is your life and the length of your days,' how much worse they would be if we were to abstain from it."

It is told that not long passed before Rabbi Akiva was caught and thrown in prison, and Pappus ben Judah was caught and imprisoned with him. He said to him: "Pappus! Who has brought you here?" He responded: "Fortunate are you, Rabbi Akiva, for having been arrested for Torah study; woe to Pappus who was arrested for idle words" (BT *Berakhot* 61b).

At their first encounter, Pappus sounds responsible and rational.[13] At a time of such decrees, it would have been prudent to study Torah in secret and certainly not to provoke the authorities by gathering large crowds. To Rabbi Akiva, however, the suspension of public instruction, which lies at the heart of national, cultural life, would have constituted a kind of collective, spiritual-cultural suicide. There was little doubt that they would be caught in the Roman nets, but suspending communal study would have been even worse. Was Pappus convinced by Rabbi Akiva's explanation? We don't know, because the talmudic legend cites no reply on his part.

The exchange continues in prison, and this time the final word is given to Pappus, who makes a clear distinction between the cruel regime that imprisons and executes at will and the actions of the condemned. It is the latter that define the significance of the punishment. For Pappus, who was arrested for idle words, the punishment was indeed a punishment. He was seized, like so many others under Roman rule, without having done anything wrong—merely for having asked Rabbi Akiva a question, received an answer, and remained silent. It was enough for the authorities that he did not dispute Rabbi Akiva's statement, and so they arrested him for his silence. Rabbi Akiva, on the other hand, was arrested for having flagrantly violated a government decree: gathering crowds and publicly teaching Torah. For Rabbi Akiva, the punishment was, in fact, a reward: "This is the Torah and this is its reward!"— in the most literal sense, not as a remonstration against heaven or a cry of pain.

The cry "Is this is the Torah" is generally understood as referring specifically to Torah study—to the diligence, knowledge, and scholarship of the Ten Martyrs.

An unusual use of "This is the Torah and this its reward" can be found in the case of Elisha ben Abuyah ("Aher"), who witnessed the martyrs' deaths and drew very different conclusions from those drawn by most of his friends and colleagues. The sight of the severed tongue of Rabbi Judah the baker in the mouth of a dog is said to have been one of the things that led Ben Abuyah to abandon his faith and deny its tenets. If "this is the Torah and this its reward," concluded Elisha, it is pointless to study Torah and observe the precepts, and there is no reward and punishment in the world.[14]

"Is this the Torah and this its reward?" (or in the affirmative: "This is the Torah and this its reward") has been used to convey various meanings and has been variously interpreted: as an expression of deep shock; a remonstration against heaven, voiced by human beings or angels; an introduction to a discussion of reward and punishment; an introduction to a discussion of theodicy; a reaffirmation of the rewards enjoyed by the righteous in this world and especially in the world to come; or a rejection of divine providence and retribution.

As noted at the beginning of this chapter, the talmudic text that recounts Moses's shock at Rabbi Akiva's "reward" does not address the issue of theodicy at all. There is one source, not a central one, that attests to Rabbi Akiva's theodicy,[15] capable of shaping interpretations of Rabbi Akiva's death—based, rather, on a broad range of relevant texts. It does not appear among the talmudic and midrashic legends that seek to tell the story of Rabbi Akiva, but derives from a later source, dedicated primarily to the issue of theodicy with regard to the deaths of the Ten Martyrs. Thus, even if we were to claim that the author of this legend had found an appropriate answer to Moses's resounding question, "Is this the Torah and this its reward?" (assuming that it does, indeed, explain the brutal killing itself from a theodicy perspective), the question of meaning would still remain. It is meaning—so central to Rabbi Akiva in his lifetime and at the heart of the earlier midrashim that deal with his philosophy and life story—that is the primary concern of the legends that describe his behavior and words at the time of his execution.

A FINAL LESSON IN THE PHILOSOPHY OF LOVE

The meaning of Rabbi Akiva's death is in fact discussed in a number of places. Some, like the following text, pertain directly to his image as the sage of love:

> When they took Rabbi Akiva to be executed, it was the appointed hour for reciting the *Shema*. As they were scoring his flesh with iron combs, he accepted the yoke of heaven, and his students said to him: "Rabbi, even now?!" He said to them: "All my days I grieved at the words 'with all your soul' (*Deuteronomy* 6:5)—even when your soul

is taken from you. I said: when will I have the opportunity to fulfil this? And now that the opportunity presents itself, will I not fulfil it?" He drew out [the word] "one" [*ehad*] until his soul departed with "one." (BT, *Berakhot* 61a)

The final lesson on the philosophy of love was given by the sage of love at the moment of his execution. His students, who had learned from him, during the years of their studies, that suffering is beloved and must be accepted and even embraced, were unable to come to terms with his death. Those who had been at his side at the time of his son's death, and even then wondered at his behavior, find it difficult to maintain their composure, but faced with their rabbi's equanimity, make an effort to control themselves. Had they wanted to cry or shout, they could not have done so in the presence of this man who, even as he was being tortured to death, accepted the yoke of heaven by reciting the Shema—with serenity, composure, and focus.

These circumstances were unlike anything they had experienced or learned with Rabbi Akiva before. Even when a person suffers terrible anguish and great misfortunes befall him, he is still a living, breathing human being, beyond the suffering and the misfortune. The meaning of suffering lies in life itself and is afforded by the living. We can thus understand and accept, albeit with great difficulty, theodicy and the acceptance of suffering, based on the distinction between the afflicted and the affliction and based on the hope that redemption may be attained through suffering and from suffering. As witnesses to the execution of Rabbi Akiva, what they experienced was the absolute, the point of no return—a situation in which one can no longer distinguish between the man and his fate, to cease to exist. All they had learned from their teacher up to this point about theodicy and the meaning of suffering was no longer applicable, because it pertained only to those who live in this world—capable, in their imaginations, in their mind's eye, of envisioning themselves alive after having been delivered from their misfortunes. Meaning is manifested in moral behavior, in observing the commandments and in living up to one's obligations in a given situation. As unbearable as it may be, it is still existence as opposed to nonexistence or to the nullification of existence that is the result of death.

They watch him as he is executed, with admiration, profound grief, shock at the violence of the event and the cruelty of the executioners, and anxiety at the imminent separation and their approaching orphanhood. Among all of these raging emotions, however, their greatest fear is that his loss will lack meaning. As faithful students who have internalized his philosophy of meaning that affords value and significance to every situation and event, they turn to him with a question-cry: "Rabbi, even now?!" Here and now, as you are being executed and are a hairsbreadth from certain death, have you not reached the point at which all meaning is lost? Do you even now hold fast to your principles? Do you even now accept God's judgement? Until when?

And Rabbi Akiva, clearly, precisely, and simply, explains to his students the meaning of his death: love. Love to the last breath! The Torah is the Torah of love and it commands us to love God—a commandment that, under ordinary circumstances, can never be fully observed. "All my days I grieved at the words 'with all thy soul.'" As the sage of love, Rabbi Akiva was keenly aware of the fact that one of the most important of the precepts of love—"And you shall love the Lord your God with all your heart, and with all your soul and with all your might" (Deut 6:5)—cannot be fulfilled in its entirety. Most people will never have the chance to observe the commandment to love God "with all your soul," even at the time of their death. Throughout his life, he mourned the almost certain incompleteness of his observance of the commandment to love God. "And now that the opportunity presents itself will I not fulfil it?" What could possibly afford more meaning, at that moment in time, his last, the point of no return that is death? "'With all your soul' (Deut 6:5)—even when your soul is taken from you!"

As the legionnaires score his flesh with iron combs to end his life in terrible agony, he accepts the yoke of heaven and teaches those around him—in word and deed—the meaning of his death. Something is missing, however, in this incredible exchange between Rabbi Akiva and his students, something very basic. Rabbi Akiva chooses not to answer their question—"Even now?"—in the simplest, most obvious way: life after death. He could have told them that there is no question of loss of meaning because the body is merely a vessel, and the soul returns to its source. At the most appropriate time imaginable, he does not discuss belief in the world to come, eschewing the relatively easy solution to the problem of meaning in his death. His emphasis is on what one can still do in this world: to complete the commandment to love God. To his mind, meaning must be sought in life itself and not beyond it.

Rabbi Akiva's avoidance of the subject of life after death at such an obvious juncture becomes even more pronounced upon examining the concepts he employs in his brief words to his students: "He said to them: 'All my days I grieved at the words "with all your soul [*nafshekha*]" (Deut 6:5)—even when your soul [*nishmatkha*] is taken from you. I said: when will I have the opportunity to fulfil this? And now that the opportunity presents itself will I not fulfil it?'"

The meanings associated with the words *nefesh* and *neshamah* (both translated "soul" here) are many and varied. The following is presented as an interpretative suggestion that need not address each and every use or inflection of these two concepts in the Bible and rabbinic literature. The basis for the discussion will be the primary meaning of these words in the first part of the book of Genesis and elsewhere in the Pentateuch. Genesis 2:7 reads: "And the Lord God formed man of the dust of the ground, and breathed into his nostrils the breath of life [*nishmat hayyim*]; and man became a living soul [*nefesh hayyah*]." The word *nefesh* is used in a similar fashion with regard to the prohibition against eating consuming blood: "Only be strong not to eat the blood, for the blood is the life [*nefesh*], and you shall not eat the life with the flesh" (Deut 12:23).

Before addressing the various homiletic interpretations of these words, I would like to note that the term *hisha'arut hanefesh* [life after death; literally "remaining of the soul"] is a borrowed one, which first appears in Jewish sources in the early Middle Ages. Earlier rabbinic sources use the term *hayyei ha'olam haba*, sometimes in the sense of life after death and sometimes in other senses. For the purposes of the present discussion, emphasis will be placed on fulfilment of the commandment to love God "with all your soul [*nafsheka*]," until the moment at which one no longer has a *nefesh* because it has been taken away. The only question that interests Rabbi Akiva is "Will I fulfil it?"—What commandment has reality presented him with that he might fulfil? And what of the soul [*neshamah*] and the world to come [or *hisha'arut hanefesh*]? Rabbi Akiva is wholly absorbed by "with all your soul" [*bekhol nafsheka*]. According to the talmudic and midrashic legends, he devotes neither thought nor speech to the matter and conveys nothing regarding the fate of the soul that is about to be taken from him. His immense effort focuses entirely on that which he can do as long as he has the "breath of life" [*nishmat hayyim*] within him—as long as he is a living soul [*nefesh hayyah*].[16] With his body, he can fully observe the commandment of love. The question of the soul and its fate is not broached at all.

This is not the first time that Rabbi Akiva's students are exposed to this view, which is in fact part of a consistent method revealed on various occasions. The most striking of these concerns Rabbi Akiva's behavior at the bedside of his teacher, Rabbi Eliezer ben Hyrcanus, who lay dying in agony.[17] His friends, Rabbi Joshua, Rabbi Tarfon, and Rabbi Elazar ben Azariah, also present at their teacher's bedside, rose above the moment, the pain and the suffering, to speak of eternal life and the immortal soul: "and my master is in this world and the next."[18] Rabbi Akiva, on the other hand, frankly and determinedly returned Rabbi Elazar to reality, with all its difficulties, as the only place in which man can find meaning—preventing him from escaping for even a single moment to the world of eternity and immortality. "Beloved is suffering" here and now because of the moral opportunity it provides for true introspection and for accepting it with love. Even at the time of his own death, he does not want to escape the final terrible moments to reassuring descriptions of the hereafter. He finds his peace in these very moments and in the moral challenge they present—a challenge that only life in this world can offer.

The circumstances intensify the moral dimension of fulfilling the commandment to love God. The Roman legionnaires score his flesh with iron combs, as they torture him to death. There is of course a kind of connection—physical contact—between the executioners and the condemned prisoner. In their every movement, in every piece of flesh they tear from his body, they represent the greatest possible moral depravity—their own and that of the regime that ordered them to do such things on a mission of hatred. (My use of the expression "mission of hatred" here, with regard to the executioners, is meant to create a parallel to the executed sage's mission of love and makes no claims regarding the actual presence of hatred.) It would have been perfectly understandable had the condemned man cursed his executioners as they tormented him, but that would have transformed the forced physical contact into a kind of dialogue on the same plane of hatred. Rabbi Akiva manages to isolate himself completely from the executioners, whose hold on his body is one-sided.[19] The text gives eloquent expression to the fact that the two sides acted entirely independently: "As they were scoring his flesh with iron combs, he accepted the yoke of heaven."

Not only does he not curse them; he does not respond to their actions at all—not even to cry out at the terrible pain they are inflicting on him. There is no dialogue whatsoever between the executioners and the prisoner, who utters neither curses nor cries nor moans. High above their low plane of moral depravity, opposite executioners and rulers who have lost their humanity, Rabbi Akiva presents another, separate plane of moral behavior, through which—in observing the commandment of loving God to the fullest at a time of suffering and in the face of death—he teaches his students and future generations the connection between morality and love. This is Rabbi Akiva's final lesson in the philosophy of love.

SOCRATES AND HIS COMPANIONS COMPARED TO RABBI AKIVA AND HIS STUDENTS

It is interesting to compare the discussion between Rabbi Akiva and his students during his execution and the conversation between Socrates and his companions as the time approached for him to drink the cup of hemlock—particularly with regard to the question of the immortality of the soul.[20] Both accounts stress the equanimity with which the two men accept their deaths, in sharp contrast to the agitation of those around them. Rabbi Akiva, who is subjected to terrible torments, accepts the yoke of heaven with composure and devotion. His students cannot allow themselves to cry out or weep in the face of their rabbi's composure. Socrates's companions burst into tears, and he rebukes them. There too it seems as if the circumstances weigh more heavily upon those who will be left behind than upon Socrates himself, who remains calm until the very end. The similarity between the two stories ends, however, at the composure with which the protagonists accept their deaths and the behavior of those around them. The discussion of the meaning of death and the source of Socrates's comfort could not be more different from that of Rabbi Akiva.

Socrates's companions come to visit him in prison on the day of his execution by poison. They try to convince him to escape and save his soul or at least to ask his judges for a pardon or a reprieve. A discussion ensues, during the course of which Socrates rejects their proposals. The event and Socrates's arguments are described at length in Plato's dialogue *Phaedo*.

The basis of the Socratic-Platonic discussion is the dichotomy between the mortal body and the immortal soul, whereby the body hinders the development of the soul as it sways human actions toward the satisfaction of physical desires. Life is thus a struggle between the desires of the body and the aspirations of the soul to join the forms—something that is possible only after death, once the soul has departed the body. Therefore, every person, and especially philosophers who have devoted their lives to approaching the forms ("ideas") and have lived the good life in practice and pursuit of knowledge, should welcome death. One may not commit suicide, that is, separate the soul from the body, or precipitate death, but death should not be feared when it comes, as the world of meaning, the world of forms, lies beyond death. Those who have nurtured their souls while still attached to their bodies—and none more than the philosopher—will attain their ultimate goal after death. This idea, expressed in the *Phaedo* and in Plato's theory of the soul in general, laid the foundations for the theology of the body and the soul found in important religious currents, particularly in the monotheistic faiths.[21]

The comparison between Socrates and Rabbi Akiva is important, due to the absence of theological discourse concerning the immortality of the soul and its significance in the description of the latter's death. Rabbi Akiva identifies the realm of human action from birth to death as the locus of meaning. Although Socrates ascribes great importance to human action and behavior in this life, he finds the locus of meaning in the world beyond death, where the soul can finally unite with the intelligible forms.

The Platonic dialogue also addresses political questions of government and law that have no parallel in the story of Rabbi Akiva's execution. Socrates, a respectable Athenian citizen, is sentenced to death by a particularly large jury, comprising five hundred and one of his city's most prominent citizens. He believes they were wrong to accept the accusations against him and to reject his own defense. Nevertheless, he recognizes the legitimacy of the Athenian political and legal systems, including eventual errors in judgement, as in his case. Rabbi Akiva's execution, on the other hand, is carried out by a foreign regime, illegitimate in his eyes and in the eyes of most of his countrymen,[22] and his behavior intensifies and highlights the immorality of his executioners.

We are thus left with the comparison to Socrates, who chooses to comfort his companions, telling them that they should not grieve at his death because death is not the end for the essence of man, which is the soul. The conclusion he draws from this is a moral one:

> [I]f the soul is really immortal, what care should be taken of her, not only in respect of the portion of time which is called life, but of eternity! And the danger of neglecting her from this point of view does indeed appear to be awful. If death had only been the end of all, the wicked would have had a good bargain in dying, for they would have been happily quit not only of their body, but of their own evil together with their souls. But now . . . there is no release or salvation from evil except the attainment of the highest virtue and wisdom. (Plato, *Phaedo* 106–7, trans. Benjamin Jowett)

In the crux of the discussion, he seeks to prove the immortality of the soul as compared to the body's ephemerality and finite existence after death. Socrates (according to Plato) presents theological/metaphysical arguments, from which he draws moral conclusions. As noted, Rabbi Akiva could easily have made the very same argument, yet he does not turn to theology, choosing rather to focus entirely on the moral argument. The moral import of Socrates's words pertains to the way in which one should approach death but make no claims regarding the continued effort to hold onto life and to continue to act in a moral fashion. The main thrust of his parting discourse is the assertion that death is merely a passage to immortality:

> [I]nasmuch as the soul is shown to be immortal . . . let a man be of good cheer about his soul, who hast cast away the pleasures and ornaments of the body . . . and has followed after the pleasures of knowledge in this life; who has adorned the soul in her own proper jewels, which are temperance, and justice, and courage, and nobility, and truth—in these arrayed she is ready to go on her journey to the world below, when her time comes.

Although Plato does not preach abstinence and those who satisfy the needs of the body are not considered sinners, such actions are ultimately meaningless—a consequence of physical existence, for as long as the soul is attached to the body, that is, for as long as one lives. After death, the soul of one who has lived a worthy life—of a philosopher who has nurtured his soul by studying, helping others, and fulfilling his duties to society as a soldier or a law-abiding citizen; of one who has told the truth and pursued justice—will attain its rightful place in the world of forms. Such a person has nothing to fear from death and should be prepared for it. It is these thoughts that Socrates shares with his companions, as his own death approaches.

On the basis of these claims regarding the body, the soul, and the different meaning death holds for each of them, he comforts his companions, telling them that that they should not grieve at the burial of his body:

> [W]hen I have drunk the poison I shall leave you . . . and then he [Crito] will suffer less at my death, and not be grieved when he sees my body being burned or buried. I would not have him sorrow at my hard lot, or say at the burial, Thus we lay out Socrates, or Thus we follow him to the grave or bury him; for false words are not only evil in themselves, but they infect the soul with evil.

Socrates does not cling to life or delay drinking the poison until the last possible minute—further emphasizing the fact that his death derives its meaning not from life itself, but from the immortality of the soul. From the moment he comes to terms with his death, Socrates no longer values life: what is another hour of life as compared to eternity?

It is in these few minutes that the difference between Socrates and Rabbi Akiva lies. Rabbi Akiva refuses to cease pursuing his moral objective in this world for even a single instant and thus clings to the most terrible moments of his life as if they were the greatest of treasures. Socrates believes that man enters this world unwillingly and must strive to live in a good and fitting manner, but there is no point in clinging to life when eternity is just around the corner. When man is about to coalesce with ultimate meaning, he can only laugh at himself for trying to give meaning to another few moments of life.

The differences between these two positions can be summed up in the words of Rabbi Jacob Kurshai,[23] teacher of Rabbi Judah ha-Nasi—without attempting, as he does, to resolve the dilemma that arises from the juxtaposition of the two positions or claiming that there is no problem at all: "One hour spent in repentance and good deeds in this world is better than the whole of life in the world to come; and one hour of satisfaction in the world to come is better than the whole of life in this world" (Mishnah, *Avot* 4, 17). In the previous Mishnah (*Avot* 4,16), Rabbi Jacob stresses the importance of action in this world: "This world is like an antechamber before the next world. Prepare yourself in the antechamber, that you might enter the banquet hall." These words correspond to the Socratic-Platonic view. In this Mishnah (4,17), Rabbi Jacob maintains the distinction between this world—the world of action, in which one must aspire to perfection through repentance and good deeds—and the next world—the world of reward and spiritual enjoyment. There is no equivalence between "repentance and good deeds," which are moral objectives, and "satisfaction," which is spiritual fulfilment because they belong to different worlds. Some have suggested another reading of the Mishnah: "One hour spent in repentance and good deeds in this world is like life in the world to come."[24]

It is thus up to man to choose: Rabbi Akiva decided in favor of one hour spent in repentance and good deeds in this world, and the proposed reading of the Mishnah concords with his view; while Socrates decided in favor of an hour of satisfaction in the world to come. In his final words, however, Socrates momentarily returns the moral argument to the fore, albeit in a rather ludicrous fashion, as if the author (Plato) did not wish to eclipse his earlier message:

> [A]nd the servant went in, and remained for some time, and then returned with the jailer carrying a cup of poison. Socrates said: "You, my good friend, who are experienced in these matters, shall give me directions how I am to proceed." The man answered: "You have only to walk about until your legs are heavy, and then to lie down, and the poison will act." At the same time he handed the cup to Socrates, who in the easiest and gentlest manner, without

the least fear or change of color or feature, looking at the man with all his eyes . . . and said: "What do you say about making a libation out of this cup to any god? May I, or not?" The man answered: "We only prepare, Socrates, just so much as we deem enough." "I understand," he said: "yet I may and must pray to the gods to prosper my journey from this to that other world—may this, then, which is my prayer, be granted to me." Then holding the cup to his lips, quite readily and cheerfully he drank off the poison. . . . He was beginning to grow cold . . . when he uncovered his face, for he had covered himself up, and said (they were his last words)—he said: "Crito, I owe a cock to Asclepius; will you remember to pay the debt?" (Plato, *Phaedo* 117–18)

Three statements link Socrates's death and the departure of his soul to the divine. The first—his enquiry (whether serious, humorous, or ironic) about poring a libation to the gods from his cup of poison. They are immortal, so the poison would not harm them. It would provoke the death of his body but, at the same time, would link his soul to the eternal, that is, to the gods. This is perhaps the serious dimension of Socrates's question: is it fitting to pour a libation to the gods from the cup of poison that will cause the death of his body and the passage of his soul to the realm of eternity? The representative of the authorities, the jailer responsible for carrying out the sentence, does not allow himself to be dragged into philosophical/theological questions, but responds matter-of-factly that the cup contains just enough poison to kill the condemned. Socrates therefore makes do with a prayer for the felicitous departure of his soul from this world to the realm of the souls. This is his second statement. Both the attempt to pour a libation and the prayer are meant to propitiate the gods and receive their blessing and assistance for a successful passage of the soul to the next world. Socrates's prayer, therefore, cannot be compared to Rabbi Akiva's recitation of the Shema, which is nether prayer nor supplication but acceptance of the yoke of heaven and utmost fulfilment of the commandment to love God.[25] Socrates petitions the gods for his own sake, while Rabbi Akiva observes God's commandments out of love, asking for nothing in return.

Socrates uttered his third statement shortly before his soul departed: "I owe a cock to Asclepius; will you remember to pay the debt?"—as if to say, "I am going on a journey to eternity with the good deeds I have accrued for my soul in my lifetime. You who continue to live still have a moral obligation." The cock in question was a thanksgiving offering to Asclepius, Greek and Roman god of healing, customarily brought by those who had enjoyed a healthy life. In this context one might say, despite the irreverence in the comparison, that Socrates too gave up his soul with an affirmation of his connection to the divine. Once again, however, Socrates's prayer is an expression of gratitude to the god for a physical benefit received rather than the disinterested fulfilment of an obligation. All attempts at comparison between the two cases are necessarily superficial. As noted above, there is a fundamental difference between Socrates's conversation with his companions and the exchange between Rabbi Akiva and his students. For Socrates, the source of meaning is the immortality of the soul—its journey and fate as it leaves the body after death. For Rabbi Akiva, on the other hand, it is the moral challenge in this world, within life itself, that constitutes meaning.

LOVE TO THE LAST BREATH

In his usual fashion, Rabbi Akiva does not focus on the theory of moral behavior, but on its practice. He often acts first and only then explains his action. For example, when one of his students was absent from the study hall for a time, he went to visit him and discovered that he was gravely ill. He cared for him with great devotion, washing and nursing him back to health—thereby saving his life. Only when the student had fully recovered did Rabbi Akiva pass from practice to theory (or to formulating the theory behind the appropriate action), teaching that one who does not visit the sick it is as if he has shed blood.[26] On other occasions as well, he combined action with teaching. So too in his final lesson in the philosophy of love—on the complete fulfilment of the commandment to love God—he incorporates both theory and practice: "He accepted the yoke of heaven . . . He drew out [the word] 'one' [*ehad*] until his soul departed with 'one.'" He actively fulfils the commandment as he explains its theoretical basis to his students: "All my days I grieved at the words 'with all your soul [*nafshekha*]'—even when your soul [*nishmatkha*] is taken from you. I said: when will I have the opportunity to fulfil this? And now that the opportunity presents itself will I not fulfil it?"

As explained above, the way in which *nafshekha* is interpreted in relation to *nishmatkha* affects our understanding of Rabbi Akiva's words. The two words may, of course, simply be seen as synonyms and no more. Such an approach is certainly legitimate, but would be inconsistent with the many varied meanings afforded by the midrash to such words as *nefesh*, *neshamah*, *ruah*. As we have already seen, both words appear in Genesis 2:7: "And the

Lord God formed man of the dust of the ground, and breathed into his nostrils the breath of life [*nishmat hayyim*]; and man became a living soul [*nefesh hayyah*]." According to the plain meaning of the verses in Genesis, as well as their midrashic interpretation,[27] the man had a "soul" [*nefesh*] when he was first created—"of the dust of the ground."

Similarly, the blood of a slaughtered animal is equated with the *nefesh*, in Deuteronomy 12:23: "for the blood is the life [*nefesh*], and you shall not eat the life with the flesh." When the "breath of life" [*nishmat hayyim*] was breathed into the man, he became a "living soul" [*nefesh hayyah*]. The *nefesh* thus pertains to earthly existence—"from below" in the words of the midrash; the life-giving *neshamah* is "from above—"[28] When Rabbi Akiva speaks of fulfilling the commandment to love God, *bekhol nafshekah* ["with all your soul"], he is referring to the act performed with the physical body, the *nefesh*—that is, with one's blood—and that is, why it pertains to life in this world. The *neshamah* enables the act by virtue of the life it gives the body and the *nefesh*, and Rabbi Akiva fulfils the commandment *bekhol nafsho*—with all his *nefesh*—until it is utterly exhausted with the departure of the *neshamah*.

He accepts the yoke of heaven, reads the Shema, and draws out the word *ehad* [one], and the completion of the commandment merges with the departure of his soul—thereby actively fulfilling the verse "and you shall love the Lord your God . . . with all your *nefesh*—even when your *neshamah* is taken from you." At that very moment, his *neshamah*—his "breath of life"—is taken, as he completes the commandment to accept the yoke of heaven and the commandment to love God with his body and his *nefesh*.

"He drew out [the word] 'one' [*ehad*] until his soul departed with 'one.'" With all the strength in his body, with all the force of his *nefesh*, with immeasurable love of God, he devotes his final breath to "one." "And you shall love the Lord your God with all your heart, and with all your *nefesh*, and with all your might"—love to the last breath.

NOTES

1. BT *Sanhedrin* 38b and parallel sources.

2. *Pesikta Zutarta* (*Lekah Tov*) on Ruth, introduction.

3. BT *Hagigah* 13a; Ben Sira 3:21.

4. Accounts of the Martyrs (not necessarily ten) can be found in the following talmudic sources: BT *Bava Batra* 10b, *Sotah* 48b, *Berakhot* 61b, *Avodah Zarah* 8b, and *Sanhedrin* 14b. The deaths of Rabbi Simeon ben Gamaliel and Rabbi Ishmael are also described in

tractate *Semahot*, chapter 5. The story of the Ten Martyrs comes from *Lamentations Rabbah* 2; it is also mentioned in the *Epistle of Sherira Gaon*. Its prominent place in cultural consciousness, however, derives from the *kinah* [lament] of the Ten Martyrs, recited in many communities on the Ninth of Av and/or on the Day of Atonement.

5. J. D. Eisenstein, *Ozar Midrashim*, s.v. "*Asarah harugei malkhut*," vol. 2, 440.

6. Ibid.

7. *Berakhot* 61b.

8. Minor Tractates, *Semahot*, 8, 12.

9. Compare the words of Rabbi Akiva: "He is severe with the righteous, and calls them to account in this world for their few evil deeds, that he might lavish happiness and abundant reward upon them in the world to come" (*Genesis Rabbah* 33,1). Similarly, Rabbi Akiva's statement, "Dear is suffering" (BT *Sanhedrin* 101a–b); see also below.

10. *Semahot*, 8, 12.

11. *Berakhot* 61b; *Yalkut Shimoni*, *Va'ethanan*.

12. *Mekhilta*, ed. M. Friedmann, 33a.

13. See also the exchange between R. Jose ben Kisma and R. Hanina ben Teradion in BT *Avodah Zarah* 18a.

14. JT *Hagigah* 2,1.

15. Quoted in Eisenstein, *Ozar Midrashim*, vol. 2, 441–42.

16. For *midrashim* that support the interpretation of *nefesh* and *neshamah* in this vein, see *Genesis Rabbah*, *Bereshit* 12 and 14.

17. BT *Sanhedrin* 101a and parallel sources.

18. Both this and the following quote are from *Sanhedrin* 101a.

19. The prisoner's isolation from his executioners invites the comparison to martyrs in other cultures and to the philosophy of nonviolence.

20. Plato, *Phaedo*, 58–118.

21. There are many comparisons between the death of Jesus and the death of Socrates. See, for example, Emily Wilson, *The Death of Socrates: Hero, Villain, Chatterbox, Saint* (Cambridge: Harvard University Press, 2007), 141–68.

22. R. Jose ben Kisma's statement, "Hanina, my brother, do you not know that this nation was appointed by heaven to rule?" (BT *Avodah Zarah* 18a), should not be seen as affording political or moral legitimacy to Roman rule, even in the speaker's opinion. Rome has served as a symbol of anti-Jewish hatred from ancient times up to the modern era. Such symbolic references to Rome abound in Jewish literature throughout the ages.

23. Some ascribe this dictum to Rabbi Akiva, although parallel sources offer no support for this view.

24. See Avigdor Shinan, *Pirkei Avot: Perush Yisre'eli hadash* (Jerusalem: Yediot Aharonot, 2009), 162.

25. There is no contradiction between this assertion and the talmudic account whereby "a heavenly voice said: 'Fortunate are you, Rabbi Akiva, for you are summoned to the next world'" (BT *Berakhot* 61b), as this was not in response to a prayer or request by Rabbi Akiva himself.

26. BT *Nedarim* 40a.

27. *Genesis Rabbah, Bereshit* 12.

28. Ibid.

Heaven on Earth: The World to Come and Its (Dis)locations

Christine Hayes

INTRODUCTION

Ancient Jewish sources from the Bible to the Talmud contain a dizzying array of ideas about a better life or world to come that features proximity to or dwelling with the divine—be it a personal life after death, a messianic period in ordinary historical time, or an eschatological era when the world as we know it is brought to a crashing end by God and an entirely new world order is established. Rather than explore any one of these ideas in detail, this essay focuses on a question that occupied proponents of all three conceptions: can the world to come—however it is imagined—be experienced, even if briefly, in this world? If so, what might that experience look like, and how might it be attained?

To be sure, some ancient Jewish sources imagine a deep disjunction between this world and the world to come. Take for example, the following Talmudic teachings. The first is attributed to the third century C.E. Palestinian sage, R. Yoḥanan:

> *b. Berakhot* 34b
> R. Ḥiyya b. Abba also said in the name of R. Yoḥanan: All the prophets prophesied about the days of the Messiah only, but as for the world to come, "No eye has seen, O God, but You, Who act for those that trust in You" (Isa 64:3).

R. Yoḥanan distinguishes here between the messianic age and the world to come and states that all of the biblical prophets' promises of a future ideal time referred not to the world to come, but to a time in the course of human history when a king anointed by God (a messiah) would once again reign in Israel. Regarding the world to come, no human has ever seen what awaits us there, not even the prophets. It is a world and a time completely apart.

A second tradition, attributed to the third century C.E. sage Rav, imagines what the world to come will be like, but does so in a way that only serves to underscore the disjunction between that world and this one:

> *b. Berakhot* 17a
> A favorite saying of Rav was: The world to come is not like this world.[1] In the world to come there is no eating or drinking

or propagation or business or jealousy or hatred or competition, but the righteous sit with their crowns on their heads feasting on the splendor of the *shekinah* [divine presence], as it says, "And they beheld Elohim, and ate and drank" (Exod 24:11).

For Rav, this world and the world to come are not alike, but radically disjunctive. In this world, our material bodies are engaged in eating and drinking and propagating; we sustain ourselves in business in competition with others, which engenders jealousy and hatred. But in the world to come, when we are free of material bodies of flesh and blood, none of these elements is present, and the righteous will be sustained by the splendor of the divine presence. Now if this world and the world to come are such distinct and disjunctive realities, we might conclude that entry into the world to come requires a complete escape from the present world—through temporary elevations out of this world or permanently, through death.

But according to some ancient Jewish sources, this world and the world to come are not so radically disjunctive. I refer not only to sources, such as *b. Ketubot* 111b, that assume there is plenty of eating and drinking in the afterlife, but to sources that posit certain points, or loci, of conjunction between this world and the world to come. Take for example, this anonymous tradition, also from *b. Berakhot*:

> *b. Berakhot* 57b
> Five things are a sixtieth part [of something else]: namely, fire, honey, Sabbath, sleep and a dream. Fire is one-sixtieth part of Gehinnom. Honey is one-sixtieth part of manna. Sabbath is one-sixtieth part of the world to come. Sleep is one-sixtieth part of death. A dream is one-sixtieth part of prophecy.

According to this text, the experience of the Sabbath anticipates in some way the experience of the world to come. If one may employ the shorthand of "heaven" for this ideal world to come, then according to this tradition, the Sabbath is a temporal point of conjunction—a meeting in time—that establishes a little piece of heaven on earth.

This essay explores the diverse ways in which different groups of ancient Jews understood the relationship between this world and some version of an ideal world to come. Some will assume an absolute disjunction between the two. The disjunctive approach declares that no experience in this world anticipates the experience of the next world. In fact, it is foolish or even dangerous to occupy oneself with such matters. But many others assume some point of connection or conjunction between the two worlds. This conjunctive approach takes two distinct forms. First, some ancient Jews who believed in the conjunction of these worlds sought to identify or create a bridge that would carry them from this world to the ideal world, certainly in death, but perhaps also in moments of transcendence that elevate one out of this life. There is a second approach, however, to experiencing the conjunction of this world and the world to come that moves in the other direction. Some ancient Jews sought not to escape the realities of this world, to travel from this world to the ideal world beyond this one, but to experience "heaven on earth." Convinced that this world and the world to come are not radically divorced from one another, these ancient Jews, particularly the talmudic rabbis, applied themselves to the task of obtaining a foretaste of the world to come while in this world by bringing the world to come into this world.

Ancient Jews developed their ideas in conversation with both the Hebrew Bible and the intellectual currents and belief systems in their immediate cultural environment. We begin, then, with a brief overview of the relevant biblical sources before moving on to Second Temple period Jewish writings from the third century B.C.E. to the first century C.E., the centuries just prior to the rise of the talmudic rabbis. These Second Temple sources emphasize a movement from this world to another, ideal world. We will then turn to classical talmudic literature and examine the strategies employed by the rabbis for moving in the opposite direction and locating heaven on earth.

BIBLICAL SOURCES ON THIS WORLD AND THE WORLD TO COME

There is no clearly articulated notion of a world to come in the Pentateuch, no promise of immortality, no life with God and celestial beings after death. In fact, the Garden of Eden story in Genesis 2–3 makes it clear that humans traded immortality for free will. While a few biblical stories refer to a shadowy region below the earth, Sheol (see for example Gen 42:38, Prov 7:27, Job 10:21–22 and 17:16), to which the life force [*nefesh*] of the deceased descends, this is not a robust concept of a world to come.

What we do find in the Hebrew Bible—and this is more relevant to the central concern of this essay—is the basic idea of two realms: the earthly realm is the abode of humans and the heavenly realm is the abode of God. And so we may ask: do biblical sources understand there to be a radical disjunction between the abode of humans (the earth) and the abode of the divine (heaven)? Or are their times, places, and experiences in which the two realms—the human and the divine—are conjoined, creating the possibility for some kind of shared experience or coexistence that might anticipate a future world to come?

In the Bible, the meeting or conjunction of heaven and earth occurs along three axes: the temporal, the covenantal, and the spatial. The first that we encounter is the temporal axis. At the creation, God sets apart one time—a day of the week—as a holy day of rest (Gen 2:1–3). Israel is enjoined to observe this Sabbath day in imitation of God (Exod 20:8–10) and as an everlasting covenant between God and Israel (Exod 31:16):

> *Exodus 31:15–17*
> Six days may work be done, but on the seventh day there shall be a Sabbath of complete rest, holy to Yahweh; whoever does work on the Sabbath day shall be put to death. The Israelite people shall keep the Sabbath, observing the Sabbath throughout the ages as a covenant for all time. It shall be a sign for all time between Me and the people of Israel. For in six days Yahweh made heaven and earth, and on the seventh day He ceased from work and was refreshed.

In Leviticus 23:3, the Sabbath heads the list of appointed times, or festivals, that are holy to God and that are to be observed as holy by Israel. Thus the temporal conjunction of heaven and earth occurs in Israel's calendar observance.

The second axis along which heaven and earth are conjoined is the covenantal axis. The two realms meet in the giving and receiving of the Torah that establishes the covenant between God and Israel. The Torah contains divine instruction or wisdom; obedience to its terms is a requirement for those who would live with God in his holy Land: "You shall faithfully observe all My laws and all My regulations, lest the Land to which I bring you to settle in spew you out" (Lev 20:22). By accepting this divine instruction and obeying the terms of the covenant, Israel secures God's protective presence in her midst.

Third, there is a spatial dimension to the conjunction of heaven and earth—the sanctuary. Exodus 25:8 is explicit on this point. God says, "And let them make Me a sanctuary that I may dwell among them." When the Israelites construct the sanctuary according to the divine direction, God's presence descends and fills the sanctuary. And in fact, the sanctuary is referred to as the tent of meeting because it was there that God would meet and converse with Moses.

In short, the Bible envisages three ways in which a piece of heaven may be found on earth: through the covenant or Torah that conveys divine instruction and enables the Israelites to dwell in God's Land, through sacred time (i.e., the Sabbath and other sacred times of the calendar), and through sacred space (the sanctuary or tent of meeting and of course eventually the Jerusalem Temple where the divine and human realms meet).

We turn now to the literature of the Second Temple period. Do these texts see the earthly realm and the divine realm as disjunctive or conjunctive? If conjunctive, how do they understand and depict the three axes of that conjunctive relationship: the covenantal or Torah axis, the temporal or calendar axis, and the spatial or sanctuary axis?

SECOND TEMPLE LITERATURE

We begin with the covenantal axis of the conjunction of the divine and human realms. Some Second Temple writings continue the biblical portrayal of the divinely revealed Torah as a body of divine wisdom given over to the people of Israel, and therefore a piece of heaven on earth. Thus, chapter 24 of the book of Sirach from the second century B.C.E. relates the journey of divine wisdom, wandering throughout all of creation and all nations in search of a resting place until, in the course of time, she came to dwell in Israel as the Torah. Wisdom says:

> 24:3 "I came forth from the mouth of the Most High, and like a mist I covered the earth.
>
> . . .
>
> 24:5 A circle of sky I encircled alone, and in the deep of abysses I walked.
>
> 24:6 In the waves of the sea and in all the earth and in every people and nation I led.
>
> 24:7 With all these I sought repose, and in whose inheritance I would settle.
>
> 24:8 Then the creator of all commanded me, and he who created me put down my tent and said, 'Encamp in Jacob, and in Israel let your inheritance be.'
>
> 24:9 Before the age, from the beginning, he created me, and until the age I will never fail.
>
> 24:10 In a holy tent I ministered before him, and thus in Zion I was firmly set.

> 24:11 In a beloved city as well he put me down, and in Jerusalem was my authority.
>
> 24:12 And I took root among a glorified people, in the portion of the Lord is my inheritance."
>
> . . .
>
> 24:23 All these things are the book of the covenant of the Most High God, a law that Moses commanded us, a heritage for the gatherings of Jacob.[2]

Wisdom permeated the cosmos and enjoyed a possession within each nation, and yet in due time she was instructed by God to set down her tent in Jacob and to dwell permanently in Zion, or Jerusalem. Verse 23 makes it clear that this Wisdom—this portion of Yahweh—is none other than "the book of the covenant of the Most High God, a law that Moses commanded us, a heritage for the gatherings of Jacob" (v. 23). The Torah is clearly viewed here as divine wisdom sent from on high to abide in Israel, a piece of heaven on earth. At the same time, however, the Torah is described in spatial terms—it has a holy tent, it encamps in the beloved city. By means of these spatial metaphors, Torah and Temple are blended into a single image of heaven on earth spatially located at the heart of the Jewish nation.

Other Second Temple texts, however, take a very different position, despairing of the possibility of experiencing heaven on earth. While these texts maintain a belief in and even a desperate yearning for the conjunction of the divine and human realms, they indicate that accessing the divine requires an ascent from the earthly realm to the divine realm where one can discover hidden divine wisdom unavailable on earth. The germ of this idea is found in Deuteronomy 29:28: "The secret things belong to Yahweh our God; but the things that are revealed belong to us and our children forever, that we may observe all the words of this Law." In this verse, Moses draws a distinction between the exoteric revelation—the words of the Law or Torah given at Sinai—and esoteric matters ("the secret things") that were not revealed and belong only to God. Certainly, some texts from this period, such as Sirach 3:21–24, warn against dabbling in the hidden and esoteric wisdom that remains with God in heaven ("Things too difficult for you do not seek . . . the things that have been prescribed for you, think about these, for you have no need of hidden matters"),[3] but others are drawn to it. For if the exoteric Torah of Moses is only part of the divine wisdom, the part needed for life in this world, then the hidden or esoteric wisdom that remains in heaven must hold the key to life in the world to come.

The desire to gain access to this wisdom that was not revealed is evident in *1 Enoch*, an unusual, composite work dating to the centuries before the Common Era. Like Sirach, *1 Enoch* contains a narrative of Wisdom's search for an abode, but the morals of the two stories couldn't be more different. As we saw, Sirach depicted the universal divine Wisdom emerging from heaven, wandering throughout the earth, and eventually establishing residence on earth in the form of Israel's Torah. *1 Enoch* relates Wisdom's story quite differently:

> 42:1) Wisdom did not find a place where she might dwell, so her dwelling was in the heavens.
>
> (2) Wisdom went forth to dwell among the sons of men, but she did not find a dwelling. Wisdom returned to her place, and sat down in the midst of the angels.[4]

According to *1 Enoch*, Wisdom searched for a home among humankind, but finding no dwelling place on earth was forced to retire to heaven, where she dwells among the angels. In Sirach, Wisdom takes the form of the exoteric Torah, but the Wisdom spoken of in *1 Enoch* is the esoteric wisdom not revealed at Sinai. How then is humankind to learn of this esoteric divine Wisdom that resides only in heaven? The book tells us: the secret treasures of divine Wisdom were made known to one righteous individual, Enoch, not through an act of revelation from heaven to earth (as in Sirach), but through a movement in the opposite direction. Enoch was taken up from the earth; he ascended to heaven where he was shown the secret divine Wisdom that resides there and can be accessed only there. His visions were recorded in a book, *1 Enoch*, and that book was transmitted to a select community of readers who alone possess the esoteric wisdom.

And what is this esoteric divine wisdom? According to *1 Enoch*, the esoteric divine wisdom that was not revealed at Sinai and can be experienced only in heaven, has a temporal and to some extent a spatial content. *1 Enoch* claims that upon his ascent, Uriel, the angel in charge of all luminaries, guided Enoch through the celestial sphere and revealed to him the "heavenly secrets," that is, the secret laws that govern the movement of the heavenly bodies (*1 Enoch* 72:1, 74:2, etc.) and determine the true 52-week, 365-day calendar (*1 Enoch* 74:12, 75:3). Uriel explains that this calendar, established at the time of creation, is observed by the divine beings in heaven, and noncompliance with the calendar by those on earth is a sinful breach of God's commands to the cosmos (78:10, 79:6, 80:1, and 82:7).[5] By obeying this divine calendar, humans participate in the temporal rhythms of a supramundane or heavenly realm. Esoteric wisdom has a second specific content in *1 Enoch* that is spatial. During his tour, Enoch is given esoteric knowledge not only of astronomical and calendrical matters but also of the heavenly palaces awaiting the holy and elect (41:1–2).[6]

We noted earlier that the Bible envisages the conjunction of heaven and earth along three axes: the covenantal (or Torah-based) axis, the temporal (or Sabbath- and calendar-based) axis, and the spatial (or sanctuary-based) axis. To be specific, the divine presence is experienced in the mundane realm by virtue of the exoteric Torah delivered from heaven; it is experienced in mundane time by virtue of the Sabbath and festivals; and it is experienced in mundane space by virtue of the sanctuary. *1 Enoch* continues these three axes but where the Bible locates each in this world, *1 Enoch* takes them out of this world altogether and locates them firmly in heaven in an esoteric, heavenly Torah and in supramundane time and space. It is only by accessing the secret and esoteric Torah that one can observe the Sabbath at the correct time and in synchrony with the angels who observe it in heaven. And it is only by accessing this esoteric Torah that one can adopt the behaviors of purity, praise, and obedience required of those who hope to reside, like the angels, in the heavenly sanctuary. In *1 Enoch*, the covenantal, temporal, and spatial dimensions of the conjunction of heaven and earth remain intact but are lifted out of this world and placed in the heavens, accessible only to those who gain entry to that realm.

RABBINIC LITERATURE

We turn now to rabbinic sources. Some rabbinic sources view this world and the next, or the earthly and heavenly realms, as disjunctive rather than conjunctive and, like Sirach, warn against dabbling in esoteric knowledge of the world beyond this one. For example:

> *m. Ḥagigah* 2:1
> The laws of sexual immorality may not be expounded in the company of three persons, nor the account of Creation [i.e., cosmogony] [be expounded] before two persons, nor the account of the Chariot [i.e., esoteric teachings about the divine] before one person unless he is a sage and understands on his own. Whoever reflects on four matters—it would be better for him had he not come into the world: What is above? What is below? What is ahead and what is behind?[7]

However, many more rabbinic texts assume some kind of conjunction between the divine and human realms. Some of these sources continue the

Second Temple focus on heaven, seeking to escape this world in order to experience heaven. But in other rabbinic sources, we see a reassertion of the biblical model that moves in the opposite direction and brings heaven down to earth. Consider the following traditions:

> *m. Avot* 4:15 (following Kaufman ms):
> R. Jacob said, "This world is like a vestibule to the world to come; prepare yourself in the vestibule that you may enter into the banqueting hall."
> He used to say, "Better is one hour of repentance and good deeds in this world than the whole life of the world to come; and better is one hour of bliss [*qorat ruaḥ*] in the world to come than all the life of this world."

According to R. Jacob, this life is a preparation or perhaps a dress rehearsal for the world to come. Just as the noise, sights, sounds, and smells of the festivities of the banquet hall can be perceived from the vestibule, so too heaven spills over into this world, providing a foretaste and creating anticipation. R. Jacob's second statement contains a three-way comparison that rates one hour of bliss in the world to come above all of the life of this world (unremarkably enough) except for repentance and good deeds; one hour of the latter is better than the whole life of the world to come (remarkably enough). This second statement is more radical than the first. Its claim is not that this world offers glimpses of the world to come but rather that by performing acts of repentance and good deeds in this world, the experience of the world to come is not only anticipated but also outperformed in this world.

The idea in R. Jacob's first teaching—that heaven's pleasures are experienced in some small or attenuated way in this world—is also found in traditions that describe activities in this world [*olam ha-zeh*] that will continue in the next world [*olam ha-ba*]:

> *b. Sanhedrin* 91b
> R Joshua b. Levi also said: Whoever utters song [of praise to God] in this world shall be privileged to do so in the next world too, as it is written, "Happy are those who dwell in your house: they forever praise you. Selah" (Ps 84:5).[8]

> *b. Sanhedrin* 92a
> R. Sheshet said: Whoever teaches the Torah in this world will be privileged to teach it in the next, as it is written, "And he who satisfies others shall himself be sated" (Prov 11:25). . . .

R. Eleazar said: Every leader who leads the community with mildness will be privileged to lead them in the next world [too], as it is written, "for he who loves them will lead them; he will guide them to springs of water" (Isa 49:10).

While these passages speak of reward for good deeds in this world, the reward is the continuation of the deed in the next world. Thus, singing God's praise, teaching Torah, and leading the community are among the common activities engaged in every day that afford an experience of the next world.

Unlike the Second Temple sources that envisage a movement out of this world in order to enter the heavenly realm, many rabbinic sources seek to locate heaven on earth. They do so along the three axes we have identified thus far—the covenantal, the temporal, and the spatial. Moreover, the heightened rhetoric of the rabbinic sources suggests that the rabbis knew that in seeking to transform rather than transcend this world, they were swimming against a tide.

We consider first the covenantal axis. The rabbis reassert the biblical depiction of the Torah as divine instruction given over to Israel and found on earth, but with a twist. In some rabbinic sources, Moses must forcibly wrest the Torah from heaven in a dramatic move that arouses the jealousy of the angels, who believe it belongs in heaven.[9] See, for example, the following midrash in which God has to disguise Moses to prevent the angels' attack:

Exodus Rabbah 28:1

"And Moses went up to God" (Exod 19:3). It is written "You have ascended on high, you have led captivity captive" (Ps 68:19). What is the meaning of "You have ascended on high"? It means you (Moses) have been exalted because you wrestled with angels on high. . . . At that moment, the angels wanted to attack Moses, but God changed the features of Moses to resemble those of Abraham and said to the angels: "Are you not ashamed to touch this man to whom you descended [from heaven] and in whose house you ate?"

Later in the same midrashic work, God prepares an escape tunnel as the raging angels come after Moses to destroy him:

Exodus Rabbah 42:4

R. Isaac said: When God said to Moses, "Go, get down" (Exod 32:7), Moses' face darkened so that he became like a blind man on account of his many troubles and did not know which way to go down. The angels sought to kill him, saying "Now is the time to slay him"; but God knew the intention of the angels. What did He do?

... The Lord opened unto him a window under his throne of glory and said to him: "Go, get down" (Exod 32:7).

In several traditions, the angels articulate the reasons for their vociferous objections to God's plan to place heaven's greatest treasure in the hands of mere mortals.[10] In *Song of Songs Rabbah* 8:11, 2, the angels fear abandonment. Arguing that the Torah belongs in heaven with them, the angels compel God to assure them that he will not abandon the heavens in order to be with his Torah on earth:

> *Song of Songs Rabbah* 8:11, 2
> When the Holy One, blessed be he, announced his intention of giving the Torah to Israel, the ministering angels said to the Holy One, blessed be he: "Sovereign of the Universe, You are he whose majesty is over the heaven; it is your happiness, your glory, and your praise that the Torah should be in heaven." He said to them: "What does it matter to you?" They said: "Perhaps tomorrow you will cause your divine presence to abide in the lower world." Then the Holy One, blessed be he, replied to them: "I will give my Torah to the dwellers on earth but I will abide with the celestial beings. I will give away my daughter with her marriage portion to another country in order that she may pride herself with her husband in her beauty and charm and be honored as befits a king's daughter. But I will abide with you in the upper world. . . .
> R. Shimeon said in the name of R. Joshua ben Levi: Wherever God made His law to abide, there He made His divine presence to abide.

In the following midrash, the angels are described as coveting the Torah for themselves:

> *Deuteronomy Rabbah* 7:9
> And should you say that I have given you the law to your disadvantage, [know that] I have given it for your benefit, for the ministering angels coveted it, but it was hidden from them, as it is said "Seeing it is hidden from the eyes of all living . . . and kept close from the flying beings of the air" (Job 28:21)—this is the angels.

Remarkably, this midrash reverses 1 Enoch's trope of a Torah hidden in the heavens away from humans and speaks instead of a Torah hidden from the angels and given to humans. In a similar reversal, the next midrash asserts that it is the angels who are unworthy of the divine Law. It is too abstruse or difficult for them and therefore God gives the Torah to humans:

Deuteronomy Rabbah 8:2

God said to Israel: "My children, the law is too abstruse for the ministering angels, but for you it is not too abstruse." Whence do we know this? From what we read [in Deut 30:11] "For this commandment which I command you this day, it is not too hard for you" [for you, but it is too hard for ministering angels].

While the Second Temple sources examined above idealized an esoteric Torah beyond the ken of humans and known only to the angels in heaven, this rabbinic source idealizes the exoteric Torah as beyond the ken of angels and known only to humans on earth.

In all of these sources, the Torah conjoins heaven and earth and does so in this world. As for the temporal and spatial dimensions of the conjunction of heaven and earth, here too some rabbinic sources focus on bringing heaven down to earth. Contrary to Second Temple sources that move in the opposite direction, it is not the heavenly calendar that is privileged. On the contrary, the earthly calendar is privileged and sets the standard to be followed by those residing in heaven, rather than the reverse. We see this in:

Pesiqta Rabbati piska 15 (parallels *b. RoshHaShanah* 8a–b, *Exodus Rabbah* 15:2, *Deuteronony Rabbah* 2:14)

R. Hoshaya taught: When the lower court makes a decision and declares "Today is the new year," then the Holy One, Blessed be He, says to the ministering angels: set up the tribunal, install the advocate, install the clerk of the court, for the lower court has decided and made fast today and this morning is the new year!

If the witnesses are delayed or if the court reconsiders and transfers it to the next day, says God, blessed be he, to the angels: take down the tribunal, and the advocate and dismiss the clerk of the court, for the lower court has made a decree saying that tomorrow should be the new year. And what is the proof? "For it is a law for Israel, a ruling of the God of Jacob" [read by the rabbis as: For a law in Israel is also a ruling, i.e., obligation, for the God of Israel] (Ps 81:5)—what is not a law for Israel is also if we may say so, no obligation for the God of Israel.

R. Pinḥas and R. Hilkiah b. R. Simon say: When all the ministering angels assemble before God and ask, "Lord of the universe, when is the new year?" he answers them: "You're asking me? I and you, we should ask the lower court." And what is the proof? "For what great nation is there that has a god so close at hand as is the

Lord our God whenever we call upon Him?" [read by the rabbis as: when we make known to him (the festivals)] (Deut 4:7).

The calendar as determined by Israel on earth is the calendar to be followed in heaven and the angels align their worship with the worship of Israel, rather than the reverse. Indeed, the power of Sabbath observance in this world to actualize the conjunction of heaven and earth may be seen in the following traditions:

b. Shabbat 118b
R. Yoḥanan said in the name of R. Simeon b. Yoḥai: If Israel were to keep two Sabbaths according to the Sabbath laws, they would be redeemed immediately, for it is said, "Thus says the Lord: 'As for the eunuchs who keep my Sabbaths . . . ' (Isa 56:4), which is followed by, 'I will bring them to My sacred mount, etc.' (ibid. v, 517)."

Two properly observed Sabbaths can bring redemption, which here is likely an indication of the world to come, since it is also said that just one Sabbath properly observed has the power to usher in the Messianic age (*Leviticus Rabbah* 3:1).

Finally, we turn to the spatial dimension of the conjunction of heaven and earth. In the Bible, of course, the spatial conjunction of heaven and earth was concentrated in the sanctuary. It was the central sanctuary in the Jerusalem Temple that attracted and housed the Shekinah or divine presence. In the Second Temple period sources reviewed above, the divine presence filled the heavenly temple to which humans seek access beyond this world. For their part, the rabbis reasserted the biblical emphasis on the central sanctuary in Jerusalem but, again, with a twist. They lived in a post-Temple era. The sanctuary was destroyed. Where, then, was the divine presence to be experienced? In what space and place on earth is heaven to be found?

Rabbinic sources provide two responses: the holy Land or the holy community.[11] According to the first, the entire Land of Israel and not simply the site of the Jerusalem Temple attracts and houses the Shekinah. The idea of the divine presence in the Land was adduced by the rabbis when asserting the importance of residing in the Land of Israel and delegitimizing Jewish life outside the Land, as may be seen in *m. Ketubbot* 13:10–11 and *t. Ketubbot* 12:12, according to which a spouse (in some versions, husband or wife) cannot be compelled to leave the Land but can be compelled to move to the Land. According to *t. Avodah Zarah* 5:2–5 it is preferable to live in the Land even in a town in which the majority of the inhabitants are non-Jews than to live outside the Land in a town in which the majority of the inhabitants are Jews. In case the point is lost, the text goes on to explain that "dwelling in the Land of Israel is deemed as important as fulfilling all the commandments in the Torah" (a view repeated in *Sifre Deuteronomy* 80). A little further on, the same passage stigmatizes those living in the Diaspora as comparable to those who have renounced God altogether and interprets Leviticus 25:38 ("I am the Lord your God, who brought you forth out of the land of Egypt, to give you the land of Canaan, to be your God") as saying "as long as you are in the Land of Canaan I will be your God, but when you are not dwelling in the Land of Canaan, it is as if I am not your God." The passage ends with the climactic assertion that "anyone who leaves the Land during peacetime and goes [to live] abroad is as if he were worshiping idols," and "Israelites who reside outside the Land are idolaters" even when they take pains to live in accordance with God's laws.[12] Only in the Land does one encounter the divine presence and experience a little heaven on earth.

Indeed, some texts go further. The Palestinian Talmud contains an extended reflection on the virtue not only of residing in the Land but also of dying in the Land. The dead in the Land will be the first to be resurrected in the messianic age. Although God intervenes to ensure that sages who die and are buried in exile will have a rapid underground transit to the holy Land, Palestinian sages scorn those who seek burial in the Land after a life lived outside the Land, and the sage Ulla is depicted as lamenting the fact that he will die in exile, with these words: "Losing the soul in the bosom of one's mother is not to be compared to losing the soul in the bosom of a foreign woman" (*y. Kil'ayim* 9:4, 32c).[13]

These sources, extolling the Land of Israel as the locus of the divine presence in a postdestruction world and indeed the point of entry to the world to come, were not uncontested. Indeed, Isaiah Gafni argues that the rabbis' hyperbole concerning the Land, and their insistence on residence in the Land, increased in intensity in the early Amoraic period, precisely in response to an enhanced self-assuredness in Babylonia.[14] And so we conclude by considering rabbinic sources that give a different account of where, in spatial terms, the divine presence may be found in this world. We begin with the Babylonian Talmud.

While the Babylonian Talmud incorporates Palestinian traditions that valorize the holy Land and residence within it, it moderates this rhetoric of loyalty to the Land with a rhetoric of what Gafni has called "local patriotism"[15] that asserts the value of the Diaspora. The result is an often conflicted discourse, exemplified in an extensive passage at the end of Bavli tractate *Ketubbot* (110b–112a).[16] The *Gemara* on this Mishnah opens with some of the heavily pro-Land Palestinian traditions already cited and closes with other strongly pro-Land traditions, attributed primarily to Palestinian authorities: "The dead outside the Land will not be resurrected" (R. Eleazar); "Whoever walks four cubits in the Land of Israel is assured of a place in the world to come" (R. Yoḥanan); and in the most explicit statement of the Land as both a necessary and sufficient condition for life in the world to come, R. Abbahu is reported as saying: "Even a Canaanite bondwoman who lives in the Land of Israel is assured of a place in the world to come." Residence alone—even for a non-Jewish, female slave (who, in the rabbis' view, occupies the lowest status before God)—suffices to secure a place in the world to come.[17] The unit ends with hyperbolic expressions of the love that certain sages feel towards the Land; they kiss its cliffs and roll themselves in its dust.

However, these pro-Land statements serve as an envelope around dueling Babylonian and Palestinian traditions in which the status of the Holy Land, particularly vis-à-vis Babylonia, is contested. For their part, the pro-Babylonian voices in this dialogue subvert Palestinian claims, elevating Babylonia to a status that is sometimes second, sometimes equal, and sometimes superior to that of the holy Land[18] and asserting that the divine presence, or Shekinah, is found in Babylonia.

Taking advantage of a Tannaitic tradition that states that the Shekinah accompanies the Israelites wherever they are exiled, Abaye and Rava and even some Palestinian authorities teach in *b. Megillah* 29a that the Shekinah is currently in Babylonia, in certain synagogues and houses of learning. Indeed, this is said to be the meaning of Ezekiel 11:16, "I have been to them a small sanctuary." According to *Midrash Tanḥuma* Noah 3, the superiority of the Babylonian yeshivot that were transferred to Babylonia from Jerusalem after the first destruction is attributed to the fact that they never saw captivity or persecution or despoilment and were never ruled by Greece or Rome, but dwelled securely in Babylonia with their Torah since the first destruction. In short, the Palestinians may have the Land, but the Babylonians have the Shekinah, synagogues and study houses, and the relatively safe and secure conditions needed for Torah learning to thrive.

Related to this idea of the attachment of the Shekinah to yeshivot is the rabbis' second response to the problem of the location of the divine presence after the destruction of the Temple: the Shekinah is connected not to a specific geographic location, such as the Land of Israel or Babylonia, but to righteous individuals wherever they might be. Hence we read:

> *Numbers Rabbah* Naso 13, 2
>
> When the Tabernacle was erected Israel said: "Let my beloved come into his garden" (Song 4:16). . . . He [the Holy One, blessed be He] sent word to them through Moses, saying, "Why do you fear? I have already, 'Come into my garden, my sister, my bride!'" (Song 5:1).
>
> R. Ishmael son of R. Yosi said: It does not say in this text, "I am come into the garden" but "I am come into my garden" (Song 5:1)—this means, into My bridal chamber; namely, into the place which has been My principal abode from the very beginning, for was not the principal abode of the *shekinah* in the terrestrial regions [i.e., on earth]?
>
> When Adam sinned, the *shekinah* withdrew to the first sky; when Cain sinned, it withdrew to the second sky; when the generation of Enosh sinned, it ascended to the third sky; when the generation of the Flood sinned, it rose to the fourth sky; when the generation of the Dispersion sinned [at the time of the Tower of Babel], it moved up into the fifth sky; when the Sodomites sinned, it rose into the sixth sky, and when the Egyptians sinned, it ascended into the seventh sky. As a counterpart to these, seven righteous men arose who brought the *shekinah* down from the celestial to the terrestrial regions. They were the following: Abraham brought it down from the seventh to the sixth; Isaac brought it down from the sixth to the fifth; Jacob brought it down from the fifth to the fourth; Levi brought it down from the fourth to the third; Kohat brought it down from the third to the second; Amram brought it down from the second to the first; and Moses brought it down from the celestial to the terrestrial region. . . .
>
> The wicked caused the *shekinah* to depart from the earth, but the righteous have caused the *shekinah* to dwell on the earth.

How different this text is from the Second Temple sources reviewed above. In the narratives related in Sirach and *1 Enoch*, divine Wisdom was portrayed as descending from heaven and seeking a home in the earth (successfully in Sirach but unsuccessfully in *1 Enoch*). By contrast, in this rabbinic narrative the direction of the movement of the divine element is reversed! The original home and principal abode of the Shekinah, or divine presence, is not in the heavens but on earth. In the beginning, the Shekinah dwelled on earth. But human wickedness caused the Shekinah to retreat to the heavens, implying that when the Shekinah is in heaven it is in exile. The Shekinah is redeemed, however, brought back to its rightful abode on earth by the actions of the righteous. Thus, beginning with Abraham, the Shekinah began the return journey until finally, with the construction of the sanctuary by the Israelites, it was safely home.

This text both affirms and undermines the importance of the sanctuary as the site of the spatial conjunction of heaven and earth. Although the passage ends with the Shekinah's descent into the sanctuary, it makes clear that the earth as a whole is the dwelling place of the Shekinah, not just the sanctuary. Moreover, it ties the Shekinah's presence or absence to human morality.

Other texts go further in explicitly connecting the Shekinah to communities or to individuals who are righteous. In *b. Megillah* 29a we read that the Shekinah leaves the Holy Land and goes into exile with the people,[19] choosing Israel the people over Israel the Land, an idea found already in the book of Ezekiel. While according to some texts, the Shekinah plays favorites, attaching only to persons of good lineage (*b. Qiddushin* 70b) or certain personal qualities (*b. Shabbat* 92a), other texts focus on the activities that draw the Shekinah. As might be expected, the Shekinah is said to be found in synagogues and houses of learning (*b. Megillah* 29a), but also:

> *b. Berakhot* 6a
>
> Rabin b. R. Adda says in the name of R. Isaac: How do you know that the Holy One, blessed be He, is to be found in the synagogue? Because it is said, "God stands in the divine assembly" (Ps 82:1). And how do you know that if ten people pray together the *shekinah* is with them? Because it is said, "God stands in the divine assembly" (Ps 82:1). And how do you know that if three are sitting as a court of judges the *shekinah* is with them? Because it is said, "among the divine beings He pronounces judgment" (Ps 82:1). And how do you know that if two are sitting and studying the Torah together the *shekinah* is with them? Because it is said, "In this vein have those who revere the Lord been talking to one another. The Lord has heard and noted it, and a scroll of remembrance has been written at His behest concerning those who revere the Lord and esteem His name" (Mal 3:1). . . . And how do you know that even if one man sits and studies the Torah the *shekinah* is with him? Because it is said, "In every place where I cause My name to be mentioned, I will come to you and bless you" (Exod 20:21).

b. Bava Batra 10a

If a man gives even the smallest coin to a beggar, he is deemed worthy to receive the *shekinah*.

b. Menaḥot 43b

R. Simeon b. Yoḥai says, "Whosoever is scrupulous in the observance of this precept [*tsitsit*, the wearing of fringes] is worthy to receive the *shekinah*."

These and other sources teach that wherever prayer, judging, Torah study, ritual observance, hospitality, kindness, and other benevolent deeds occur, there too the Shekinah is to be found. The actions and activities of humans create a space in the mundane world into which the Shekinah enters, thereby actualizing the conjunction of worlds and locating heaven on earth.

CONCLUSION

Ancient Jews prior to the rise of Islam did more than imagine a better world to come. They sought not only to gain access to it after death but to experience it, even if fleetingly, while yet living. To do so they identified points of conjunction between heaven and earth along three axes: a covenantal axis centering on Torah or wisdom as the bridge between the two, a temporal axis centering on the Sabbath and festivals as the bridge between the two, and a spatial axis centering on the sanctuary or other holy sites as the bridge between the two. While some Second Temple Jews privileged the esoteric Torah hidden in heaven, the Sabbath and festivals as observed in heaven, and the pure sanctuary in heaven as sites for accessing an experience of the next world, a set of texts within rabbinic literature pushed against this trend. Privileging the exoteric Torah given over to Israel on earth, the Sabbath as determined and observed on earth, and earthbound spaces such as the Land and even righteous human communities or individuals as opportunities for accessing an experience of the next world, the rabbis sought to bridge the gap between this world and the world to come so as to locate "heaven on earth."

NOTES

1. Following the Oxford ms.

2. Translations of Sirach are based on the translation of Benjamin G. Wright as found in Albert Pietersma, et al., eds., *A New English Translation of the Septuagint* (New York: Oxford University Press, 2007), with standardization of proper names such as Moses and Jacob.

3. The full passage reads: "Things too difficult for you do not seek, and things too strong for you do not scrutinize. The things that have been prescribed for you, think about these, for you have no need of hidden matters. With matters greater than your affairs do not meddle, for things beyond human understanding have been shown to you. For their presumption has led many astray, and their evil fancy has diminished their understanding." For a discussion of this passage and the claim that "hidden matters" in Sirach refers to knowledge of past occurrences and future events, see Yair Furstenberg, "The Rabbinic Ban on *Maaseh Bereshit*: Sources, Contexts and Concerns," in *In the Beginning: Jewish and Christian Cosmogony in Late Antiquity* (Texts and Studies in Ancient Judaism; ed. S. Kattan, et al.; Tübingen: Mohr Siebeck, 2013), 39–63, esp. 45–47.

4. Translations of *1 Enoch* are based on George W. E. Nickelsberg et al., eds., *1 Enoch: A New Translation, Based on the Hermeneia Commentary* (Minneapolis: Fortress Press, 2004).

5. See Maxwell J. Davidson, *Angels at Qumran: A Comparative Study of 1 Enoch 1–36, 72–108 and Sectarian Writings from Qumran* (Sheffield: Sheffield Academic Press, 1992), 310; also, Christoph Berner, "The Four (or Seven) Archangels in the First Book of Enoch and Early Jewish Writings of the Second Temple Period," in *Angels: The Concept of Celestial Beings—Origins, Development and Reception* (Deuterocanonical and Cognate Literature Yearbook 2007; ed. F. V. Reiterer, et al.; Berlin: Walter de Gruyter 2007), 395–411; esp. 400.

6. This knowledge is referred to as the "books of zeal and wrath" as well as the "books of haste and whirlwind" received by Enoch (39:2).

7. For a full discussion of this passage and a persuasive explanation of the inclusion of the laws of sexual immorality in this list, see Furstenberg, "The Rabbinic Ban."

8. This passage does not appear in some witnesses due to *homoioteleuton*.

9. The following five texts are cited in connection with a different thesis in Christine Hayes, "'The Torah Was Not Given to Ministering Angels': Rabbinic Aspirationalism," in *Talmudic Transgressions: Festschrift for Daniel Boyarin* (ed. C. Fonrobert, et al.; Leiden: Brill, 2017).

10. For the similar second to third century C.E. gnostic myth of the opposition of the evil planets to the soul's ascent to heaven in order to bring the powers of light to earth, see Peter Schäfer, *Rivalität zwischen Engeln und Menschen. Untersuchungen zur rabbinischen Engelvorstellung* (Berlin: de Gruyter, 1975), 219; for the idea that the angelic opposition to Moses reflects a Jewish adaptation of this gnostic myth, see Joseph P. Schultz, "Angelic Opposition to the Ascension of Moses and the Revelation of the Law," *Jewish Quarterly Review* 61 (1971): 282–307, 288. For more on the angelic opposition to the revelation, see Hindy Najman, "Angels at Sinai: Exegesis, Theology and Interpretive Authority," *Dead Sea Discoveries* 7:3 (2000): 313–33.

11. For a clear discussion of the tension generated by the lack of congruence between Israel the holy Land and Israel the holy people, see Richard Sarason, "The Significance of the Land of Israel in the Mishnah," in *Land of Israel: Jewish Perspectives* (ed. L. Hoffman; Notre Dame: Notre Dame University Press, 1986), 109–38.

12. The relevant parts of the passage are *t. Avodah Zarah* 5:3–6.

> 3. One should rather dwell in the Land of Israel even in a town in which the majority of the inhabitants are Gentiles, than outside the Land even in a town in which all the inhabitants are Jews.
>
> —This [ruling] implies that dwelling in the Land of Israel is deemed as important as fulfilling all the commandments in the Torah, and all who are buried in the Land of Israel it is as if they were buried beneath the altar [of the temple in Jerusalem]. . . .
>
> 5 And [Scripture also] states, "[I am the Lord your God who brought you forth out of the land of Egypt] to give you the land of Canaan, and to be your God" (Lev 25:38) [which implies] that as long as you are in the Land of Canaan I will be your God, but when you are not dwelling in the Land of Canaan, it is as if I am not your God. . . .
>
> R. Simeon b. Eleazar says, "Israelites who reside outside the Land are idolaters. How so? If it gentile threw a party for his son and went and invited all the Jews dwelling in his town, even if they should eat and drink [only] their own [food and drink], and their own attendant should stand ready to serve them, they still worship idols, as Scripture states "[. . . lest you make a covenant with the inhabitants of the Land, and when they play the harlot after their gods and sacrifice to their gods] and one invites you, you eat of his sacrifices" (Exod 34:15).

13. The same metaphor appears in *y. Moed Qatan* 3, 81c, where a priest is severely chastised for proposing to leave the holy Land—even temporarily—to perform the mitzvah of levirate marriage on behalf of his deceased brother. "Your brother," he is told, "left [the Land] and God is to be blessed for killing him; do you wish to follow in his steps? He abandoned his mother's bosom and embraced a foreign bosom—would you now commit the same sin?" According to an alternative tradition, the brother's sin is described as abandoning his mother's bosom and embracing a foreign bosom.

14. Isaiah Gafni, *Land, Center and Diaspora: Jewish Constructs in Late Antiquity* (Sheffield: Sheffield Academic Press, 1997), 71–72.

15. Ibid., 12–13, 41–57.

16. An excellent analysis of this unit may be found in Jeffrey Rubenstein, "Coping with the Virtues of the Land of Israel: An Analysis of Bavli Ketubot 110b–112a," in *Israel-Diapora Relations in the Second Temple and Talmudic Periods* (ed. I. Gafni; Jerusalem: Shazar Institute, 2004), 159–88. Relevant excerpts from this extensive unit are as follows [PA= Palestinian *Amora*; BA = Babylonian *Amora*]:

> Rab Judah [BA] said: Whoever lives in Babylon is deemed as though he lived in the Land of Israel; for it is said in Scripture, "Away, escape, O Zion, you who dwell in Fair Babylon" (Zech 2:11).

Abaye [BA] stated: We have a tradition that Babylon will not witness the sufferings [that will precede the coming] of the Messiah. . . .

R. Eleazar [PA] stated: The dead outside the Land will not be resurrected; for it is said in Scripture, "And I will give glory in the land of the living" (Ezek 26:20) [implying] the dead of the Land in which I have my desire will be resurrected, but the dead [of the Land] in which I have no desire will not be resurrected.

Abba b. Memel [PA] objected: "Oh, let your dead revive, let corpses arise" (Isa 26:19); does not [the expression] "let your dead revive" refer to the dead of the Land of Israel, and "let corpses arise" to the dead outside the Land; while the text, "And I will give glory in the land of the living" (Ezek 26:20) was written of Nebuchadnezzar concerning whom the All-Merciful said, "I will bring against them a king who is as swift as a stag"? The other replied: Master, I am expounding another Scriptural text: "Who gave breath to the people upon it, and life to those that walk thereon" (Isa 42:5). . . .

Now as to R. Abba b. Memel, what [is the application] he makes of the text, "Who gave breath to the people upon it"? He requires it for [a teaching] like that of R. Abbahu [PA] who stated: Even a Canaanite bondwoman who [lives] in the Land of Israel is assured of a place in the world to come. . . .

"and life to those that walk thereon." R. Jeremiah b. Abba [BA] said in the name of R. Yoḥanan [PA], that [this teaches that] whoever walks four cubits in the Land of Israel is assured of a place in the world to come.

Now according to R. Eleazar [PA], would not the righteous outside the Land be revived? R. Ilai [PA] replied: [They will be revived] by rolling [to the Land of Israel].

R. Abba Sala the Great demurred: Will not the rolling be painful to the righteous? Abaye [BA] replied: Cavities will be made for them underground.

17. Residence also takes priority over fulfilling the commandment to be fruitful and multiply as we learn from the story about the man who remained unmarried rather than leave the Land in order to marry a particular woman.

18. Thus, immediately following the first set of pro-Land teachings, the *Gemara* tells the story of Rav Zera who evaded Rav Judah because he wanted to emigrate to the Land, but Rav Judah had taught that "whoever goes up from Babylon to the Land of Israel transgresses a positive commandment" since it is God who will effect the restoration of the exiles. Rav Judah cites a tradition that locates Babylonia just below the Land in status: "As it is forbidden to leave the Land of Israel for Babylon, so it is forbidden to leave Babylon for other countries." Rabbah and R. Joseph go further in asserting Babylonia's superiority

to the Land in some respects: "all countries are like dough (an indeterminate admixture as opposed to fine flour) towards the Land of Israel, and the Land of Israel is like dough towards Babylonia." The two are equated by Rav Judah: "Whoever lives in Babylon is deemed as though he lived in the Land of Israel," and Abaye maintains that Babylonia will not witness the sufferings that will precede the coming of the Messiah.

19. The passage reads:

> It has been taught: R. Simon b. Yoḥai said: Come and see how beloved are Israel in the sight of God: to every place to which they were exiled the *shekinah* went with them. They were exiled to Egypt and the *shekinah* was with them, as it says, "Lo, I revealed Myself to your father's house in Egypt" (1 Sam 2:27). They were exiled to Babylon, and the *shekinah* was with them, as it says, "for your sake I was sent to Babylon" (Isa 43:14). And when they will be redeemed in the future, the *shekinah* will be with them, as it says, "Then the Lord your God will return [with] your captivity" (Deut 30:3).

On this text as an expression of local patriotism, see Gafni, *Land*, 55–56.

Olam Ha-ba in Rabbinic Literature: A Functional Reading

Dov Weiss

INTRODUCTION

The Hebrew phrase *olam ha-ba* [the next world] first appears in rabbinic literature.[1] It is not found in the Hebrew Bible or Second Temple Hebrew writings.[2] Typically, the rabbinic term *olam ha-ba* is juxtaposed with *olam ha-zeh* [this world]. But what exactly does *olam ha-ba* mean? What world does it refer to? A physical one or a spiritual? Here, the rabbinic sources are vague.

At times, it seems to refer to the messianic age, to the time of resurrection, when all of the dead will rise again and return to their original bodies. At other times, the term denotes the place to which every (worthy) individual soul (re)turns after death. In this latter case, *olam ha-ba* would exist in present time—though on a different realm. This connotation would be roughly synonymous with *Gan Eden* [Garden of Eden]. And, still yet, on other occasions one gets the sense that the rabbis themselves are not sure what they mean by *olam ha-ba*. They simply have in mind another world that is different from this one.[3] Like *olam ha-ba*, a similar amorphous phrase used by the rabbis is *le-atid lavo* [the future to come].

According to either explanation—whether *olam ha-ba* refers to the messianic age or a spiritual life after death—the concept in rabbinic literature transformed Judaism. It became a supreme article of Jewish faith. Remarkably, the term *olam ha-ba* appears over two thousand times in rabbinic literature, yet the Hebrew Bible contains no notion of an individual receiving rewards and punishments after death. And the belief in bodily resurrection emerges only in the latest books of Tanakh, most notably in Daniel 12.[4] For the most part, reward and punishment in the Hebrew Bible is relegated to the mundane pre-messianic physical world.[5] Thus, with their intense emphasis on *olam ha-ba*, the rabbis in the first few centuries of the Common Era were able to restructure the primary arena of religious life. This world was understood to be merely a prelude to the more significant next world. The following rabbinic texts make this point: (1) The Mishnah in *Avot* (4:16) has Rabbi Jacob declare: "This world is like a hallway before the World to Come. Prepare yourself in the hallway so that you may enter the banquet hall." (2) Midrash *Tanhuma* claims that God gave Israel the Torah and mitzvoth only so that they could merit *olam ha-ba*.⁶ (3) A late rabbinic midrash on Exodus compares *olam ha-zeh* [this world] to a man and woman who are engaged but the all-the-more-important *olam ha-ba* symbolizes the actual marriage.⁷ That same midrash also compares this world to the first tablets of law [*luchot*] that were smashed by Moses, and the next world to the second tablets that were to be eternal.⁸

The rabbinic decision to place *olam ha-ba* at the center of their religious consciousness did not go unnoticed by many medieval Jewish theologians, such as Sa'adia Gaon, Judah Halevy, and Bahya Ibn Pakuda.⁹ And the apparent absence of *olam ha-ba* in the Hebrew Bible disturbed these medieval thinkers, for they wondered: if the rabbis regarded *olam ha-ba* as embodying the very aim of Jewish life, why did the Hebrew Bible never explicitly mention it? Interestingly, this medieval Jewish anxiety became inverted in contemporary times, when, in most denominations (excluding the Ultra-Orthodox) this world, *olam ha-zeh*, stood—and continues to stand—at the core of religious life.¹⁰ Post-Enlightenment, modern Jews are typically not interested in afterlife speculations. In short, whereas medieval Jewish theologians were consumed with afterlife speculation—and anxious about its apparent absence in the Hebrew Bible—modern Jews, by stark contrast, are obsessed with this world and anxious about the centrality that the next world occupies in rabbinic and medieval Jewish literature.

The modern Jewish sidelining of *olam ha-ba* has also affected the academic study of ancient Judaism, as scholars of rabbinic literature have given relatively little attention to *olam ha-ba*. None of the great rabbinics scholars of the twentieth century, such as Ephraim Urbach, Abraham Joshua Heschel, Arthur Marmorstein, and Max Kaddushin, devote a separate section of their theological books to *olam ha-ba*.¹¹ Admittedly, the term *olam ha-ba* or a discussion of the afterlife appears here and there, but their works do not provide a systematic or comprehensive analysis of a religious category that is so fundamental to rabbinic thinking. While the phrase *olam ha-ba* can be found close to two thousand times in rabbinic literature, a quick database search of contemporary academic articles on the subject reveals very little by way of scholarship. To be sure, Ephraim Urbach, the great systemizer of rabbinic theology, has a multipage discussion on *olam ha-ba*, but this reflection appears only in the context of describing God's justice system.¹² Reading Urbach, one would come away with the mistaken impression that the rabbis imagined *olam ha-ba* to be merely a place where humans are judged. But, of course, the rabbinic view of *olam ha-ba* is richer than that.

Strikingly, two lesser-known scholars of ancient Judaism, Claude Montefiore (1858–1938) and Herbert Loewe (1882–1940), admit this very point when defending their pithy and highly disorganized chapter on *olam ha-ba*.[13] They maintain that the rabbis "thought about [*olam ha-ba*] in terms and conceptions most of which have become obsolete and remote for us today, and so their ideas are of small interest or profit."[14] Similarly, the founder of Reconstructionist Judaism, Mordechai Kaplan (1881–1983), in *Judaism as a Civilization* argues:

> We are so far removed from the world-outlook and thought-habits of the pre-enlightenment days that, with the best of intentions to know and understand the past, we find it hard not to read into it our own ideas. We are habituated to the modern emphasis upon improvement of life in this world as the only aim worthy of our endeavors. We take for granted that, if we do our best here, we can afford to let the hereafter take care of itself. So much a part of our thinking has this modern conception of human life become that we can scarcely conceive that not long ago the center of gravity of human existence for Jews, Christians and Mohammedans alike, lay not in this world, but in the world to come.[15]

Notwithstanding Kaplan's commitment to modernity and his attendant rejection of the miraculous and supernatural realms, Kaplan celebrates *olam ha-ba* not because it actually exists but because of how the concept functioned for the rabbis. Kaplan posits: "[T]he traditional conception of the world to come expresses man's discontent with the things as they are and his yearning for the things as they ought to be. From this viewpoint, the important element in this belief is not the fantastic picture of the ideal world, but the inner urge of which it was an expression."[16]

In short, according to Kaplan, rabbinic writings on *olam ha-ba* reflect rabbinic dreams, desires, and aspirations. In what follows, I will use Kaplan's functional method of interpretation to make sense of the rabbinic descriptions of *olam ha-ba*.

SIX PRIMARY FUNCTIONS OF *OLAM HA-BA*

Broadly speaking, rabbinic teachings on *olam ha-ba* can be grouped into six functions. After outlining the first five of them quickly, I will explore the sixth one, the moral function, in greater detail.

JUDICIAL

The first and most crucial function of *olam ha-ba* in rabbinic literature is judicial: *olam ha-ba* provided a defense of God, a theodicy.[17] Although righteous people suffer in this world, they could now be thought of as duly compensated in the next world. Inversely, although some wicked people prosper in this world, they would be duly punished in the next world. In short, *olam ha-ba* squares everything away; debts will be paid and rewards will be procured. The most famous rabbinic articulation of this theology is when the Babylonian Talmud claims that all of a person's deeds in this world will be replayed back for him/her in the next world.[18]

The judicial function of *olam ha-ba* has three basic versions: one moderate, one extreme, and one intermediate. The moderate position envisions God primarily rewarding and punishing in this world, but subsequently, if necessary, slightly adjusting each person's accounts via punishments and rewards in the next world. This method guarantees that full justice will be ultimately implemented. The radical view, attributed to Rabbi Yaakov in the Babylonian Talmud (*Kiddushin* 39b) is that God rewards (and punishes) people only in the next world.[19]

Between the moderate and radical positions, we have the famous view attributed to Rabbi Akiva that God reluctantly rewards the wicked in this world—but God does so only in order to punish the wicked more harshly in the next world; inversely, God punishes, lovingly, the righteous in this world so as to protect them from incurring a more painful punishment in *olam ha-ba*.[20] Rabbi Akiva's position assumes that divine rewards and punishments in the next world are far more potent than the rewards and punishments of this world. Rabbi Akiva, thus, radically reverses the biblical picture. In the Bible, the righteous are rewarded in this world, and the wicked are punished in this world. Now, the righteous are punished in this world, and the wicked are rewarded in this world. As a consequence of this theology, Rabbi Akiva's followers argued that human suffering in this world should be regarded as a sign of divine love, for only the truly righteous are punished in this world.[21]

HERMENEUTICAL

The second function for *olam ha-ba*, the interpretive one, provided the rabbis with a new hermeneutical tool to read biblical passages that, ostensibly, have nothing to do with reward and punishment. This binary of *olam ha-zeh* and *olam ha-ba* is often employed to explain strange or redundant biblical words and phrases. At times, the rabbis situate *olam ha-zeh* and *olam ha-ba* as opposites: for example, they would argue, unlike this world where suffering occurs, the next world would be full of pleasure.[22] At other times, the rabbis use the binary of *olam ha-zeh* and *olam ha-ba* to express continuities or foreshadowing: for example, just as there are Torah academies in this world, so too there will be Torah academies in the next world, albeit even greater ones.[23]

MYSTICAL

The third function of *olam ha-ba* in rabbinic literature is what I would call the mystical one. In these instances, the rabbis use *olam ha-ba* as a method to satisfy their spiritual yearnings of having an unmediated encounter with God in a world where God is hidden. For example, *Sifre Deuteronomy* posits that the dead will be able to see God in *olam ha-ba*.[24] Or a more moderate version from *Leviticus Rabbah*, which asserts that that whereas in this world only select individuals can see God, in *olam ha-ba* everyone would see God.[25] A teaching in *Pesikta de-Rav Kahana* maintains that whereas in this world the priests purify the impure, in the next world God would assume the role of purifier.[26] Also in *Pesikta de-Rav Kahana* it is said that God would directly teach Torah to all of Israel.[27] Two more examples: the Jerusalem Talmud has God dancing with the righteous in *olam ha-ba*.[28] And, *Ecclesiastes Rabbah* presents us with a picture of God leading the *olam ha-ba* choir.[29]

POLEMICAL

The fourth function is polemical. Here, the rabbis invoke *olam ha-ba* as a theological weapon to express their animosity toward specific nations or peoples, such as their immediate Jewish rivals or gentiles. Most famously, a Mishnah in *Sanhedrin* declares that Epicureans, and those who reject the resurrection of the dead or that Torah is from Heaven, will lose their place in *olam ha-ba*.[30] Many scholars, such as Menachem Kellner, read this Mishnah as a critique of the Sadducees, who rejected the afterlife and the Oral Torah.[31] Or consider the *Tosefta* in *Sanhedrin* that has Rabbi Eliezer posit that "none of the gentiles will have a place in the World to Come."[32] One final instance: the rabbis use *olam ha-ba* as a method to express their disgust at particular biblical villains and at wicked generations such as the people of Sodom, Korach and his followers, the generation of the Flood, and the spies.[33]

RHETORICAL

The fifth function, the rhetorical one, represents the inverse of the polemical function. In these cases, the rabbis invoke *olam ha-ba* not to lambast others, but to motivate or threaten righteous Jews to comply with various rabbinic ethics and laws. They appropriate *olam ha-ba* as a placeholder or carrier to express their deepest values and concerns. Examples of actions that would cause a person to forfeit his or her *olam ha-ba* include desecrating holy objects, disgracing the holidays, embarrassing a fellow Jew, teaching an incorrect halachah,[34] eating meat that is not slaughtered,[35] eating pork,[36] making use of the tetragrammaton,[37] acting jealously, having desires, seeking honor,[38] ceasing to learn Torah, neglecting to tend to the needs of Torah sages,[39] sleeping in the morning, drinking in the afternoon, speaking like a child, or attending the synagogues of simpletons.[40] On the positive side of the rhetorical function, *Midrash Mishlei* states that any Jew who walks six feet in the Land of Israel will receive a share in *olam ha-ba*,[41] while *Avot de-Rabbi Nathan* contains an entire list of *olam ha-ba* achieving actions that include being a good friend and a good neighbor.[42]

ETHICAL

The sixth function of *olam ha-ba* is ethical. In these cases, the rabbis use the afterlife as a method to subtly express moral discomfort with a biblical idea or received Jewish tradition. They accomplish this by declaring the problematic Jewish principle inoperative for the next world. Stated differently, *olam ha-ba* provided the rabbis, among other things, with a moral safe haven: although a troubling law or theology might not be eradicated in this world, at least it could be so in the next.[43] This ethical response does not solve the moral problem, but minimizes it.[44] In what follows, I present three such examples in some detail.

The first example revolves around the rabbinic concept of the *Yetser Hara* [the evil inclination]. As Ishay Rosen-Zvi has shown, the various strata of rabbinic literature convey different conceptions of the *Yetser Hara*.[45] For R. Ishmael and his school, the *Yetser Hara* is not an essential component of the human being, as it was for R. Akiva. It is rather an external and independent entity housed within the human heart. Moreover, for R. Ishmael, the *Yetser Hara* does not drive a human being to sin by manipulating a person's emotions or desires, but rationally incites him or her to disobey God.[46]

According to Rosen-Zvi, the position of Rabbi Ishmael and his students emerged as the dominant one in the post-Tannaitic period as these sages regarded the evil inclination as fundamentally evil. Because of that, not unexpectedly, a moral-theological problem arose: why would God create something that is evil or harmful to humanity? Does this not imply that God is evil, or at least is responsible for evil? Indeed, some late antique thinkers, such as Marcion (85–160 c.e.), Celsus (second century c.e.), and Adimantus (fourth century c.e. student of Mani) all railed against the idea that the biblical God implanted an evil desire in the hearts of humanity, beginning with Adam.[47] They argued: if God created this sinful force, why should humanity suffer the consequences? God, therefore, must be unjust. These types of critiques might have reached the rabbis and naturally would have only exacerbated the theological crisis. Either way, the rabbis were confronted with this theological-moral dilemma. Many early rabbinic texts attempt to solve the problem.[48] For example, *Sifre Deuteronomy* (ca. third century c.e.) maintains that God provided a method by which an individual could overcome the deleterious effects of the evil inclination: the study of Torah. Only through it could humanity defeat the evil inclination's power.[49]

Other rabbinic texts ignore this solution and evince a profound discomfort and unease with an evil entity created by God. But they invoke *olam ha-ba* as a method to mitigate the problem. So, for example, *Exodus Rabbah* has God making this distinction: "In this world [Israel] made idols because of the evil inclination in them, but in the future world I will uproot from them the evil inclination."[50] About a dozen or so rabbinic texts make this type of distinction.[51]

Using *olam ha-ba* to mitigate problematic Jewish principles also emerges in response to the biblical notion, first found in the context of the Decalogue (Exod 20:5), where God announces that, as a "jealous God," He will "visit the guilt of the parents upon the children, upon the third and upon the fourth generations." This theology posed serious ethical problems for select rabbis who struggled with how the Torah could endorse a theology that punishes an innocent person for the sins of another. How does this punitive doctrine comport with God's attributes of mercy and kindness? Moreover, the need for Jewish—and for that matter Christian—biblical exegetes to respond to this problematic idea was heightened by the fact that late antique thinkers, from Marcion onward, were wont to cite the doctrine of inherited punishment to argue for the immorality of the Old Testament and the Old Testament God.[52]

Some early rabbinic texts ignore the ethical problems and simply affirm the theology of transgenerational punishment. Others, like *Mekhilta de-Rabbi*

Ishmael, posit that a child of the third generation would be punished for the sins of his grandparent only if there were a continuous line of evildoers from the grandparent to the grandchild. If the grandparent, parent, or child were righteous, then the child would not be punished for any of his or her ancestors' sins. By limiting the applicability of inherited punishment to those who continue in their parents' evil ways, this Tannaitic text resolves the implicit moral problem: innocent children are not punished for the sins of their parents or grandparents.[53]

Other rabbis reject this solution and continue to insist—along with a simple reading of Scripture—that righteous children indeed suffer for the sins of the parents. One of them, Rabbi Yossi, however, mitigates the moral problem by limiting the theological doctrine to this world only: "[If a person's] deeds are good but his father's deeds are not good. His father causes him to suffer (lit. not to enjoy) in this world, but his [own] deeds cause him to enjoy the next world [עולם הבא]."[54]

One last example of where *olam ha-ba* acts as an ethical reflex involves a specific type of inherited punishment that has real-life consequences. And that is the case of *mamzer*, a bastard child that is the product of incest or an extramarital affair. Tragically, this child can never marry a standard (non-*mamzer*) Jew. No doubt, this law clashes with the moral principle of individual responsibility that the rabbis elsewhere promote. Consequently, *Leviticus Rabbah* attributes the following question to Daniel the Tailor: "If the parents of these *mamzerim* committed transgression, what concern is it of these poor sufferers [i.e., the children]?"[55] Strikingly, according to Daniel the Tailor, when Ecclesiastes 4:1 speaks of "all the oppressions that are done under the sun," it refers specifically to children who are *mamzerim* due to no fault of their own. Amazingly, this late rabbinic text depicts this challenging Torah law as "oppressive."

Yet, here too—as in the other two cases—the midrash has God declare that the "next world" will provide respite for the "oppressed" children: "It shall be My task to comfort them. For in this world there is dross in them, but in the World to Come ... they will all be pure gold."[56] Needless to say, these types of distinctions—between this world and the next world—do not appear in the Bible itself.[57] Notably, in each of these three aforementioned examples—evil inclination, inherited guilt, and *mamzer*—the exegetical grounding is forced, thus highlighting the rabbinic agenda to minimize the moral-theological irritant.[58]

In conclusion, the rabbis use *olam ha-ba* as a category to place their hopes, fears, anxieties, and yearnings. However, not all of them adopted the mythic speculations of their colleagues. There was some rabbinic pushback against these types of theologizing. For instance, in the Babylonian Talmud (*Sanhedrin* 99a), we have two forms of critique: the first, attributed to the early Palestinian *Amora*, Rav Yochanan, challenges the very notion that we can know what *olam ha-ba* will bring:[59] "R. Hiyya b. Abba said in R. Yohanan's name: All the prophets prophesied [all the good things] only in respect of the Messianic era; but as for the world to come 'the eye has not seen, O Lord, beside You, what he has prepared for him that waits for him' [Isaiah 64:3]."

The second critique of *olam ha-ba* speculation, attributed to the early Babylonian *Amora* Samuel, relies on the belief that *olam ha-ba* will be exactly the same as *olam ha-zeh*, with only one difference: the Jewish people will no longer be controlled by foreign nations; they will have political independence. "Samuel said: This world differs from [that of] the days of the Messiah only in respect of servitude to [foreign] powers."

DEDICATION

This article is lovingly dedicated to the memory of Stewart Harris. *Yehi Zichro Baruch* [May his memory be for a blessing].

NOTES

1. See Efraim E. Urbach, *The Sages: Their Concepts and Beliefs* (Jerusalem: Magnes Press, 1975), 4.

2. On the relative lateness of Judaism's embrace of the afterlife, see George Foot Moore, *Judaism in the First Centuries of the Christian Era: The Age of the Tannaim* (Cambridge: Harvard University Press, 1954), 291.

The prerabbinic Ethiopic (non-Hebrew) equivalent, *alam zayekawwen* [the world which is come to come], can be found in *1 Enoch* 71:15. See *Outside the Bible: Ancient Jewish Writings Related to Scripture*, vol. 2 (ed. Louis H. Feldman, James L. Kugel, and Lawrence H. Schiffman; Philadelphia: Jewish Publication Society, 2013), 1399 notes to 71:15. To be sure, while the technical term *olam ha-ba* emerged in the rabbinic period, the Jewish notion of a separate life for the soul after death long predated the rabbinic period.

3. See Max Kadushin, *The Rabbinic Mind* (2nd ed.; New York: Blaisdell Pub. Co., 1965), 363–65; Urbach, *The Sages*, 651, 52.

4. The tenet of bodily resurrection also surfaces as a Jewish theology in 2 Maccabees 7 and *1 Enoch* 51:1–2, 102:4–103:8. These Second Temple texts, however, were not considered sacred for traditional Jews through the millennia. For an analysis of corporate resurrection

in the Hebrew Bible, see Jon Douglas Levenson, *Resurrection and the Restoration of Israel: The Ultimate Victory of the God of Life* (New Haven: Yale University Press, 2006).

5. Note, famously, that the Sadducees in the Second Temple period rejected the existence of *olam ha-ba*. See Josephus, *The Jewish War* chapter 7, and Mishna *Sanhedrin* 10:1.

6. *Midrash Tanhuma* (Buber) *shelah* 28.

7. *Exodus Rabbah* 15:31.

8. *Exodus Rabbah* 41:6.

9. Baḥya ben Joseph ibn Paḳuda, *The Book of Direction to the Duties of the Heart* (ed. Menahem Mansoor; The Littman Library of Jewish Civilization; London: Routledge & K. Paul, 1973), 258; Sa'adia Gaon, *The Book of Beliefs and Opinions* (trans. Samuel Rosenblatt; Yale Judaica Series; New Haven: Yale University Press, 1976), 326 ff; Judah Halevy, *The Kuzari (Kitab Al Khazari): An Argument for the Faith of Israel* (trans. Hartwig Hirschfield; New York: Schocken Books, 1964), 80.

10. See Mordecai Kaplan, *Judaism as a Civilization: Toward a Reconstruction of American-Jewish Life* (Philadelphia: Jewish Publication Society of America, 1994), 8–15. Even in twentieth century modern Orthodox circles, the focus of religious life revolved around this world. See Joseph Dov Soloveitchik, *Halakhic Man* (Philadelphia: Jewish Publication Society of America, 1983), 30–32.

11. Abraham Joshua Heschel, *Heavenly Torah: As Refracted through the Generations* (trans. Gordon Tucker; New York: Continuum, 2005); Max Kadushin, *Organic Thinking: A Study in Rabbinic Thought* (New York: Jewish Theological Seminary of America, 1938); Kadushin, *The Rabbinic Mind*; Arthur Marmorstein, *Studies in Jewish Theology* (London: Oxford University Press, 1950); and *The Old Rabbinic Doctrine of God* (Farnborough: Gregg, 1969); Urbach, *The Sages*.

12. Urbach, *The Sages*, 436–44.

13. C. G. Montefiore and H. Loewe, *A Rabbinic Anthology* (New York: Schocken Books, 1974).

14. Ibid., 580.

15. Kaplan, *Judaism as a Civilization*, 8, 9.

16. Ibid., 402.

17. See David Charles Kraemer, *Responses to Suffering in Classical Rabbinic Literature* (New York: Oxford University Press, 1995), 39, 40.

18. BT *Ta'anit* 11a.

19. Also see BT *Hullin* 142 and *Tanhuma* (ed. Buber) *Pekude* 7.

20. See *Genesis Rabbah* 33:1 and *Pesikta de-Rav Kahana* (ed. Mandelbaum) 9.

21. On this rabbinic notion, see *Mekhilta de-Rabbi Ishmael*, *baḥodesh* 10, and *Sifre Deuteronomy* 32. The dictum is often repeated by his students in rabbinic literature

(e.g., BT *Bava Metzi'a* 85a and BT *Sanhedrin* 101a). On Rabbi Akiva's understanding of suffering, also see E. P. Sanders, "Akiba's View of Suffering," *Jewish Quarterly Review* 63 (1972–1973): 332–52; Urbach, *The Sages*, 444–48. Also see the related maxim attributed to Rabbi Judah the Prince in *Avot de-Rabbi Nathan* (ed. Schechter version a, 28) that if people get pleasure in this world, they will lose an equal amount of that pleasure in the next world. Interestingly, the German pietists of the thirteenth century would radicalize this notion even further by willfully afflicting themselves so as to incur greater pleasures in the next world. See chapter three of Ivan G. Marcus, *Piety and Society: The Jewish Pietists of Medieval Germany* (Leiden: Brill, 1981).

22. BT *Pesachim* 50a. For other examples of rabbinic texts that contrast *olam ha-ba* and *olam ha-zeh*, see especially *Leviticus Rabbah* 13:3, BT *Bava Metsia* 85b, and *Midrash Psalms* 91.

23. *Ecclesiastes Rabbah* 5. For other examples of *olam ha-zeh* as foreshadowing *olam ha-ba*, see *Genesis Rabbah* 62:2; BT *Bava Batra* 15b, 16b; *Pesikta de-Rav Kahana* (ed. Mandelbaum) 12; and *Midrash Psalms* 84.

24. *Sifre Deuteronomy* 357. See also *Midrash Psalms* 13.

25. *Leviticus Rabbah* 1.

26. *Pesikta de-Rav Kahana* (ed. Mandelbaum) 4.

27. *Pesikta de-Rav Kahana* (ed. Mandelbaum) 12 and echoed in *Tanhuma vayigash* 11. Also see *Tanhuma* (ed. Buber) *miketz* 4, which posits that in the next world all of Israel will become prophets.

28. JT *Megillah* 2:4, 73b. See also *Song of Songs Rabbah*, 7 and *Midrash Psalms* 48. Other examples of the mystical function of *olam ha-ba* include the saying of God's real name (BT *Pesachim* 50a, *Midrash Psalms* 91) and God's direct blessing to all of Israel (*Pesikta Rabbati* 5).

29. *Ecclesiastes Rabbah* 1.

30. *Mishnah Sanhedrin* 10:1. See also *Leviticus Rabbah* 13:2, which declares that idolaters have no share in the world to come.

31. Menachem Marc Kellner, *Must a Jew Believe Anything?* (London; Portland: Littman Library of Jewish Civilization, 1999).

32. *Tosefta Sanhedrin* 13:1. R. Joshua challenges Rabbi Eliezer's view, arguing that righteous gentiles will receive a share in *olam ha-ba*. Also see *Mekhilta de-Rabbi Ishmael, nezikin*, 10, which declares that gentiles have no redemption in the "time to come." Strikingly, some rabbis even wanted to rob Solomon of his *olam ha-ba* until a heavenly voice intervened (see *Tanhuma*, Buber, *metsorah* 1).

33. See *Mishnah Sanhedrin* 10:3, *Tosefta* (ed. Zuckermandel) 13:6, 8, 9.

34. *Mishna, Avot* 3:11.

35. *Lev. Rabbah* 13:3.

36. *Eccl. R* 1.

37. *Avot Rabbi Nathan*, version a, 12.

38. *Avot de-Rabbi Nathan*, version b, 34.

39. *Avot de-Rabbi Nathan*, version a, 36.

40. *Avot de-Rabbi Nathan*, version b, 34.

41. *Midrash Mishlei* 17.

42. *Avot de-Rabbi Nathan*, version a, 14.

43. In the ninth century, Sa'adia Gaon (882–942 C.E.) attempted to prove the existence of an afterlife because otherwise God would be unjust: "We are confronted by the fact that God, the just, ordered the killing of the young children of the Midianites (Num 31:17) and the extermination of the young children of the Generation of the Flood (Gen 6–9). We note also how He continually causes pain and even death to little babes. Logical Necessity, therefore, demands that there exist after death a state in which they would obtain compensation for the pain suffered prior thereto." Sa'adia Gaon, *The Book of Beliefs and Opinions* (trans. Samuel Rosenblatt; New Haven: Yale University Press, 1976), 330. In this passage, Sa'adia acknowledges that God's decision to wipe out, inter alia, the generation of the Flood, minus Noah and his family, if taken at face value, was immoral. Even if every adult acted violently and with corruption (Gen. 6:12)—and that itself is a huge assumption—what could justify God's destruction of small children? To defend God, Sa'adia posits the necessity of the afterlife: although killed in this world, children will be rewarded in the next one. (Sa'adia ignores *Mishnah Sanhedrin* 10:3: "The generation of the Flood does not have a share in the World to Come [עולם הבא]." Cf. *Tosefta Sanhedrin* 13:2, 6.) Remarkably, for this Jewish theologian, God's killing of children, or His commanding of it, proves the existence of the afterlife; for if the soul does not survive death, then God would be deemed immoral and unjust, which for Sa'adia, as a staunch defender of God's justice, would be rationally impossible.

44. See Heschel, *Heavenly Torah*, 694.

45. Ishay Rosen-Zvi, "The Torah Speaks to the Evil Inclination: The School of Ishmael and the Origins of the Evil Inclination," *Tarbiz* 66 (2007): 41–79; and "The Evil Inclination in Amoraic Literature," *Tarbiz* 67 (2008): 71–107.

46. Rosen-Zvi, "Torah Speaks," 45–60.

47. Jacob Albert van den Berg, *Biblical Argument in Manichaean Missionary Practice: The Case of Adimantus and Augustine* (Leiden; Boston: Brill, 2010), 117, 18; Adolf von Harnack, *Marcion: The Gospel of the Alien God* (Durham: Labyrinth Press, 1990), 58, 68, 69; Origen, *Contra Celsum* (trans. Henry Chadwick; Cambridge: Cambridge University Press, 1980), 370, 71; Edward Young, "Celsus and the Old Testament," *Westminster Theological Journal* 6 (1944): 186.

48. These texts are analyzed by Daniel Boyarin, *Carnal Israel: Reading Sex in Talmudic Culture* (New Historicism 25; Berkeley: University of California Press, 1993), 61–67.

The most radical Christian-like explanation appears in *Avot de-Rabbi Nathan* (version b) 42: God implanted the Evil Inclination in humanity as a punishment to Adam for eating the Tree of Knowledge.

49. Using various formulations, post-Tannaitic texts also present this teaching. See, for example, BT *Kiddushin* 30b, BT *Avodah Zarah* 5b, BT *Bava Batra* 16a, *Avot de Rabbi Nathan* (version a), 16.

50. *Exodus Rabbah* II 41:7.

51. See *Genesis Rabbah* 48:11, 89:1; *Exodus Rabbah* II 41:7, 46:4; *Numbers Rabbah* II 17:6; *Deuteronomy Rabbah* 2:80, 6:14; *Pesiqta Rabbati* 29; *Tanhuma yitro* 17; *Tanhuma* (Buber) *bereishit* 40; *Tanhuma* (Buber) *kedoshim* 15; *Tanhuma* (Buber) *shelah* 31; *Tanhuma* (Buber) huqqat supplement #1; *Tanhuma* (Buber) *va-ethanan* 2; *Seder Eliyahu Rabbah* 3, 16; *Ecclesiastes Rabbah* 2:1, 12:1.

52. See, for example, van den Berg, *Biblical Argument*, 107–8; von Harnack, *Marcion*, 69; Julian, *Against the Galileans* (trans. R. Joseph Hoffmann; Amherst: Prometheus Books, 2004), 102; Samuel Thrope, "Contradictions and Vile Utterances: The Zoroastrian Critique of Judaism in the Skand Gumanig Wizar" (Ph.D. diss., University of California, Berkeley, 2012), 170.

53. *Mekhilta de-Rabbi Ishmael, bahodesh*, 7.

54. *Avot Rabbi Nathan* (version b, 22). A similar solution can be found in *Ecclesiastes Rabbah* 4:1.

55. *Leviticus Rabbah* 32:8. See also the position of Daniel the Tailor cited in *Ecclesiastes Rabbah* 4:1 and the debate between R. Yossi and R. Meir in JT *Kiddushin* 3:13.

56. *Leviticus Rabbah* 32:8.

57. See also *Midrash Psalms* 19:13, which records a debate as to whether there will be Gehinnom in the next world; in *Leviticus Rabbah* 19:5 a view is presented that there will be no Attribute of Justice [*midat hadin*] in the future world.

58. *Ecclesiastes Rabbah* 1:6 and BT *Nedarim* 8b (in the name of Reish Lakish) claim that there will be no Gehinnom in the next world. See also *Midrash Psalms* 19.

59. Also see *Midrash Mishlei* 13.

Dining In(to) the World to Come
Jordan D. Rosenblum

The ancient rabbis believe in two worlds: their present, lived reality, which they refer to in Hebrew as *olam ha-zeh*, or "this world"; and a future, not-yet-experienced realm, which they call in Hebrew *olam ha-ba*, or "the world to come." It is in *olam ha-ba* that the just receive their divine reward and the wicked incur their divine punishment. The world to come thus solves the problem of theodicy, or divine justice. Since present, lived reality does not always accord with rabbinic ideals, the future realm of *olam ha-ba* establishes an alternate universe in which the real and the ideal resolve from discord into harmony. The world to come is how the rabbis explain theologically problematic but empirically observed paradoxes encountered in this world. For example, why do good things happen to bad people, while bad things happen to good people? Why is a young child afflicted with cancer or killed in a car crash? And why do reality television shows bring fame and fortune on the amoral and the rabbinically reprehensible?

While other essays in this volume explore additional aspects of the dual rabbinic realms of this world and the world to come, some of which also intersect with food, I focus in this essay on two specific, and interrelated, questions: (1) What diet in this world merits entrance into the world to come; and (2) Upon entering this future realm, what menu awaits therein? In doing so, I argue that consideration of dining into and in *olam ha-ba*, the world to come, is a mechanism for the ancient rabbis to justify their preferred dietary practices in *olam ha-zeh*, this world.

DINING INTO THE WORLD TO COME

In the Hebrew Bible, certain foods are permitted, while others are tabooed. Explicit rationales for the inclusion or the exclusion of various foodstuffs, however, are almost never found in biblical texts. The rabbis, like other both Jewish and non-Jewish ancient commentators, seek to explain the meaning behind these often unjustified practices.[1] One example of this phenomenon is encountered during a conversation about why God chose to give the Torah to Israel (i.e., to Jews) rather than to any other nation. In the midst of this discussion, the following parable appears in *Leviticus Rabbah* 13:2:

[A] Rabbi Tanḥum bar Hanilai said:

[B] This may be compared with the case of a physician who went to visit two sick persons, one who would live, and another who would die.

[C] To the one who would live, he said: "This and that you may not eat."

[D] But to the one would die, he said to them:[2] "Whatever he wants [to eat], bring it to him."

[E] Thus, of the [other] nations of the world, who are not destined for the life of the world to come, [it is written in regard to them,] "[Every moving thing that lives shall be food for you;] as the green herbs, I have given you all" (Gen 9:3).

[F] But to Israel, who are destined for the life of the world to come, [it is written,] "These are the *living things* [*ha-ḥayyah*] that you may eat from among all of the quadrupeds on the land" (Lev 11:2).[3]

Using the parable, a common rabbinic interpretive mechanism, this text discusses a physician who has two patients: one presents with merely a minor malady and the other with a fatal illness. To the one who will survive, the doctor prescribes a careful dietary regimen, since that patient will heal and recover. To the one who will not survive, however, the doctor permits all foods, since a dying person need not count calories, worry about how much sodium she is eating, or order the heart-healthy entrée.[4] After all, there is no reason to skip dessert if these are your last few meals in this world.

Gentiles are the terminal patient in this parable. Destined to die in this world, but not be revived in the world to come, they can eat "all." Hence, Genesis 9:3 allows them to eat everything. Jews, on the other hand, are the living patient in this parable. Destined to live beyond this world and to enter the world to come, they cannot eat "all." It is for this reason that in Leviticus 11:2 their divine doctor commands them to only eat "living things" [*ha-ḥayyah*].[5]

I have purposely translated "living things" differently from how it is usually rendered when translating the biblical verse in its original context, simply as "creatures." Playing on the dual meaning of the Hebrew word *ha-ḥayyah*, which literally means "living things," the rabbis understand God, the divine physician, to command Jews to eat only living things, which in turn will grant Jews life in the world to come. Gentiles do not eat only living things, and thus they are denied access to the world to come.[6]

This text presumes the chosenness of Israel, who alone enters the world to come.[7] Of course, this is not the only domain in which the rabbis presume that Israel is a special, chosen, and divinely set-apart people. It is for this reason, for example, that since the early rabbinic period, the daily morning liturgy includes a blessing praising the fact "that [God] did not make me a Gentile."[8] Chosen for a special diet with special benefits, Jews are rewarded. Meanwhile, like the child who was not chosen for the kickball team in gym class, Gentiles must remain eternally on the sidelines and watch while others enjoy the fun.[9]

As a biological necessity, eating is a matter of life or death. For the rabbis, eating is also a matter of eternal life or death. One key reason for the biblical food laws is therefore to guarantee that, by following these dietary prescriptions, Jews ingest the essential vitamins and nutrients to assure them entrance into the world to come.[10] Eating "all" food sustains Gentiles in this world, but eating only "living things" sustains Jews both in this world and in the world to come.

Though Jews must fastidiously observe the proper rabbinic diet in order to guarantee their acceptance into the world to come, the rabbis are careful not to renounce the permitted pleasures of this world. According to one tradition, for example:

[A] Rabbi Ḥezekiah [said] Rabbi Cohen [said] in the name of Rav:

[B] In the future, man must give a summary and account concerning all [permitted foods] that his eyes beheld, but he did not eat.

[C] Rabbi Lazar considered this teaching and set aside funds so that he could eat every [permitted] thing once a year.[11]

The world to come promises to be a culinary extravaganza.[12] That being said, the rabbis do not want Jews to forget that there are myriad delicious foods available for consumption in this world.[13] In fact, these very permitted foods combine to form the diet necessary for entrance into the buffet found in the world to come. A good rabbinic Jew should not completely forsake this world. To reformulate a famous biblical pseudo-quotation:[14] eat all rabbinically permitted foods, drink all rabbinically permitted drinks, and be merry in all rabbinically permitted manners, for tomorrow you die in this world, but through engaging in a rabbinically permitted lifestyle, you will live eternally in the world to come.

DINING IN THE WORLD TO COME

Though proper diet merits one entrance into the world to come, upon arrival, two important culinary changes occur: (1) previously forbidden foods are now permitted, and (2) previously mythical foods are now existent. Taken together, this means that the world to come features a cornucopia of cuisines unimaginable in this world.

The world to come is a realm of reversals. The wicked are punished; the good are rewarded; and perhaps most shockingly of all, nonkosher food is now kosher. In a fascinating reversal, foods forbidden to Jews in this world will be permitted in the world to come. The reward reaped by the pious rabbinic Jew for not eating nonkosher food in this world, therefore, is not only entrance into the world to come, but the opportunity to enjoy these formerly forbidden foodstuffs for eternity. As *Leviticus Rabbah* 13:3 makes abundantly clear: Why are Jews commanded not to eat forbidden food in this world?

> [A] In order that you may eat it in the time to come.
>
> [B] For this reason, Moses cautioned Israel, and said to them:
>
> [C] "These are the *living things* [*ha-ḥayyah*] that you may eat" (Lev 11:2).[15]

The time to come, in Hebrew *la'atid labo'*, is a common variant rabbinic term for the world to come. This text contains another future-food-related exegesis of Leviticus 11:2, wherein the divine doctor is now the divine teacher. Acting on behalf of God, Moses declares only some foods suitable for ingestion by the Israelites in order to teach Israel the vital rabbinic virtue of self-restraint.[16] To observe the rabbinic food laws is therefore to embody rabbinic theology relating to diet, eschatology, and ethics. Israel must refrain from placing pork on its plate in this world in order to cultivate self-restraint; and, in doing so, Israel shall enjoy piles of pork on its plate in the world to come. Or, to pun a common English idiom: a piggy saved is a piggy earned.

In fact, the Hebrew word for pig, *ḥazir*, contains this very lesson hidden within it etymologically. "Why is [pig] called by the name '*ḥazir*'? Because it is destined to restore [*lehaḥazir*] greatness and sovereignty to its rightful owner."[17] In this text, "pig" stands in for all nonkosher animals. However, casting the pig to play this role is quite important. In antiquity, as in today, pig is understood to represent the most nonkosher animal. It therefore often serves as a synecdoche for the entire category of "nonkosher." Further, "pig" was a common rabbinic metonym for Rome, Romanness, and Roman authority.[18]

So Rome, or "The Pig," currently possesses greatness and sovereignty. However, that is only in this world. In the world to come, greatness and sovereignty will be restored to their rightful owner, the Jews. And how does the Hebrew word for pig, *ḥazir*, teach this lesson? In Hebrew, the infinitive "to restore" is *lehaḥazir*. Pig, *ḥazir*, and "to restore," *lehaḥazir*, therefore share the same Hebrew root letters, *ḥ-z-r*, a linguistic connection that the rabbis also pun in other texts.[19] This shared root is understood to be instructive: in this world, Jews, who cannot eat pig, are ruled by Rome, or "The Pig." As non-Jews, however, Romans cannot transcend this world; as such, "The Pig" shall not enter into the world to come. In the world to come, a world without "The Pig," Jews will once again rule themselves. Restored to power, Jews may then eat pig, which represents both protein and power, both now rightfully theirs. But today, in this world, both the literal and the figurative pig is best avoided.

As we have just seen, the world to come features a smorgasbord that would put even the fanciest Las Vegas buffet to shame. In addition to famously nonkosher foods like pork and shellfish, the righteous, deserving diners in the world to come will be allowed to dine on formerly mythical beasts, like the Behemoth, a land creature; the Leviathan, a sea creature; and the lesser-known Ziz, a bird.[20] According to some traditions, God created these mythical creatures for the specific future purpose of feeding those who merit entrance into the world to come.[21] According to another tradition, found on *b. Bava Batra* 74b–75a, God created male and female Leviathans and Behemoths and then realized that, should they mate, they and their kin would be capable of complete world domination. (They are, after all, enormous sea and land creatures.) Turning lemons into future lemonade, God castrated both the male Leviathan and the male Behemoth, and then dealt with their potential mates: in the case of the Leviathan, Mrs. Leviathan is killed; in the case of the Behemoth, Mrs. Behemoth is "cooled," which suggests a removal of her sexual drive, rendering her functionally sterile. This text implies that the male Leviathan and the male Behemoth are allowed to roam the world, without companion or mate. They cannot propagate; they can only wait.

The female Leviathan and the female Behemoth, however, are both "preserved for the righteous in the time to come."[22] Further, the future banquet at which the Leviathan's flesh shall be served is understood to have a specific guest list: not just Jews, but *talmidei ḥakhamim*, or rabbinic scholars.[23] The remainder of the Leviathan carcass will be sold in the Jerusalem markets, suggesting that nonscholars may enter into the world to come and that Jerusalem will still hold markets in the world to come, but also implying that if one wishes to have a seat at the best table and to eat the best food for eternity, then he[24] should aspire to a life of Torah study. As is a common practice throughout rabbinic literature, the rabbis once again remind their audience of the importance of busying oneself in the study of rabbinic texts. Otherwise, even if you are righteous enough to merit entrance into the world to come, you will spend eternity shopping for and eating second-rate cuts of Leviathan and Behemoth meat.

Further, according to *Leviticus Rabbah* 22:10:

> [A] Rabbi Menaḥma and Rabbi Bebai and Rabbi Aḥa and Rabbi Yoḥanan [said] in the name of Rabbi Yonatan:[25]
>
> [B] As compensation for what I have forbidden you [in this world], I have permitted you [in the world to come].
>
> [C] As compensation for the prohibition of fishes,[26] the Leviathan will be a pure fish.[27]
>
> [D] As compensation for the prohibition of fowl,[28] the Ziz will be a pure bird. . . .
>
> [E] And why do they call it "Ziz"?
>
> [F] Because it has many kinds of tastes, [the taste of] this [*zeh*] and [the taste of] that [*zeh*].
>
> [G] As compensation for the prohibition of beasts [*behemah*], the Behemoth [will be eaten on] a thousand mountains.[29]

The rabbis imagine God as offering what psychologists term delayed gratification, in which a mild pleasure or small reward now is deferred in order to receive a significantly greater pleasure or reward at a later time.[30] The divine reward for following biblical food taboos was built into the system by God at Creation. This conceptualization provides a subtle rabbinic rationalization for unjustified biblical culinary regulations. Why should a Jew not eat a fish without fins and scales or a biblically forbidden bird, such as the raven, in this world? Because to do so is to forfeit forever an opportunity to dine on an even better meal in the world to come. Why eat a McDonald's cheeseburger today when you can feast on Behemoth burgers on "a thousand mountains" for all of eternity? Why eat bland chicken not slaughtered according to rabbinic regulations, when you know that one day the nuanced flavors of the Ziz will caress your palate? These mythical creatures provide a sense of purpose to unjustified biblical law. They whet the theological palate.

CONCLUSION

As a realm of reversal, retribution, and redemption, the world to come rebalances the rabbinic scales of justice. It also serves as a mechanism to explain the unexplainable in this world. This is especially true in regard to the biblical food laws. The rabbis divide all biblical commandments into two categories: (1) *mišpatim*, which are based on logical principles; and (2) *ḥukim*, which are illogical in nature. The rabbis categorize the biblical food laws as *ḥukim*, and hence, though they must be followed like any other biblical commandment, they lack a logical justification.[31] A rabbinic Jew must engage in these practices simply because God said so.[32]

The role that diet plays in regard to dining into and dining in the world to come therefore serves as an important rabbinic means of justification for a seemingly illogical set of divine commandments in this world.[33] Though illogical, dietary rules are central to daily practice; for this reason, that which is unjustified demands justification. The function of dietary practice in dining into and dining in the world to come offers significant explanatory value for the function of dining practices in this world.

Faithfully following these illogical divine commandments promises a good rabbinic Jew an opportunity to earn the golden ticket, allowing entrance into Chef God's eternal banquet of mythical and magical mouthwatering foods. Much like Charlie in Willie Wonka's Chocolate Factory, a Jew in this world is presented with temptation. After all, according to one rabbinic source:

[A] A person should not say: . . . I do not want to eat pig meat. . . .

[B] But [rather, a person should say]: I want [to perform this prohibited act, but] what can I do, for my father in heaven decreed concerning me thusly?[34]

As Charlie discovered inside Willie Wonka's Chocolate Factory, rejecting one illicit offer can lead to a far greater reward. Acknowledging gastronomic temptation, the proper rabbinic Jew must make the theologically correct decision and delay his or her gratification in this world. By doing so, the faithful rabbinic Jew merits entrance into the world to come, wherein he or she reaps the reward of delayed gratification: not only is the formerly prohibited now permitted, but previously unimaginable delicacies are now on the dinner menu.

NOTES

1. I discuss this process in *The Jewish Dietary Laws in Late Antiquity* (New York: Cambridge University Press, 2016). The core of this essay draws from a section therein (see 135–39).

2. The plural pronoun [*la-hem*] here either anticipates the application of the parable (wherein the dying person is compared to the other nations), is addressed to the ones

taking care of the patient, is a typographical error (the singular form appears in one manuscript), or the plural form should appear in both instances (as it does in some manuscripts) and merely suggests the general application of this parable.

3. Ed. Margulies 276, emphasis added. See also *Exodus Rabbah* 30:22, *Ecclesiastes Rabbah* 5.6.1, *Tanhuma Shemini* 10. The translation of Leviticus 11:2 is based on that of Jacob Milgrom, *Leviticus 1–16: A New Translation with Introduction and Commentary* (Anchor Bible 3; New York: Doubleday, 1991), 643, 645–46 (with an important difference, which I discuss below). Unless otherwise noted, all translations are my own.

In addition to in *The Jewish Dietary Laws in Late Antiquity* (see 136–37), I have also written about this text in Jordan D. Rosenblum, "Justifications for Foodways and the Study of Commensality," in *Commensality: From Everyday Food to Feast* (ed. Susanne Kerner, et al.; New York: Bloomsbury Academic, 2015), 189–94; and "Jewish Meals in Antiquity," in *A Companion to Food in the Ancient World* (ed. John M. Wilkins and Robin Nadeau; New York: Wiley Blackwell, 2015), 353–54.

4. Though in a different context, a similar metaphor is used by the early Christian author Augustine (*On the Profit of Believing*, 29).

5. Some rabbinic slaughter regulations are derived from the same wording of this passage (e.g., *b. Hullin* 42a).

6. For other discussions about Gentiles eating everything only in this world and only Jews entering the world to come, see *Pesiqta Rabbati* 16:6, *Ecclesiastes Rabbah* 1.9.1. Converts receive entrance to the world to come and can partake of the food therein, as is implied in regard to the Leviathan in *y. Megillah* 1:13, 72b (see *y. Megillah* 3:2, 74a, *y. Sanhedrin* 10:6, 29c). On this text, see Shaye J. D. Cohen, "The Conversion of Antoninus," in *The Talmud Yerushalmi and Graeco-Roman Culture I* (ed. Peter Schäfer; Tübingen: Mohr Siebeck, 1997), 141–72.

7. For a discussion of how this general concept functions throughout the rabbinic corpus, see Sacha Stern, *Jewish Identity in Early Rabbinic Writings* (New York: E. J. Brill, 1994), 42–46, 200–202, and *passim*.

8. *t. Berakhot* 6:18 (ed. Lieberman 1:38); see also *b. Menahot* 43b.

9. On the rabbinic limitation of the applicability of kosher laws only to Jews, see Jordan D. Rosenblum, *Food and Identity in Early Rabbinic Judaism* (New York: Cambridge University Press, 2010), 68–73. For a text that depicts Gentiles unsuccessfully trying to alter their diet in order to enter the world to come, see *Ecclesiastes Rabbah* 1.9.1.

10. Speaking more generally, *b. Yoma* 39a notes that if one makes himself impure in this world, then he is impure also in the world to come (an exegesis of Lev 11:43); in contrast, if one makes himself sanctified in this world, then he is sanctified also in the world to come.

11. *y. Qiddushin* 4:12, 66b (ed. Schäfer and Becker 3:432); see also *b. Eruvin* 54a. On making sure to eat food that one likes (perhaps with repercussions in the world to come), see *Avot d'Rabbi Natan* A26:19. For further discussion of one's yearly food budget, see *b. Betzah* 15b–16a.

12. This belief, which appears often in rabbinic texts (e.g., *Pesiqta Rabbati* 41:5, *b. Ketubbot* 111b, and several texts noted in this essay), is not unique to the rabbis. Other Jews in antiquity held the same belief, though each group interpreted this future practice based on its own theological assumptions. For example, see the messianic banquet described in the Dead Sea Scrolls (e.g., 1Q28a 2:11–22). It should be noted that not all rabbis agreed with these views. For example, Rav argues that there is neither eating nor drinking in the world to come (*b. Berakhot* 17a). Most rabbis, however, presume not only eating and drinking, but sumptuous feasting therein.

13. On how the rabbinic gaze functions in this narrative, see Rachel Neis, *The Sense of Sight in Rabbinic Culture: Jewish Ways of Seeing in Late Antiquity* (New York: Cambridge University Press, 2013), 115.

14. This "quote" jumbles Isaiah 22:13 and Ecclesiastes 8:15.

15. Ed. Margulies 279 (emphasis added). Also see *Midrash Tehillim* 146:4, which contains traditions both supporting and arguing against the permission of eating in the world to come flesh that is forbidden in this world. I thank Dov Weiss for this reference.

16. In general, see Michael L. Satlow, "'Try to Be a Man': The Rabbinic Construction of Masculinity," *Harvard Theological Review* 89:1 (1996): 19–40.

17. *Ecclesiastes Rabbah* 1.9.1.

18. For the history of this association, see Jordan D. Rosenblum, "'Why Do You Refuse to Eat Pork?': Jews, Food, and Identity in Roman Palestine," *Jewish Quarterly Review* 100:1 (2010): 95–110.

19. For example, see Jordan D. Rosenblum, "The Night Rabbi Aqiba Slept with Two Women," in *A Most Reliable Witness: Essays in Honor of Ross Shepard Kraemer* (ed. Susan Ashbrook Harvey, et al.; Brown Judaic Studies 358; Providence: Brown Judaic Studies, 2015), 67–75 (esp. 73–74).

20. See, e.g., *Leviticus Rabbah* 13:3 (which includes their method of slaughter, with reference to *m. Hullin* 1:2), 22:10. See also *Pesiqta Rabbati* 16:4, *Pesiqta Rabbati* 48:3, *Tanhuma Beshallah* 24, *b. Bava Batra* 74b–75a, and above, n. 6. For an excellent discussion that sets these, and additional, traditions into their ancient context, see Debra Scoggins Ballentine, *The Conflict Myth and the Biblical Tradition* (New York: Oxford University Press, 2015), 150–66.

21. See *Pesiqta Rabbati* 48:3; Ballentine, *Conflict Myth*, 165.

22. *b. Bava Batra* 74b. See Ballentine, *Conflict Myth*, 163–64. The term "preserved" is different for each animal in this text, as more literally the female Leviathan is "salted" and the female Behemoth is "kept/guarded." Perhaps Mrs. Leviathan is "salted" because she is killed (at least in this world), and salting is a common method for preserving meat.

23. *b. Bava Batra* 75a. On converts eating Leviathan meat, see above, n. 6.

24. Throughout, I am careful to use the gendered pronouns that most accurately reflect ancient rabbinic opinions. For example, I use the male pronoun here because the rabbis

gendered Torah study as a male activity (see Satlow, "Try to Be a Man"). However, when the gender is not specific or can include either gender, then I use gender neutral and/or inclusive pronouns.

25. The names of these rabbis are not consistent in the manuscripts. On the redemptive value for citing the names of those who uttered a rabbinic tradition, see *b. Hullin* 104b.

26. In Leviticus 11:9–12 and Deuteronomy 14:9–10. Pure sea creatures must have both fins and scales.

27. On the Leviathan as a pure fish, also see, e.g., *b. Hullin* 67b.

28. In Leviticus 11:13–19 and Deuteronomy 14:11–20. Biblical texts offer no explicit criteria for inclusion or exclusion of fowl from the category of pure (and hence permitted for ingestion). Later interpreters claim that the category of excluded fowl are birds of prey (e.g., *b. Hullin* 65a [commenting on *m. Hullin* 3:6], *b. Niddah* 50b).

29. Ed. Margulies 522–23. On the thousand mountain tradition for the Behemoth, see Psalm 50:10, *Pesiqta Rabbati* 48:3.

30. See, e.g., Walter Mischel, *The Marshmallow Test: Mastering Self-Control* (New York: Little, Brown and Company, 2014).

31. See *Sifra Ahare Mot* 13:10 (see also *b. Yoma* 67b).

32. When I delivered this essay, I had not yet read the recent book by fellow contributor Christine Hayes: *What's Divine About Divine Law?: Early Perspectives* (Princeton: Princeton University Press, 2015). In this excellent volume, Hayes contextualizes the claims I make herein within the broader scope of the rabbinic corpus. While we worked in parallel and without knowledge of each other's recent scholarship, we agree on most related issues. I also would like to thank Christine Hayes for offering useful feedback on the version of this essay that I delivered at the conference.

33. This is a major reason why many of the texts I cite in the body of this essay are from *Leviticus Rabbah*, a rabbinic commentary on the book of Leviticus, which contains the *locus classicus* for the biblical food laws (Lev 11; see also Deut 14).

34. *Sifra Qedoshim* 11:22 (ed. Weiss 93b).

What's for Dinner in *Olam Ha-ba*? Why Do We Care in *Olam Ha-zeh*?: Medieval Jewish Ideas about Meals in the World to Come in R. Bahya ben Asher's *Shulhan Shel Arba*

Jonathan Brumberg-Kraus

May it be Your will, Lord our God and God of our ancestors that just as I have stood up and dwelled in this sukkah so may I merit next year to dwell in the sukkah of the hide of the Leviathan. (Jewish blessing upon leaving the sukkah at the end of the holiday of Sukkot)

Any modern discussion of Jewish traditions about rewards in the world to come must confront both the mixed messages the sources themselves present us and our contemporary skepticism about the plausibility of any supernatural realms for rewards and punishments after death. A case in point is the contradictory rabbinic traditions about meals for the righteous in the world to come. On the one hand, the righteous are promised a banquet of Leviathan, Bar Yuchnai, and Behemoth in a tent made of Leviathan's skin. But Rav says, "In the world to come, there is no eating and drinking." Rabbenu Bahya ben Asher, the fourteenth century Spanish biblical exegete and kabbalist, devotes the fourth and final "Gate" of his short treatise on Jewish eating practices, *Shulhan Shel Arba* [Table of Four], to address this apparent contradiction about meals prepared for the righteous in the world to come.[1] R. Bahya thus not only attempts to resolve the problem of the mixed messages of our sources, but in doing so, I suggest, he also hints to us moderns, who are sure only about this world, why speculating about the world to come nevertheless might still be of some value.

Since R. Bahya wrote *Shulhan Shel Arba* as a guide for meals in this world, the question arises: How does talking about, imagining, and knowing about what meals are like in the next world affect our practice and enjoyment of our meals in this world? Moreover, as Caroline Walker Bynum points out in her discussion of medieval Christian traditions about the resurrection of the dead more or less contemporary with R. Bahya's account of meals in the world to come, we moderns, even beyond our general skepticism about any sort of afterlife, are embarrassed particularly by the "extreme literalism and materialism" of these accounts.² Just as R. Bahya insists the meal of Leviathan, Bar Yuchnai, and Behemoth reserved for the righteous will be an actual meal of kosher fish, fowl, and beef flesh eaten and enjoyed by our physical bodies in a big sukkah made out of Leviathan's skin, so Christian theologians in the twelfth and thirteenth centuries worried about whether our resurrected bodies will wear clothes; if Christ's foreskin will be restored; whether we'll eat and taste, smell nice aromas, or touch other bodies in heaven; or what will happen to cannibalized bodies at the resurrection of the dead.³ Will they rise as part of the people that ate them or separately as the persons they were before they were sliced, diced, and eaten?⁴

Medieval Christian artistic representations of the resurrection of the dead seem particularly preoccupied with the reassembling of dismembered body parts in at this time! Bynum suggests that bizarre as such hypermaterialistic accounts of resurrected bodies seem to us today, they are not so different in purpose from contemporary popular talk about Star Trek "teletransportation," future growing of new bodies attached to cryogenically preserved brains, and people with organ transplants and their families feeling that they've somehow absorbed their donor's personality. Namely, they reflect concern for and assumptions about "personal identity and survival."⁵ In medieval terms, these issues are usually framed in terms of body/soul dualism: does our personhood reside in the form and matter of our physical bodies or in our souls that persist after our death? However, as we shall see, R. Bahya and other medieval Jewish thinkers were quite insistent that our bodies and souls are not really separated in the world to come: both our bodies and souls get to experience the rewards of the world to come, since both worked together in this world to earn them.

And the proof is in the pudding (so to speak) that actual tasty meaty meals are reserved for the righteous in the world to come. Similarly, our bodies and souls will also dine on the intellectual meals of the "splendor of the Shekinah" (albeit in radically transformed bodies but bodies nonetheless). After the resurrection of the dead, we'll be clothed in a new kind of body without ordinary measure and dimensions, which allows our souls infinite enjoyment of and nourishment from the light of God's presence. So what does all this mean for us to talk about these meals now in *olam ha-zeh*—this world?

For most certainly, Rabbenu Bahya provided his account of Jewish traditions of meals in the world to come in his *Shulhan Shel Arba* as talking points *for meals in this world*.⁶ And so he says:

> With these words the enlightened will discern *when they're eating, may they make themselves holy* and their minds burnished fully. With these words engaged, *may they be at their table; raise their table's renown* so that "all shall say 'Glory!'" Let their hearts be made pure, to withstand any test. "*By these raise up the table*," so that "before the Lord" is its label.[7]

Such talk about body- and soul-rewarding meals in the world to come while at meals in this world is intended to cultivate what Jonathan Haidt calls the "emotion of elevation," or what Leon Kass describes in *The Hungry Soul* as the transformation of our physical hunger for food from "*Fressen* to *Essen* . . . to sanctified eating."[8]

DISTINCTION BETWEEN TWO MEALS IN THE WORLD TO COME

In order to resolve the apparent contradiction between the Talmudic traditions that specify the menu of the meal reserved for the righteous in the world to come and the baraita of Rav that "in the world to come there will be no eating and drinking," R. Bahya distinguishes between two kinds of meals that will occur in the future to come: (1) the banquet reserved for the righteous after they die when the Messiah comes, and (2) a second banquet after the general resurrection of the dead at the end of time. He makes the sequence of these two meals quite clear in his entry on "The Bridegroom Over the Table" in his book *Kad Ha-Kemach*:

> And thus we have found that our sages z"l interpreted the future: In the future the Holy One Blessed Be He will make a meal for the righteous. And we ought to believe that *this meal will be an actual physical meal*, for the foods are the pure foods prepared from the time of the six days of creation. And they are: Leviathan from the fishes, and from the birds Bar Yuchnai, and from the beasts "Behemoth upon a Thousand Hills" [Ps 50:12]. And perhaps they will be "offsprings" of the supernal light like the manna in the desert, which are more refined and whose goal is to elevate [those who eat them], because the flow of wisdom and capacity to conceive intelligible things will be greater in them then than at any other time. *And after these meals that will be at the end of time, there will be another time made anew, and this is the time of the resurrection of the dead, and in it*

> *they will be nourished and enjoy the radiance of the Shekhinah, and they will not revert to the dust*, as our rabbis z"l interpreted, "The dead, whom The Holy One Blessed be He will resurrect, will not revert to the dust." [*b.Sanhedrin* 92a], but rather they will exist eternally like the ministering angels, and they will enjoy themselves in the seven *huppot*, as our sages z"l interpreted in Seder Eliahu, "Seven huppot will the Holy One Blessed Be He make for the righteous in the future to come [*le-atid la-vo*], as it is said, 'and the Lord will create over all of Mt. Zion and over its places of assembly a cloud by day and smoke and the glow of a flaming fire by night, for over all the glory will be a *huppah*.'"[9]

This idea is not unique to him. Before him in the twelfth century, R. Abraham ibn Ezra in his commentary on Daniel 12:12 says:

> In my opinion, the righteous who died in exile will be resurrected when the Redeemer comes. . . .They will then partake of the Leviathan, Ziz, and the Behemoth and will die a second time, only to be again resurrected in the Age to Come, in which they will neither eat nor drink but luxuriate in the splendor of the *Shekhina* [God's Presence].[10]

R. Bahya in *Shulhan Shel Arba* goes into a little more detail about the difference between the two meals and their sequence, emphasizing the different kinds of bodies the righteous will have for these two meals, to account for Rav's saying that "there will be no eating or drinking":

> So in the future Israel will merit two statuses in their body and soul. Bodily meals of fine and pure foods which I mentioned, and an intellectual meal for the soul alone of the holy spirit, for so all Israel will ascend to the level of prophecy.
>
> And now I will explain to you in what follows about the world of souls, which will come to human beings after their separation from the world, and the matter of the world to come, which is *after* the resurrection and the matter of the joy that the soul has in all these worlds together. Know that the intellectual meal is for the body and soul at the time of the resurrection of the dead, because the routine for the body will be cancelled completely, and another routine—marvelous and new—will replace it, and moral rot [*zohama'*] will cease from the world, and the Accuser will be swallowed up, "there is no adversary [*satan*] and no mischance," "the Lord will make something new on earth," and the souls will be made anew "like the eagle is renewed,"[11] all of them shall be new, "the work of

the Artist's hand," so much the more so than with vessels of glass. Then the "children of the resurrection of the dead" whose body and their soul have been renewed shall take delight in the intellectual meal in the world to come, which is after the resurrection, in which there is no bodily meal at all, and it is regarding this meal that our rabbis z"l said, "Rav was accustomed to say, 'In the world to come, there is no eating and no drinking, no envy, no hatred, and no rivalry, but rather the righteous will sit with crowns on their heads and enjoy the splendor of the *Shekhinah*.'"[12]

R. Bahya also interprets the expression "Until Shiloh will come" in Jacob's blessing for Judah in Gen 49:10 to "refer to the *two* redemptions: the first, which is nearer in time, and the last, which is more distant."[13]

FIRST, THE LEVIATHAN BANQUET

According to R. Bahya, these are the characteristics of the food of first banquet—the Leviathan banquet—in the future to come and of the bodies of the righteous who eat it. On the menu for the first banquet is the big fish Leviathan, the big bird Bar Yuchnai (or Ziz), and the big cow Behemoth.[14] These foods are special not only because of their enormous size, but also because they are kind of a magical "offspring of the light" [*toldot ha-or*] suggesting a heavenly origin. Similarly, manna, "the bread from heaven," is also an "offspring of the light" that has special powers to refine the intellect. Thus manna prompted an intellectual response when it first fell miraculously from heaven: *Man hu?* [What is it?], hence its name "manna."[15] It's what Joel Hecker calls "brain food" in his discussion of similar traditions in the *Zohar*.[16] It is related to the Shekinah's light, the light at the beginning of Creation.

Thus the rabbinic traditions that Leviathan, et al., were reserved for the banquet of the righteous from the time of the six days of creation are understood to allude to them being an "offspring" of the primordial light of the Shekinah. Moreover, as "light food," it provides a temporary glow from the heads of those who eat it, like the rays from the light on which Moses was nourished during his forty days of fasting on Mt. Sinai or the "halo effect" on the righteous at the Leviathan banquet when they're described as having "crowns on their heads." Nevertheless, this "light food" is still physical and material, enjoyed by body and soul together. The banquet is kosher. R. Bahya insists that Leviathan is a kosher fish, an appropriate reward for the righteous who kept kosher in this world. That said, my student artist/collaborator

Rosemary Liss, who composed illustrations in the style of medieval illuminations for my English translation of *Shulhan Shel Arba*, was inspired by contemporary cinematic representations of "Leviathan" as a kraken, and so she imagined Leviathan differently. [17]

Moses, the *shihulah kardona*, will cater this meal as I mentioned above. Here's the full reference from *Shulhan Shel Arba*:

> And thus they said in a midrash about Moses our Teacher (may he rest in peace): *shihula kardona*—the skinner for preparing a meal, "who was pulled out"—the explanation of *shihula*, is Moses, which is from the Aramaic [*shihaltay*] for the Hebrew, "I drew him out" (Exod 2:10). And a "skinner" (for preparing a meal) is a type of butcher or cook. So here the goal of the intention of these bodily meals is to be a device to refine the body and matter and to sharpen the mind so that it will attain knowledge of the Creator (May He be blessed) and meditate upon the purely intelligible beings, and then the souls by this looking of their bodies will become fit for the intellectual banquet from which the ministering angels themselves who are near the Shekinah eat—for then the soul will perceive the brilliant light which it is impossible to perceive as long as it is stuck in matter.[18]

The righteous diners themselves are composed of material bodies and souls, more or less the same bodies they had in this world, to eat this fleshy but light food. Nevertheless, I suspect R. Bahya's reference to Moses as a "skinner" and the "I drew him out" etymology of his name hint at the power of food at this meal to catalyze the bodily transformation of the righteous to dine "without eating and drinking" at the next, "intellectual meal" after the resurrection of the dead. That is, at this meal, the righteous souls are somehow "skinned" and "drawn out" of their ordinary this worldly bodies.

INTELLECTUAL MEAL AFTER THE RESURRECTION OF THE DEAD

At the intellectual meal in the world to come, there is "no eating or drinking," but R. Bahya qualifies this to mean no eating or drinking as we ordinarily understand it. For at this meal, the Messiah/descendent of David will raise a cup of blessing. As the much later Chasidic song, "Shnirele Perele," about this banquet puts it: *meshiekh ben dovid zist oybn on, halt a beckher in der rekhter hant, makht a brockhe afn gantsn land* [the Messiah, son of David, is above us. He holds a goblet in his right hand and gives his blessing to the whole earth]. It's an enormous overflowing cup [*kos revayah*], with a capacity of 221 logs. According to R. Bahya, this is an allegory for a different kind of consumption—"not eating and drinking" per se, but still something requiring both body and soul to enjoy. Otherwise, according to R. Bahya, there would be no need to specify "no eating or drinking," since of course our presumption for embodied souls was that consumption would involve some kind of eating or drinking.

But unlike the light food of the earlier meal, those nourished by this "food"—the splendor of the Shekinah—experience an eternal glow. Unlike the temporary glow, the rays of light shooting out of his head Moses acquired during his forty days of being nourished by the Shekinah on Mt. Sinai, this halo is like "the light Moses earned in the cleft of the rock." As R. Bahya says:

> And this is the light that Moses our Rabbi (peace upon him) earned in "the cleft of the rock," "the reflecting mirror" out of which he was able to prophesy, and thus earned the "radiation from the skin of his face" that was as bright as "the face of the sun." And in an interpretation they said, "a variety of the upper light is the globe of the sun" because the light of this level is the level of Moses' prophecy, and the globe of the sun, which is a variety of this, is the "radiation from the skin of his face." And this is what is written, "rays [*karnayyim*] given off from every side, and therein His glory is enveloped," that is, the "radiation from the skin of his face." This came directly from the hand of the Holy One Blessed be He to Moses, and this radiation is the fruit of what was his in this world, *distinct from the eternal radiance that would be his in the world to come, and that is the level of the upper light.* If so, then the word *karnayyim*—"rays"—includes both the fruit and the eternal radiance. And all this was because of the tablets—*luhot*—that he was holding. And so this is hinted at in the word "*LU'a"H*," which is an acronym of the words in Habakkuk 3:4: *karnayyim mi-yado Lo Ve-sham Hevyon 'uzo*. And they said in a midrash, "[They saw] the rays of the skin of his face," *all the majesty that Moses got was but temporary fruit, a gift he earned, but the eternal radiance would be his in the world to come, as it is said, "rays [karnayyim] from His hand to him."*[19]

In other words, the dual form of the word *karnayyim* [rays] refers both to the temporary radiance Moses experienced as his reward while alive on

Mt. Sinai in this world, and the eternal radiance he and the rest of the righteous can experience after the resurrection of the dead in their transformed bodies, as their reward in the next world. With both of these radiant rewards comes a prophetic, visionary capacity, like the "real eating" suggested by the experience of the Israelite elders and Moses at Mt. Sinai: "They had a vision of God and they ate and drank" (Exod 24:11).[20] However, the visionary capacity that will occur at the intellectual meal after the resurrection of the dead will be so far superior to that which even Moses experienced while in this world that it "cannot be pictured." We cannot picture it now:

> because of our being sunken in the world of thick and coarse bodies, which are totally thickness and coarseness, while the world of souls are totally elevation, refinement, and purity. Indeed, the two are opposites; it's impossible to think of what we are diametrically opposed to. Just as for fish, because they exist in the element of water, and need it to exist and live, it would be impossible for them to turn to the element of fire because it is its opposite, so these two worlds are opposites, and "every man is proved dull, without knowledge" of the quality of the world to come while in this world, and even the wisest of the wise are fools about this.[21]

And yet paradoxically, R. Bahya attempts to depict it nevertheless:

> However, we know in general through what we can infer through reason and from the Torah "which makes wise the simple" that just as the body enjoys and takes delight [*mitaden*] in a pleasant aromatic meal according to the body's standards of pleasure, so the soul will enjoy and take delight in this upper world. . . . So even though the power of the body is weak and unable to picture in the heart the existence of the upper beings and their delight that is without measure, the power of the upper beings and their perfection is not diminished by lesser beings, composed of matter, who are unable to conceive of them, just as the human wisdom and virtue is not diminished by a fool or beast who cannot imagine or conceive of it.[22]

This is what Jewish tradition refers to as "Gan Eden" because this meal is where souls "*mitad'nim*" [take delight] without limit in the splendor of the Divine Presence. This indeed is the "Real Eating," the *akhilah vada'it*, R. Bahya discusses at length in the Second Gate of *Shulhan Shel Arba*, though there his examples refer primarily to the kinds of "real eating" of which humans are capable within the limits of their body/soul bundles in this world.

IN TRANSFORMED BODIES: "THE FULL VESSEL THAT CAN CONTAIN, BUT THE EMPTY ONE CANNOT"

But the bodies we'll have to "eat" the intellectual meals of "Gan Eden" after the resurrection of the dead will be dramatically transformed. First of all, they will be much, much bigger. This is a reversal of the contraction of Adam and Eve's bodies (and the "downsizing" of their descendants as well) after the sin in the Garden of Eden. R. Bahya knows this because of rabbinic traditions about the heavenly Jerusalem where the windows are so high that we would have to be supersized to be able to use them. But even more importantly, our new bodies will have an unbounded capacity to take in the light.

Here's how R. Bahya tries to describe the new and improved resurrected body's capacities in analogies and parables:

> However, its way of taking delight there is not measured like bodily things, which have measures and dimensions, but the upper beings have no measure and dimension because their status is great, beyond conception, and their way of taking delight deeper than any measure.
>
> Come and see how the way of the Holy One Blessed be He is not the way of flesh and blood. For flesh and blood, an empty vessel can contain something, a full one cannot. But it is not so for the Holy One Blessed be He. *The full vessel can contain, the empty one cannot*, as it is said, "If only they would surely hear." The explanation of this is that insofar as bodily things have measure and dimension, when they are empty they can be filled, but when one fills it, they cannot contain any more since they are already filled to their capacity, and nothing with a capacity can contain something more than its capacity. But among the upper things, full contains, since it has no measured capacity.[23]

I find this imaginative conceptualization of dimensionless bodies that the righteous will acquire after the resurrection of the dead particularly striking, with no temporal or spatial limits to the shiny goodness of the Divine Presence one takes in.

R. Bahya mention of "upper beings" here alludes to his discussion of the hierarchy of beings with which he begins his book to set the scene of God's original differentiation of upper from lower beings at the beginning of time by means of the way they eat:

> "This is the table which is before the Lord," who spreads the heavens like a canopy for a tent, sets earth over water, and feeds the creatures of His home in three divisions: "the bottom, middle, and topmost

> decks." In the highest realm are the ministering angels nearest to Him: the *cherubim*, the *seraphim*, the *ofanim*, and the *arielim*. They are attendants in His palace; in legions they feast on the light of His presence, from the flowing light of His own radiance. The middle realm is the "vest of the heavens," an assembly of fire and water—rains constraining and constrained—by day and night God restrains them. The eyes of their minds see [*tzofim*] their Master's delight as their food, far sweeter to them than choice honey [*tzufim*]. They hunger for the Cause of their existence; the pillars supporting their realm are suspended by the arm of His wisdom, and quake at His rebuke. But the lowest dwelling, a circle radiating from its midpoint, has measurable dimensions. Our food is not their food. Their food is conceived in their mind, when they see the face of their Maker. Our food is meager bread, water, and tears, gotten by hard work and toil.[24]

For R. Bahya, this inequitable hierarchy is the cosmic consequence of Adam's sin in the Garden, when:

> it was decreed for him that he would earn his bread only by the sweat of his brow, and that man be humbled and brought low. He traded pleasure ['*oneg*] for plague [*nega*'], got hard work instead of rest. *His wisdom spoiled and his stature was diminished.* It caused him weakness instead of strength; instead of wheat, thorns came forth. *Instead of eternal life, death; instead of light, the shadow of death.* With all this the Lord raised the power of the upper beings, and worsened the power of the lower beings.[25]

So the new bigger and better bodies with their unlimited capacities promised to the righteous with the resurrection of the dead are clearly meant to elevate them from their human status to an angelic status (and diet), which they lost when Adam sinned and he and Eve were exiled from the Garden of Eden. In the future they will get the angels' uncomplicated and direct access to the nourishing powers of the Divine Presence. What kind of people with what kind of historical memories and experiences imagines as their future reward bodies without borders, uninterrupted connection to their "real food" source, elevation from their humble status, restoration to their "original" exalted status, and return from their exile from the primordial Garden of Eden?

WHY DO WE CARE NOW?

Any reflection about the world to come, whether medieval or modern, tells us as much about the hopes, fears, desires, and aspirations of those in this world who imagine them (or deny or repress them) than the actual status (if any) of those in the world to come. Moreover, as far as we know, only we in this world receive the emotional and intellectual benefits (or disadvantages) of talking or not talking about the specifics of the world to come. Perhaps the most conventional explanation for why descriptions of the next world are important for us in this world, particularly those that emphasize rewards and punishments, is that they offer an emotionally satisfying resolution to the problem of theodicy, or the blatant injustice we often see in this world. It is patently obvious that many wicked people go unpunished in this world and many good people seem to get more than their fair share of suffering and little material reward for their efforts; the world to come will make this all right and confirm our faith that justice triumphs, even if we don't see it now. But this works only for those who actually find a next world plausible.

And though R. Bahya certainly assumes rewards and punishments are part of what occurs in the world to come, what he says specifically about it (and what he doesn't) suggests he is interested in more than theodicy. Yes, he insists on recompense for both body and soul for the righteous in the next world, if not in this. But while he focuses on the specifics of the rewards, namely, the delightful meals in the world to come, in *Shulhan Shel Arba* at least, he pays almost no attention to the punishment of the unjust. There are no tours of hell in this book, though his rabbinic sources certainly could have provided them.

Rather, R. Bahya stresses how the meals in the world to come are the restoration of the world as God had originally intended it, as he says in his interpretation of the phrase *b'alma di-vara herutay* from the Kaddish.[26] He also tends to stress the quality of the next world's "knowability," as if what he says about it were a sacred secret or revelation that we in this world both tremble before and are attracted to know, a *mysterium tremendum et fascinans*. He uses some of the typical phrases mystics use to effect a kind of conspiratorial attentiveness in those of his audience who want to view themselves as enlightened, that he's about to divulge something fraught and significant. It's like he's often saying, I've got a secret, and now I'm going to tell you. Even though words are inadequate to express it, I'm going to do it anyway.

R. Bahya even hints that what he's revealing about the world to come might come from near-death experiences (NDEs). For example, R. Bahya says God's reply to Moses, that a "man may not see me and live," might actually mean that:

> "while alive they [human beings with material bodies] do not see, but upon their death they do see." And this is after the separation of the soul from its material form. And it is possible to specify further that "upon their death" means when they are about to die, as in the topic they discussed in *Midrash Deuteronomy Rabbah, Parashat Ekev*.[27]

And R. Bahya goes on to say:

> "How abundant is the good that You have in store for those who fear You."[28] It happened that when R. Abbahu was about to die, he saw the gift of his reward, what the Holy One Blessed be He was going to give him in the time to come, and all the good prepared for the righteous themselves in the time to come. So when he saw all these consolations which had been prepared, he exclaimed, "All these are for Abbahu!" and immediately he desired to die, and began reciting: "How abundant is the good that You have in store for those who fear You."[29]

In other words, the reward for the righteous upon death is as much the "gift" of the insight and enhanced cognitive capacity the moment of their death gives them as it is the content of the vision they see with it. But R. Bahya is in effect sharing the visions of what might have come from near-death or deathbed experiences with those living in this world now, so one doesn't necessarily have to die first to receive at least some benefit, some taste of this heightened insight.

R. Bahya also suggests this enhanced cognitive capacity is the same as the insight of mystical ascent that heroic prophetic ancestors like Moses and Enoch experienced. Moses and Enoch were vouchsafed secret revelations about the soul's rewards after death that are not mentioned explicitly in the Bible, which were concealed from the masses who couldn't understand them but which were nevertheless necessary for their salvation:

> Torah does not specify explicitly anywhere the matter of the Garden of Eden being destined for the soul as a reward for the mitzvot, but does specify the bodily things destined for Israel when they return most certainly to their land, when they will have "all their rains in their season" [Lev 26:4] and with the abundance of blessing and happiness . . . because the Torah was given to the masses of *all* of Israel, and the masses would not be able to understand the destined intellectual things.[30]

Again, the secret knowledge revealed to prophets like Moses and Enoch, such as that "Gan Eden" in the Torah is code for "the world of the souls," is shared with the enlightened in this world, who can now discern it through their intellect. That is what R. Bahya means when he says:

> It should be clear to the enlightened that the world of souls is the "Garden of Eden" for the soul, but Scripture mixes it in the general list of things destined for the body, and depended on the intellect of the enlightened to discern it from them, that it would not be hidden from him as it would be from the masses.[31]

While one could take this at face value as an assertion of the social class hierarchy of enlightened Jews over "the masses" of Jews, to say to one's audience "this is a secret that only the enlightened know but the masses don't" and then immediately reveal the secret in effect confers onto anyone in R. Bahya's audience the elevated status of "the enlightened." Here is an example of the conspiratorial attentiveness I mentioned above that the rhetoric of mysticism typically evokes by prefacing its "revelations" with phrases like "I've got a secret," in order to include its audience as sharers in an extraspecial, elite knowledge.[32]

TRANSFORMATIVE ECSTATIC EXPERIENCE OF "SUPER BODIES"

That said, I don't want to gloss over the importance of at least one striking aspect of the content of these visionary NDEs possibly alluded to in R. Bahya's Fourth Gate of *Shulhan Shel Arba*. Namely, R. Bahya discusses at length how bodies are transformed into what might be called "super bodies," bodies unbounded by the normal physical and temporal boundaries of this world, often bathed and glowing in light. We can find these phenomena cross-culturally in different religions. As a modern scholar of comparative religion, Jeffrey Kripal, puts it:

> Human beings have consistently reported moments in which the body functions as a window or star-gate into other dimensions of reality. Indeed in religions we encounter paradoxical descriptions—such as a "spiritual body," a "subtle body," a "rainbow body," an "energetic body," a "diamond body," a "glorified body," a "resurrected body," and so on. In art, moreover, the body literally *glows*. . . . Many religious traditions then have understood, and no doubt experienced, the human body in truly fantastic ways that overflow and transcend our present biomedical models, which assume of course that all the action stops at the skin.[33]

These moments of expansive insight are typically described as life changing by those who report them. Kripal calls these experiences "super sexualities" because they are often mentioned in accounts of illumination during sexual experiences, but they share features with both NDEs in general and with R. Bahya's descriptions of "bodies" at meals in the world to come. Kripal, drawing upon the research of Jenny Wade, gives her list of features of these "sexual spiritual events," of which four in particular are pertinent:

- streams of liquid light shooting out of the top of the head or skull;
- past-life memories or visions, often compared to "watching a movie";
- the stopping of time and a sense of eternity;
- the experience of every cell in the body vibrating at an extremely high frequency, *which in turn leads to an out-of-body experience and of being both inside and outside the body.*[34]

These also overlap with some of the characteristics typical of NDEs, that is, "separation from the body, sometimes accompanied by a 'spectator perspective,'" encounters with "beings of light," and, as we alluded to above, an "indescribable" experience of being immersed in light and love in which "cognitive and affective characteristics are fused," "a sense of receiving special messages or hidden truths," and "for some . . . an instantaneous, timeless, and comprehensive vision of the totality of existence."[35] Moreover, they nearly always have a profound personal effect on the way those who have them see and conduct their lives after such experiences: "transforming aftereffects, such as loss of the fear of death, newfound zest for everyday life, and renewed dedication to the values of empathetic love, lifelong-learning, and service to others."[36]

The association between NDEs and other visionary experiences of transformed, enlightened super bodies that occur for extraordinary individuals or for ordinary individuals experiencing extraordinary events in this world should be clear. Moreover, it is likely that R. Bahya's description of transformed soul/bodies nourished on the light of the Shekinah at meals in the world to come are projections, at least in part, of such visionary experiences. It certainly is not unheard of for medieval kabbalistic literature to be composed in part from ecstatic or visionary experiences, that is, through automatic writing.[37] It should also not be surprising that R. Bahya's descriptions of transformed bodies and their enhanced capacities in the world to come are similar to those found cross-culturally in other accounts of NDEs and the afterlife:

> As Gregory Shushan has suggested, mythologies surrounding death and the afterlife are unusually similar across cultural and temporal boundaries in ways that other types of mythologies are not . . . because mythologies of the end are "correlates" (which is not to say

literal descriptions) of actual human experiences of death,[38] whereas mythologies of the beginning can be only speculative. . . . Everyone everywhere dies, but no human being was present at the Big Bang.[39]

On the other hand, R. Bahya's particular choice of language to describe the transformed bodies of the righteous as soul-bodies without boundaries—"like a full vessel that can contain [more]"—may reflect particular Jewish cultural and historical social experiences of the general human experience of death.[40] Might not the promise of such rewards express the sublimated social anxieties of a people whose boundaries in their historical memory are constantly being violated, whose present social and political impact in this world seems quite diminished in comparison to the dignity they deserve as faithful members of God's elect? Living under Christian and Muslim rule subject to laws designed to humiliate them and thus "prove" their theological inferiority, Jews in this world imagine bodies whose boundaries are irrelevant, bodies restored in the world to come to their original enormous size before Adam's sin in the Garden of Eden. This restoration of Jews' stature (i.e., status) is markedly different from contemporary Christian mythic imagination of transformed bodies in the afterlife.

Medieval Christian art and theological speculation about the next world are preoccupied with the reassembly of fragmented bodies in their depiction of the resurrection.[41] While both R. Bahya's Jewish and medieval Christian depictions of transformed bodies insist on the "material continuity and personal survival" of this world's embodied souls when they are resurrected in the next world, they imagine the this worldly "problem" that bodily resurrection "solves" differently. Perhaps the reassembly of fragmented bodies reflects sublimated Christian social anxieties about the constant religious divisions breaking up the Christian empires, while Jewish resurrection is more concerned with returning Jews to their exalted religious status.

Or maybe Jewish imagination of unlimited bodily capacity to consume meals in the world to come expresses psychological longing for unblocked, unbounded, and unmediated relationship with other persons: where the line between diner and dinner, lover and beloved dissolves. Where we are personally redeemed from exile and alienation from our Creator. Where our bodies aren't fragmented, but we feel ourselves as fragments from the whole of which we were originally an integral part. The "real eating" described in the world to come and as a visionary experience is a metaphor for the union or reunion of us creatures with our Creator that crosses even the boundary of death. Indeed R. Bahya concludes all that he has to say in his book

Shulhan Shel Arba about meals in the world to come and in this world with a comforting blessing to this effect: "May he encompass us with favor; in the 'bundle of life' may He hide us, in the path of life may He guide us, and grant us what is written, 'For God is our God forever; He will guide us even beyond death' (Psalm 48:15)."[42]

Speaking words of Torah about the world to come, especially words of Torah about meals while tasting them, has the power to elevate us emotionally and spiritually at our tables in this world.[43] So R. Bahya says at the end of his book:

> With these words the enlightened will discern when they're eating. May they *make themselves holy* and their minds burnished fully. With these words engaged, may they be at their table; *raise* their table's renown so that "all shall say 'Glory!'" [Ps 29:9]. Let their hearts be made pure, to withstand any test. *"By these raise up the table"* [Exod 28:28], so that *"before the Lord"* [Exod 41:22] *is its label.* This table is greater than the table of kings, "he shall be permitted to join those attending" [Zech 3:7], and *to be lifted* in honor to gaze on [*ye-hazeh*, lit., "have a vision of"] the face of David "among the lilies grazing" [Song 6:3] to earn *"the three-legged table" of gold ablazing.*[44] They will earn the physical and intellectual meals, and be counted among the *benei aliyah* [the elite, who have literally "gone up"].[45]

Creative imaginative conversations in the sacred language of Torah about the elevating topics of God, our higher soul selves, sacred visionary or NDEs, and the material and spiritual nourishment we remember from the past that is promised to the righteous in the future, while enjoying meals in the company of friends in the present, are a kind of perfect storm of experiences that have the cumulative effect of elevating the basic physical acts of eating we need to do to stay alive through the emotions of elevation they evoke. Self-conscious experiences of thinking aloud about the Torah of meals in this world and the world to come are fused with the concrete experiences of eating and drinking at the table. Thus R. Bahya scripts ritual performances of textual study at meals to heighten its users' awareness of their experience of imaginative "midrashic" reinterpretations of Jewish traditions.[46] But if these traditional visions of the world to come and our modern conversations about them can "only" imagine our life after death, and not conclusively prove it, what's the point of engaging in them? Why should we care about an imagined *olam ha-ba* in *olam ha-zeh*?

In her book *The Life of the World to Come*, Carol Zaleski has a wonderful reply to this objection:

Certainly it is true that such imaginings will at present tell us more about our own assumptions and longings than they do about the heavenly society. And yet we have a right to them. The effort to starve out the will to imagine has not produced the humane fruits it was expected to bring. If anything, the contrary has been the case: totalistic efforts to create utopia on earth and to suppress pie-in-the-sky thinking have ended by creating hell on earth.

The social psychologist Robert Jay Lifton makes a convincing case for the need for symbols of immortality that provide a sense of continuity in the face of death. He finds that when individuals or societies are prevented from cultivating images of death that promised continued life or transcendence, their moral energy is soon sapped, and "psychic numbing" sets in. . . .

The common achievement of symbols of immortality is to offer the individual a wider cosmos within which to dwell, nourished by a rich network of social, natural, and spiritual connections. They overcome isolation, and are therefore both reasonable and adaptive, rather than illusory and regressive.[47]

It is reasonable and adaptive, not to mention morally compelling, for us Jews, for all of us as humans, to exercise our imagination to maintain an expansive view of what the world and we could be, and not be restricted by the boundaries of what our human sense perceptions, reason, and mortality limit us to assume. Not like the empty cup in this world of flesh and blood, which can contain only as much as its physical capacity allows, but rather like the full cup in the world to come, which always has room for more.

NOTES

1. All references to R. Bahya ben Asher Hlava, *Shulhan Shel Arba*, are from the Hebrew edition in *Kitve Rabenu Bahya* (ed. Charles Ber Chavel; Jerusalem: Mosad ha-Rav Kuk, 1969), henceforth cited as *SSA*. English translations are from my *Shulhan Shel Arba by Rabbenu Bahya Ben Asher Hlava*. Online: http://acadblogs.wheatoncollege.edu/jbk/.

2. Caroline Walker Bynum, "Material Continuity, Personal Survival and the Resurrection of the Body: A Scholastic Discussion in Its Medieval and Modern Contexts," in *Fragmentation and Redemption: Essays on Gender and the Human Body in Medieval Religion* (New York: Zone Books, 1992), 241.

3. Ibid., 243.

4. Ibid., 244.

5. Ibid.

6. As R. Bahya says in the preface of *Shulhan Shel Arba*:

> my heart compelled me to write about this in brief in a book, and to include in it some sacred words *so that it could be at your table, by your right hand, for you to read in it all that is required at your meal*. And if at the time you are eating, your faith is reassured by this book of mine, and according to its words, you will be sure attain the level of the pious ones who are perfect in their qualities. (*SSA*, 460)

7. "The Fourth Gate," *SSA*, 513.

8. Jonathan Haidt, "The Positive Emotion of Elevation," *Prevention & Treatment* 3:1 (2000); Jonathan Haidt, "Elevation and the Positive Psychology of Morality," in *Flourishing: Positive Psychology and the Life Well-Lived* (ed. Corey L. M. Keyes and Jonathan Haidt; Washington, DC: American Psychological Association, 2003); Leon Kass, *The Hungry Soul: Eating and the Perfecting of Our Nature* (Chicago: University of Chicago Press, 1999).

9. "Groom Over the Table," *Kad Ha-Kemach* (*SSA*, 187–88).

10. Commentary to Daniel 12:2, quoted in Neil Gillman, *Death of Death: Resurrection and Immortality in Jewish Thought* (Woodstock: Jewish Lights, 1997), 170.

11. R. Bahya knows of traditions that associate phoenix-like characteristics to the eagle [Heb., *nesher*], as in his comment to Genesis 2:19 in *Be'ur 'al ha-Torah* (ed. Charles Ber Chavel; Jerusalem: Mosad ha-Rav Kuk, 1966–1968).

12. "The Fourth Gate," *SSA*, 506.

13. R. Bahya also takes "Shiloh" to be a reference to Moses as the "caterer" of the first meal that will prepare the bodies of the righteous for the second, intellectual meal after the resurrection of the dead. This is based on a pun on the Aramaic version of the Biblical etymology for Moses's name. The etymology that the Torah has is provided by Pharoah's daughter: "*Moshe* because I drew him out [*mashiti-hu*] of the water." However, the Aramaic for *mashiti-hu*, *shihaltay*, is related to the word *shihulah* [as in *shihula kardona*—the skinner for preparing a meal], which sounds like "Shiloh"; hence Shiloh refers to Moses, according to the midrash R. Bahya brings in support of this. See below.

14. See Jordan Rosenblum's essay in this volume.

15. R. Bahya, *Bi'ur*, 2:147.

16. Joel Hecker, *Mystical Bodies, Mystical Meals: Eating and Embodiment in Medieval Kabbalah* (Detroit: Wayne State University Press, 2005), 108.

17. See http://acadblogs.wheatoncollege.edu/jbk/files/2010/12/liss_ssa6.jpg.

18. "Fourth Gate," *SSA*, 504.

19. Ibid., 513.

20. See Jonathan Brumberg-Kraus, "'Real Eating:' A Medieval Spanish Jewish View of Gastronomic Authenticity," in *Authenticity in the Kitchen: Proceedings of the Oxford*

Symposium on Food and Cookery (Totnes: Prospect Books, 2006), 119–31, and "The Ritualization of Scripture in Rabbenu Bahya's Shulhan Shel Arba'," *World Congress of Jewish Studies* 13 (2001): 1–17. There I discuss R. Bahya's interpretation of Exodus 24:11 and "real eating" as a paradigm of prophetic, visionary experience of God.

21. "Fourth Gate," *SSA*, 508.

22. Ibid.

23. Ibid.

24. "Preface," *SSA*, 457.

25. Ibid., 457–58.

26. "Fourth Gate," *SSA*, 501.

27. Ibid., 505.

28. Psalm 31:20.

29. "Fourth Gate," *SSA*, 505.

30. Ibid., 509.

31. Ibid., 510.

32. I heard this many years ago in a conversation with David Halperin about the rhetoric of esotericism.

33. Jeffrey J. Kripal, *Comparing Religions: Coming to Terms* (Malden: Wiley Blackwell, 2014), 192.

34. Ibid., 193, referring to Jenny Wade, *Transcendent Sex: When Lovemaking Opens the Veil* (New York: Paraview Pocket Books, 2004), emphasis mine.

35. Carol Zaleski, *The Life of the World to Come: Near-Death Experience and Christian Hope: The Albert Cardinal Meyer Lectures* (New York: Oxford University Press, 1996), 19.

36. Ibid.

37. Daniel Chanan Matt, ed., *Zohar: Annotated & Explained* (Woodstock: SkyLight Paths, 2002, xxiv). Kripal, *Comparing Religions*, 288–89, suggests that some traditional literary texts about the afterlife, like Plato's Story of Er or the *Tibetan Book of the Dead*, are "based on actual experiences, perhaps passed on orally and fashioned into folklore and eventually into religious doctrines."

38. Or of "little death" [*le petite mort*, the French euphemism for orgasm], to account for NDE's similarities to religious experiences of "super sexuality."

39. Kripal, *Comparing Religions*, 288.

40. Ibid., 293–94: "NDE events display near universal features (like supernatural environs, deceased humans, or beings of light) but also real cultural differences."

41. Bynum, "Material Continuity," esp. 269–96.

42. "Fourth Gate," *SSA*, 514.

43. By "elevate," I mean it precisely in the sense that Haidt uses it in his discussion of the "emotion of elevation ("The Positive Emotion of Elevation," 3):

> Love and a desire for affiliation appears to be a common human response to witnessing saints and saintly deeds, or even to hearing about them second hand. If disgust is a negative emotion that strengthens ego boundaries and defenses against a morally reprehensible other, then elevation is its opposite—a desire to affiliate with those who are morally admirable.

Intense experiences of the emotion of elevation tend to have "potentially life-altering effects," leading those who feel it to "perform pro-social and affiliative actions" (3, 4), that is, acts of loving-kindness. Significantly, witnessing the care, comfort, and support given to the families of those who are dying is one of Haidt's examples of events that evoke the emotion of elevation and its lasting social consequences.

44. An allusion to what is referred to in B. *Ta'anit* 25a: "The righteous will in time to come eat at a golden table with three legs." See R. Bahya's Preface, where he explains this idea in his discussion of the fourth reason he gives for calling his book *Shulhan Shel Arba*. There's an untranslatable wordplay here with the Hebrew word *ro'e* ["grazing" or "shepherd"] and the Aramaic word *ker'a* ["leg"]: "David among the lilies grazing [*ro'e*] to earn the table of three legs [*ker'a*]."

45. "Fourth Gate," *SSA*, 513. *Benei aliyah* translated literally means "sons (or children) of ascent."

46. Brumberg-Kraus, "The Ritualization of Scripture."

47. Zaleski, *Life of the World to Come*, 48.

The Dybbuk: The Origins and History of a Concept

Morris M. Faierstein

Approximately a century ago, Shlomo Zanvil Rapoport, better known by his pen name, S. An-sky, began to write a play he called *Between Two Worlds*. The play was a love story surrounded by a story of dybbuk possession.[1] An-sky's interest in the dybbuk came from his ethnographic work, collecting and preserving East European Jewish folk traditions that were quickly disappearing. The play premiered on December 9, 1920, in Warsaw, and the rest is history. It became the most popular Yiddish play, quickly translated into Hebrew and a number of other languages, and performed all over the world. It remains the great icon of Yiddish theater. A side effect was that the subject of the dybbuk was popularized as a folk motif. Despite this popularity, or perhaps because of it, the subject of dybbuk possession did not become the subject of serious scholarly inquiry. The few scholarly studies that have been published take An-sky's play as their starting point and assume it represents an accurate understanding of the concept and its history.[2] This study will endeavor to reconsider the concept of the dybbuk through an examination of the primary sources that discuss this concept without prior assumptions or theories. It will also trace the historical development and evolution of the dybbuk concept.

Tales of people being possessed by demons and other evil spirits can be found in Jewish literature as early as the first century C.E. Talmudic and midrashic literature also contain such stories,[3] but these stories did not attract significant attention or comments in the post-talmudic medieval Jewish tradition. The classic models of possession in Christianity were the stories of possession of people by demons and by Satan, and their exorcism by Jesus in the New Testament.[4] Following Jesus's example, stories of possession and exorcism were often encountered in the lives of Christian saints. The ability to exorcise or subdue a demonic spirit or even to vanquish the works of Satan was a sure sign of sainthood. Stories of demonic possession and connection to Satanic forces, which came to be known as witchcraft, grew in the course of the medieval period and reached a high point in the sixteenth and seventeenth centuries in the midst of the religious and political conflicts arising from the Protestant Reformation and the Catholic Counter-Reformation.[5]

In the Jewish tradition, aside from the talmudic stories of demonic possession, it was only in sixteenth century Safed that we hear of cases of people being possessed and needing exorcism. A new type of entity appeared, the soul of a Jewish man who had committed a sin whose punishment was that the soul would be trapped between this world and the next and would have to wander until expiation was found for the sin. There is no evidence in the literature of a female dybbuk. Hayyim Vital explicitly stated that the soul of a woman cannot become a dybbuk because women do not participate in the process of *gilgul*. Rather, their souls are sent directly to gehenna, where they are punished for their sins.[6] There is also no evidence that the soul of a non-Jew could be a dybbuk.[7]

The soul of the sinner condemned to *gilgul* was originally called an "evil spirit" [*ruah rah*] in the early possession stories from Safed. It has been the conventional wisdom that the term *dybbuk*, meaning that which is attached, began to be used instead of "evil spirit" at the end of the seventeenth century.[8] More recently, Sara Zfatman has demonstrated that this terminological transition took place later, in the first part of the eighteenth century. The first reference to the term *dybbuk* that she found is in a story of an exorcism in Speyer in 1715.[9] For the purpose of clarity, I will use the term *dybbuk* even where it is historically anachronistic.

THEORETICAL ORIGINS OF THE DYBBUK CONCEPT

The theoretical bases for the concept of the dybbuk are two kabbalistic concepts, *gilgul* [transmigration or metempsychosis] and *ibbur* [impregnation]. The concept of *gilgul* is first found in the early kabbalistic work, *Sefer Bahir*, and then expanded in the *Zohar*, the great classic of medieval Kabbalah. The punishment of *gilgul* was originally related in kabbalistic literature to transgressing the laws of levirate marriage. The person who refused to marry his sister-in-law and perpetuate the memory of his brother by having a son with her or participating in the ritual of *halitzah*, which would allow her to marry someone else, was punished with *gilgul*. That is, his soul would wander the earth endlessly and he would never find rest or find expiation for his other sins. Gradually, the range of sins that necessitated the punishment of *gilgul* and that could be expiated through it was expanded.

There is a midrashic exemplum, "The *Tanna* and the Dead Man," that is probably the earliest description of a case of *gilgul* and its resolution, even though the term *gilgul* is not attached to this story. Various versions of this story are cited in a number of post-talmudic and medieval sources, including the *Zohar*.[10] An early version of this story is found in tractate *Kallah Rabbati*:

> Come and hear; R. Akiba went to a certain place [a cemetery] where he met a man [i.e., a ghost] carrying a heavy load on his shoulder with which he was unable to proceed, and he was crying and groaning. He asked him, "What did you do [in your lifetime]?" He replied, "There is no forbidden act in the world which I left undone, and now guards have been set over me who do not allow me to rest." R. Akiba asked him, "have you left a son?" He answered, "By your life! Do not detain me because I fear the angels who beat me with fiery lashes and say to me, 'Why do you not walk quickly?'" R. Akiba said to him, "Tell me whom have you left?" He replied, "I have left behind my wife who was pregnant." R. Akiba then proceeded to that city and inquired, "Where is the son of So and So?" [The inhabitants] replied, "May the memory of that wicked person be uprooted." He asked them the reason and they said, "He robbed and preyed upon people and caused them suffering; what is more, he violated a betrothed girl on the Day of Atonement." He made his way to the house and found the wife about to be delivered of a child. He waited until she gave birth to [a son], circumcised him and when he grew up, took him to the Synagogue to join in public worship. Later R. Akiba returned to that [cemetery] and [the ghost] appeared to him and said, "May your mind be [always] at rest because you have set my mind at rest."[11]

Later versions of this story are much more detailed and have many similarities to the interrogations of the dybbuk found in some of the dybbuk tales from the seventeenth century and later. However, this story, which is the prototype for the concept of *gilgul*, only brings us halfway to the concept of the dybbuk. The second aspect that is also crucial to the dybbuk is the concept of *ibbur*, impregnation of a soul within the body of another person. As we will see, *ibbur* remained a theoretical concept until we get to the kabbalists of Safed.

Another definition of *gilgul* that evolved entailed the soul being reborn into a new body and being given the opportunity to atone for a sin that had not been completely expiated in the original lifetime of the soul. A famous example is the story of the ten Rabbinic Martyrs who were killed by the Romans at the end of the Bar Kochba rebellion. According to the medieval *Midrash Bereshit Rabbati*, by Rabbi Moses ha-Darshan, the death of the ten martyrs was a punishment for the sin committed by Joseph's ten brothers, who were present when they sold him into slavery. This is found in an extended commentary on Genesis 37:26. The rabbis were the *gilgulim* of the ten brothers.[12] An extended discussion of this type of *gilgul* can also be found in Hayyim Vital's mystical diary, *Sefer Hezyonot*, which will be discussed below.

A dybbuk was a soul that had committed particularly heinous crimes that could not be atoned for merely by being transmigrated into a new body, where it could atone for its original sin. The dybbuk was trapped in a limbo, wandering between heaven and gehenna, between this world and the next, until expiation was found and the soul could be judged and sent to gehenna for its punishment and then on to the Garden of Eden for its reward. *Ibbur* was considered a much more esoteric subject than *gilgul* and was not the subject of significant discussion. The term *ibbur* was always preceded by the term *sod* [the secret of], and any discussion of the concept and its significance was strongly discouraged. For the most part, *ibbur* was restricted to the righteous and considered a reward rather than a punishment.[13]

Before the fifteenth century, the concepts of *gilgul* and *ibbur* were only abstract concepts found in rabbinic and kabbalistic literature. With the dissemination of kabbalistic texts and ideas the concept of *gilgul* became the subject of debate and disagreement between kabbalists and rationalist Jewish philosophers.[14] The philosophers rejected the concept of *gilgul*, under the influence of philosophical traditions going back to Aristotle's concept of the soul. It is noteworthy that Christianity and mainstream Islam also rejected the concept of transmigration. Christian theologians of all denominations, Protestant and Catholic, repeatedly rejected the concept of transmigration and the possibility of possession by the souls of the deceased.[15] Sunni Islam also does not accept the concept of transmigration, but some offshoots of Shi'ite Islam, like the Druze, Alawites, and Ismailis, accept the concept of transmigration.[16] In other words, belief in possession by a dybbuk is impossible in the Christian and mainstream Muslim traditions. It is a uniquely Jewish concept. Of course, transmigration is a key concept in Hinduism and Buddhism along with the religions that emanate from them. However, the understanding of this concept in these religions is different from its understanding in Judaism, and an analysis is beyond our present purview.

GILGUL AND *IBBUR* IN SAFED

The first reports of actual cases of possession, based on the concepts *gilgul* and *ibbur*, appeared in the literature of the kabbalistic revival in Safed. Why did the Safed kabbalists give life to the concept of dybbuk possession, and what purpose did it serve in their reinterpretation of Jewish belief and practice? Why did this concept move from the theoretical to the actual only in Safed? There are no reports of the appearance of a dybbuk prior to the Safed events. Central to answering this question are the concepts of *gilgul* and *ibbur* and how they were implemented by the kabbalists of Safed. The aspect of *gilgul* that most interested the kabbalists of Safed is the idea of soul families and family trees.[17] This concept asserts that there is a familial relationship between souls that can impact a person's present life and behaviors. One of Luria's mystical talents was that he could also look at someone's forehead and tell them about the history of their soul, not only about their previous *gilgulim*, but also identify to which soul families they belonged.

In the fourth part of his mystical diary, *Book of Visions*, Hayyim Vital discusses in great detail what he was told by R. Isaac Luria about the origins and history of his soul, tracing it back to Adam's sons, Cain and Abel. Surprisingly, Vital's soul is traced back to Cain, rather than to Abel, as one might normally expect. Luria also told Vital about his prior *gilgulim*, starting with Rabbi Vidal de Tolosa (second half of the fourteenth century), author of the *Maggid Mishneh*, an important commentary on Maimonides' great halachic work, *Mishneh Torah*. Vital then went through several more *gilgulim* in undistinguished people, each of whom committed a sin relating to blood that was not atoned for. It was now Vital's turn, and he needed to exert himself to finally atone for the sin first committed by Rabbi Vidal de Tolosa.[18]

This was important because a *Yihud* or unification, which is a form of *ibbur*, was efficacious when one tried to unite their soul with the soul of a deceased worthy who was from the same soul family. *Yihud* of two souls that have a familial connection is one version of positive *ibbur*. The concept of *ibbur* asserts that it is possible for the soul of a deceased person to enter the body of a living person and communicate with the living person's soul and mind. There are two types of positive *ibbur*, and one of negative *ibbur*, and all three, *Yihud* and the two types of *ibbur*, are represented in the literature of Safed. Of the three, the negative one, dybbuk possession, is the best known, but the positive ones were the more important ones for the kabbalists of Safed. The most important practitioner of *Yihudim* was Isaac Luria, who regularly visited the grave of Rabbi Simeon bar Yohai, the purported author of the *Zohar*, the canonical text of the kabbalistic tradition. Rabbi Simeon's grave was in Meron, not far from Safed. Luria also saw himself, and was seen by his disciples, as a *gilgul* of Rabbi Simeon, which further enhanced his aura of authority.[19] Not only was Luria a *gilgul* of Rabbi Simeon, but his disciples were also seen as the *gilgulim* of Rabbi Simeon's disciples mentioned in the Zohar.[20]

In addition to the *Yihudim* of Luria and his disciples, there was another type of positive *ibbur* possession in Safed. In this type of *ibbur*, the person being possessed did not directly invite the possession, but it was for a positive purpose and the person was not harmed. The best known example is the *Maggid*, the heavenly messenger who guided Rabbi Joseph Karo in many ways throughout his life. The messages and instructions of the *Maggid* are contained in Karo's book, *Maggid Mesharim*.[21] Another example of maggidic possession is found in Hayyim Vital's mystical diary, the *Book of Visions*. It tells the story of the heavenly messenger who possessed the daughter of Raphael Anav and brought a number of messages for Hayyim Vital, with her acting as the medium.[22]

MAGGID AND *DYBBUK*

About the same time that the phenomenon of maggidic possession appeared in the sixteenth century, another type of possession appeared, by a malevolent spirit that came to be known as a dybbuk and that could be seen as the negative inverse of the *maggid*. Rather than bringing positive revelations, it brought discord and the revelation of sins and misbehavior on the part of participants and observers. As Moshe Idel has observed, it is no accident that Rabbi Joseph Karo, the best known person possessed by a *maggid*,[23] was also the first exorcist of a dybbuk. The two phenomena were two sides of the same coin, the result of attempts by kabbalists in the sixteenth century to access divine revelations by magical means.[24]

DYBBUK POSSESSION IN SAFED

The negative form of *ibbur* is what we call dybbuk possession. In this circumstance, a soul that has been condemned to the punishment of *gilgul* finds a vulnerable human host and takes it over. Dybbukim, when questioned, often mentioned the pain of wandering and their desire to find rest, which can be found only in a host. The dybbuk not only took over control of the host's body, but also took over the ability to speak and move, and the host became a puppet that was controlled by the dybbuk. While the details of how and why a dybbuk entered a person are interesting, our interest here is in the larger social and cultural significance of dybbuk possession.

The Safed literature contains seven stories of dybbuk possession. Certain things stand out about this group of stories. The people being possessed were four men and three women. Two of the males were described as young boys, and one was eighteen years old. The fourth man was Rabbi Hayyim Vital, Luria's most important disciple.[25] The three females are described as a woman, the daughter of someone, and a widow.[26]

Another characteristic of the Safed exorcism stories is that relatively little attention is paid to the actual events in most of the Safed descriptions. There are no detailed descriptions of what happened at an exorcism in Safed in the literature produced by the Safed kabbalists themselves. The event of possession is mentioned and that an attempt at exorcism was made. Half the time the exorcism failed, and the person being possessed died as a result of the process of forcing the dybbuk to leave. In one case, R. Isaac Luria could not go, so he taught his disciple, R. Hayyim Vital, what to do and sent him to deal with the matter alone. In another case, Vital records that he became angry at a dybbuk for not showing the proper respect he felt was due him. After slapping the dybbuk and rebuking him, he concludes his account with, "and then I exorcised him."[27] It would seem that getting proper respect was more important for Vital than exorcising a dybbuk.

THE PURPOSE OF DYBBUK STORIES IN SAFED

There does not seem to be any larger purpose in these stories. Unlike other stories about Luria, they do not reflect positively on his mystical powers and abilities, which seems to be the purpose of most of the other stories preserved about him. What then was the significance and meaning of these dybbuk possession stories for the kabbalists of Safed? If the purpose were to glorify Luria's magical and mystical powers, one would have expected a much higher success rate for the exorcisms that Luria attempted. Rather, I would suggest that they are related to the important role that the concepts of *gilgul* and *ibbur* played in Safed Kabbalah. These two interrelated concepts were central to the process of validating and authenticating the apparently new ideas and practices of the Safed kabbalists.

By the second half of the sixteenth century, a combination of factors, including the codification of Jewish law in Rabbi Joseph Karo's *Shulhan Arukh*[28] and the printing press, which made many more works available, had the effect of canonizing certain ideas and practices. This gave them an air of authority that made religious innovation more difficult than it had been before the age of print. Yet, in spite of the increasing difficulties of religious innovation and creativity, Isaac Luria and the circle of kabbalists in Safed were able to revolutionize both the study of Kabbalah and more importantly the practice of Judaism. The new religious practices and rituals created or "rediscovered" by the Safed kabbalists in the *Zohar* and other medieval kabbalistic texts transformed Judaism in the following centuries.[29]

THE SOURCE OF ISAAC LURIA'S RELIGIOUS AUTHORITY

Central to understanding how this innovation occurred is the question of Isaac Luria's religious authority. There were two stages in Luria's career, and in each of them a different reason was offered to support the religious authority and sanctity of Luria's teachings. The first phase was the six years in Egypt that began when he obtained a manuscript of mystical writings and ended with his heavenly mentor, Elijah the prophet, telling him that the time had come for him to go to the land of Israel and become a teacher of mysticism. During these six years he spent his time in a hut near the Nile studying with Elijah, who taught him the meaning of the esoteric manuscript that he had obtained. Thus, his ideas had the approval and support of his heavenly mentor.[30]

Luria arrived in Safed in early 1570 C.E. That summer, Moses Cordovero, who had been considered the greatest kabbalist of Safed before Luria's arrival, became ill. Before his death his disciples asked him, who would be his successor? He responded that it would be the one who would see the pillar of fire over his grave. At the funeral, Luria said that he saw a pillar of fire in a certain place in the cemetery and that should be the site of Cordovero's grave. Luria had fulfilled the sign that Cordovero had told his disciples to look for. Within a few months of his arrival in Safed, Luria became the dominant figure in the Safed kabbalistic community that had been established approximately thirty-five years earlier. His kabbalistic teachings supplanted those of Cordovero and became the dominant school of kabbalistic thought.[31]

There is no evidence of any claims to revelations from Elijah during his period in Safed. Aside from his personal charisma, which undoubtedly was great, what was the religious authority that gave the great weight necessary to move the community to accept his teachings and innovations in religious practice over those of his predecessors? An additional problem is the belief among kabbalists that true innovation in Kabbalah ended with Nahmanides (d. 1270 C.E.).[32] I believe the answer is to be found in his claim to be a *gilgul,* a transmigration of Rabbi Simeon bar Yohai, the author of the *Zohar*, the most authoritative work of Kabbalah, and the use of the concepts of *gilgul* and *ibbur*, which were combined in the concept of *Yihud* as the explanation and validation of his spiritual and charismatic authority.

YIHUDIM

The process of *Yihudim* [unifications] was that Luria would prostrate himself on the grave of his soul mate, Rabbi Simeon bar Yohai, and through a series of prayers and mystical incantations invite the soul of the deceased to come down from heaven and unite with the kabbalist's soul in his body. When this union was effected, the kabbalist could communicate with the other soul and acquire information about future events or obtain a better understanding of a text that was not clear. R. Shloimel Dreznitz, author of the first hagiography of R. Isaac Luria, quoted a description of Luria's practice of *Yihudim*:

> He [Luria] used to stretch himself out on the tomb of R. Simeon bar Yohai, and he knew how to cleave spirit to spirit, and to concentrate on binding and raising up his soul with that of R. Simeon until he brought about unity above. Afterwards, R. Simeon's soul descended into his body, and R. Simeon would speak with him, revealing to him all that he had learned in the academy on high, as a man speaks with his neighbor.[33]

Were one to see R. Isaac Luria as he engaged in one of his *Yihudim* in Meron, one would see little beyond Luria lying on the grave, praying and perhaps some small bodily movement. On the other hand, the positive and negative public manifestations of *gilgul* and *ibbur*, that is, dybbukim and *maggidim*, were public events that the community could see and hear. They helped reinforce Luria's claims to spiritual authority. Having seen a dybbuk possess someone or hearing from eyewitnesses about Karo's *maggid* gave greater credence to the idea that Luria could meditate on the grave of a great talmudic figure, like Rabbi Shimon bar Yohai, and come back with new interpretations and teachings that derived from a heavenly source that vouched for its authenticity and authority. The dybbuk stories in Safed did not play a central role in developing the status of Rabbi Isaac Luria as a holy man. Rather, they supported and added further validation of his status as a religious authority whose innovations were supported by the heavenly and ancient authority of his earlier incarnation and soul mate, Rabbi Simeon bar Yohai, the author of the holy *Zohar*.

THE DYBBUK IN THE SEVENTEENTH CENTURY

The subsequent history of the dybbuk concept and its relation to the Safed incidents is complicated. Many of the relevant Safed stories concerning dybbukim were found in documents that remained in manuscript and were not published until much later, some as late as the middle of the twentieth century. For example, Hayyim Vital's *Sefer Hezyonot*, the single most important source of dybbuk stories in Safed, was not published in a complete edition until 1954.[34] Thus, most of what was subsequently known about dybbuk possession was based on two documents first published in the seventeenth century.

The first source is a letter written by R. Elijah Falcon, a disciple of Luria's, who was expelled by Luria from his group of disciples.[35] Falcon wrote a long letter in which he described in great detail an exorcism that occurred in Safed in 1571. He also appended a second shorter exorcism story. He circulated copies of this letter to a number of Jewish communities. His motivations in sending this letter are not clear, and we do not know to which communities he sent this letter. However, copies of this letter have survived in a number of sources. The first published version of his whole letter was in Manasseh Ben Israel's work *Nishmat Hayyim*, which defended the immortality of the soul and was published in Amsterdam in 1652. The story of the possession and exorcism was published in the context of being another piece of evidence attesting to the immortality of the soul. The second story in Falcon's letter appeared in the Yiddish *Mayse Bukh*, first published at Basel in 1602. This is the first published account of a dybbuk.[36] Another important witness to the circulation of Falcon's letter is *Divrei Yosef*, a chronicle by Joseph Sambari, composed in Damascus in the 1670s, but not published until the 1990s.[37]

The second description of a dybbuk is found in Rabbi Yosef Shlomo Delmedigo's *Ta'alumot Hokhmah*, published by his disciple, Samuel Ashkenazi, at Basel in 1629. Among the things published in this kabbalistic miscellany were three letters by R. Shloimel Dresnitz and an appendix that described the possession and exorcism of a dybbuk. Dresnitz was a kabbalist from Moravia who went to Safed in the 1590s to learn more about the new kabbalistic developments there. He stayed and married the daughter of one of Luria's disciples. He also sent a series of letters to his friend, Rabbi Issachar Ber of Kremnitz, in Poland describing what he had heard about Luria and his greatness. These letters became the basis of the hagiographical account of Luria's life known as *Shivhei ha-AR"I*. At the end of the third letter there is a dybbuk story, similar in many ways to Falcon's account.[38]

These two accounts by Dresnitz and Falcon became the basis for many of the future dybbuk stories and traditions. The relationship of these two documents to the actual events in Safed that they purport to describe is not entirely clear. Further analysis and comparison of these two accounts is necessary before a decision can be made with regard to their historical accuracy. There are significant differences between these two accounts and the accounts of possession and exorcism found in the writings of Hayyim Vital and other Safed kabbalists that were not published until the late nineteenth or even twentieth century.

One thing that jumps out when one compares the Safed accounts to these two letters is the brevity and lack of detail in the Safed accounts and the prolixity and great detail of these letters. In addition, motifs, concepts, and procedures first found in these two texts became stereotypical aspects of almost all the later stories of possession and exorcism, but are not found in the Safed texts. For example, the intense interrogation of the dybbuk that is a central part of the Falcon letter is not a feature of the Safed stories. Isaac Luria had the unique ability to discern the sources and sins of souls and did not need to interrogate the dybbuk. Introducing smoke under the nose of the possessed person to drive out the dybbuk is also not found in Safed. It is noteworthy that both of these motifs are important in stories of Christian stories of demonic exorcisms. A closer comparison between the details of the Safed stories with the Dresnitz and Falcon accounts is an important desideratum. The Falcon account, in particular, has aspects that raise questions about its authenticity.

The second half of the seventeenth century also produced the first dybbuk account that is most likely fictional. Sarah Zfatman found an interesting Yiddish pamphlet that is known in only one copy that has survived, called "The Exorcism of the Evil Spirit in Koretz." Her study of this story demonstrated that it had no historical basis and must be considered to be a fictional account. The pamphlet has no date, but the physical evidence of the pamphlet dates it to the end of the seventeenth century in Eastern Europe.[39] More recently, Zfatman has discussed several more dybbuk stories reported in the same period and geographical area in a major monograph.[40] Unlike the Koretz story, the story of a dybbuk in Nikolsburg, Moravia, in 1696 included well-known historical figures, and the story was widely reported and may have become a model for later dybbuk stories.[41]

One aspect of this story that stands out is the Sabbatean connection of some of the figures involved in this episode.[42] This relationship to Sabbateanism may be the key to understanding the significance of this dybbuk incident.

From its beginnings, this movement sought to demonstrate its legitimacy by modeling itself on the Safed kabbalistic revival. Prophecy and direct contact with the divine world were central aspects of Sabbateanism,[43] and like in Safed, a dybbuk would be a vivid illustration that direct contact between the mundane and heavenly worlds was still possible. In other words, the dybbuk played a similar role for the Sabbateans in late seventeenth century Moravia as it did for the kabbalists in Safed a century earlier.

The Sabbatean relation to the dybbuk is confirmed by the significant role it played in the writings of Rabbi Elijah ha-Cohen of Izmir, known by his nickname, Ittamari. He was born in the middle of the seventeenth century, lived in Izmir, and died in 1729. He is best known as the author of the famous ethical work *Shevet Musar*, but he was a prolific author who wrote a large number of homiletical and ethical works, most of which were published after his death. He never served as a rabbi, but was a popular and influential preacher, who was influenced by Kabbalah.[44] Recent scholarship has suggested that he was a moderate follower of the false messiah, Sabbetai Sevi.[45] He gives the following explanation as his reason for his interest in dybbukim: "I the author say that it is a mitzvah to publicly inform the public about the concept of *gilgul* and to inculcate this in their minds that through the concept of *gilgul* many difficult questions can be resolved that cause a person to turn from God, because of the [problem of] the righteous who suffer, and similar things. Through the concept of *gilgul*, these problems will be resolved, and the wise will understand the matter."[46]

With the rise of Chasidism, the ability to exorcise a dybbuk became one of the attributes of the Chasidic *zaddiq*. The hagiographical biography of Israel Baal Shem Tov (Besht), the founder of Hasidism, *Shivhei ha-Besht*, was directly modeled on *Shivhei ha-Ari*, that of Isaac Luria.[47] *Shivhei ha-Besht* included an important story of his encounter with and domination of a dybbuk. According to one story, when the Besht and several others entered the room where a possessed woman was found, the spirit possessing her greeted each according to his deeds and status. However, the spirit said to the Besht that it was not afraid of him because it knew that he had been forbidden by heaven to utilize holy names and to practice as a *baal shem* before his thirty-sixth birthday.[48] In turn, the Baal Shem Tov became the model for future Chasidic leaders, and exorcism stories proliferated and became a standard part of Chasidic hagiography. Accounts of dybbuk possession and exorcism were part of later Chasidic hagiography, chapbooks, and popular folklore. It is also noteworthy that most of the dybbuk stories in Chasidic hagiography are secondhand accounts, stories told about earlier figures and not firsthand accounts of events witnessed by the narrator of the story.[49]

An-sky's play is a combination of several of these factors with a heavy dose of influence from Russian theatrical adaptations of Romeo and Juliet, as has been demonstrated by a number of authors in the important collection of essays on An-sky edited by Steve Zipperstein and Gabriella Safran.[50] It may be good theater, but in no way does it reflect the historical reality of dybbuk possession. The full history and meaning of the dybbuk concept remains to be explored.

NOTES

1. Concerning the play and its reception history, see Michael C. Steinlauf, "The Dybbuk," in *YIVO Encyclopedia of Jews in Eastern Europe* (ed. Gershon Hundert; New Haven: Yale University Press, 2008) 1: 434–36. Concerning An-sky's life and work, see Steven Zipperstein and Gabriella Safran, eds., *The Worlds of S. An-sky: A Russian Jewish Intellectual at the Turn of the Century* (Stanford: Stanford University Press, 2006); Gabriella Safran, *Wandering Soul: the Dybbuk's Creator, S. An-sky* (Cambridge: Belknap Press of Harvard University Press, 2010).

2. Two recent studies of this type are Jeffrey H. Chajes, *Between Worlds: Dybbuks, Exorcists and Early Modern Judaism* (Philadelphia: University of Pennsylvania Press, 2003); Rachel Elior, *Dybbuks and Jewish Women in Social History, Mysticism and Folklore* (Jerusalem: Urim, 2008).

3. See the sources cited in Gedalyah Nigal, *Dybbuk Stories in Jewish Literature* [Hebrew], (Jerusalem: Reuben Mass, 1983; 2nd ed., 1994), 265–66. Other rabbinic sources are Bernard Mandelbaum, ed., *Pesikta de Rav Kahana* (New York: Jewish Theological Seminary, 1962) 1:74; *Midrash Tanhuma, Hukat,* 8; *Midrash Numbers Rabah,* 19.8.

4. Among the references to demons and their exorcism in the New Testament are: Mark—1:34, 1:39, 5:8, 7:26, 16:9; Matthew—4:10, 8:16, 8:31–32, 9:34, 12:24, 12:26–27; Luke—4:35, 4:41, 8:29, 11:14, 11:18–20, 13:32.

5. Concerning demonic possession and its relation to witchcraft in early modern Europe, see Moshe Sluhovsky, *Believe Not Every Spirit: Possession, Mysticism, & Discernment in Early Modern Catholicism* (Chicago: University of Chicago Press, 2007); Brian P. Levack, *The Witch-Hunt in Early Modern Europe* (London: Longman, 1987).

6. Hayyim Vital, *Sefer ha-Gilgulim* (Vilna, 1886), chapter 13. Cited in Moshe Hallamish, *An Introduction to the Kabbalah* (Albany: State University of New York Press, 1999), 283.

7. *Zohar*, II: 96a–98b; Hayyim Vital, *Etz Hayyim* (Jerusalem, 1962), Gate 5, chapter 2.

8. Gershom Scholem, "Dibbuk-Dybbuk," in *Encyclopedia Judaica* (Detroit: Macmillan Reference USA, 2007) 5:643–44.

9. Sara Zfatman, *Leave Impure One: Jewish Exorcism in Early Modern Ashkenaz* [Hebrew] (Jerusalem: Magnes Press, 2015), xiv, note 7.

10. David I. Shyovitz, "You Have Saved Me From the Judgment of Gehenna": The Origins of the Mourner's Kaddish in Medieval Ashkenaz," *AJS Review* 39:1 (April 2015): 55–58. He quotes a medieval version of this story and notes 28–30 cite the previous scholarship regarding this story.

11. *Kallah Rabbati*, 2.9. Quoted from A. Cohen, *The Minor Tractates of the Talmud* (London: Soncino, 1965) 2: 434–35.

12. Benjamin was not there and therefore not liable. Concerning the origins of this story see Ra'anan S. Boustan, "The Contested Reception of *The Story of the Ten Martyrs* in Medieval Midrash," in *Envisioning Judaism: Studies in Honor of Peter Schäfer on the Occasion of his Seventieth Birthday* (ed. Ra'anan Boustan, et al.; Tübingen: Mohr Siebeck, 2013) 1: 383–90.

13. Three basic studies of *gilgul* are Gershom Scholem, "Gilgul: The Transmigration of Souls," in *On the Mystical Shape of the Godhead: Basic Concepts in the Kabbalah* (New York: Schocken Books, 1991), 197–250; Hallamish, *Introduction to the Kabbalah*, 281–309; Rachel Elior, "The Doctrine of Transmigration in *Galya Raza*," in *Essential Papers on Kabbalah* (ed. Lawrence Fine; New York: New York University Press, 1995), 243–69. Concerning the concept of *ibbur*, see Moshe Idel, "The Secret of Impregnation as Metempsychosis in Kabbalah," in *Verwandlungen* (ed. Aleida and Jan Assmann; Munich: Wilhelm Fink Verlag, 2006), 341–79.

14. The pioneering study of this controversy is Ephraim Gottlieb, "The Controversy about Gilgul in Candia in the 15th Century" [Hebrew], in *Studies in the Literature of Kabbalah* [Hebrew] (ed. Joseph Hacker; Tel Aviv: Rosenberg School of Jewish Studies of Tel Aviv University, 1976), 370–96. A more recent and comprehensive study of the controversy in the fifteenth and sixteenth centuries is Brian Ogren, *Renaissance and Rebirth: Reincarnation in Early Modern Italian Kabbalah* (Leiden: Brill, 2009).

15. Levack, *The Witch-Hunt*, 167–68.

16. See Paul E. Walker, "The Doctrine of Metempsychosis in Islam," in *Islamic Studies Presented to Charles Adams* (ed. W. B. Hallaq and Donald E. Little; Brill: Leiden, 1991), 219–38.

17. Hayyim Vital, *Sha'ar ha-Gilgulim*, is largely devoted to description of and analysis of these soul families. A particularly interesting discussion, where Vital describes in great detail his own soul family and his own transmigrations, is found in Hayyim Vital, *Book of Visions*, in *Jewish Mystical Autobiographies: Book of Visions and Book of Secrets* (ed. and trans. Morris M. Faierstein; New York: Paulist Press, 1999), 156–243.

18. Faierstein, *Jewish Mystical Autobiographies*, 161–63.

19. Lawrence Fine, *Physician of the Soul, Healer of the Cosmos: Isaac Luria and His Kabbalistic Fellowship* (Stanford: Stanford University Press, 2003). Chapter 9 has a comprehensive discussion of Luria as a transmigration of Rabbi Simeon bar Yohai and its implications.

20. Faierstein, *Jewish Mystical Autobiographies*, 172.

21. The primary study of Karo and his *Maggid* is R. J. Z. Werblowsky, *Joseph Karo: Lawyer and Mystic* (Philadelphia: Jewish Publication Society, 1977).

22. The story is found in Faierstein, *Jewish Mystical Autobiographies*, 57–62, and 65–73.

23. Earlier figures that claimed maggidic revelations were Karo's teacher, Rabbi Joseph Taitatzak and the anonymous author of the *Book of the Responding Angel* [*Sefer ha-Meshiv*]. Concerning Taitatzak, see Gershom Scholem, "Rabbi Joseph Taitatzak and the Revelations attributed to Him [Hebrew]," *Sefunot* 11 (1971–1978): 69–112. Regarding the *Sefer ha-Meshiv*, see Moshe Idel, "Inquiries in the Doctrine of *Sefer ha-Meshiv* [Hebrew]," *Sefunot* 17 (1983): 185–266. However, it is important to remember that both of these works remained in manuscript until the recent publications by these scholars and thus their influence was minimal at best.

24. Moshe Idel, "Jewish Magic from the Renaissance Period to Early Hasidism," in *Religion, Science, and Magic: In Concert and in Conflict* (ed. J. Neusner, et al.; New York: Oxford University Press, 1989), 106–11.

25. Concerning Vital's possession see, Morris M. Faierstein, "The Possession of Rabbi Hayyim Vital by Jesus of Nazareth," *Kabbalah: Journal for the Study of Jewish Mystical Texts* 37 (2017): 29–36.

26. A list of these possession stories can be found in Morris M. Faierstein, "*Maggidim*, Spirits, and Women in Rabbi Hayyim Vital's *Book of Visions*," in *Spirit Possession in Judaism: Cases and Contexts from the Middle Ages to the Present* (ed. Matt Goldish; Detroit: Wayne State University Press, 2003), 187.

27. Faierstein, *Jewish Mystical Autobiographies*, 73.

28. For an overview of the significance and influence of the *Shulhan Arukh*, see Isadore Twersky, "The *Shulhan Arukh*: Enduring Code of Jewish Law," in *The Jewish Expression* (ed. Judah Goldin; New York: Bantam, 1970), 322–43.

29. This transformation is described in Morris M. Faierstein, *Jewish Customs of Kabbalistic Origin: Their History and Practice* (Boston: Academic Studies Press, 2013).

30. Concerning Luria's life in Egypt, see Lawrence Fine, *Physician of the Soul, Healer of the Cosmos: Isaac Luria and His Kabbalistic Fellowship* (Stanford: Stanford University Press, 2003), 19–39.

31. Fine, *Physician of the Soul*, is the most comprehensive biographical study of Luria and describes his life in Safed in great detail.

32. Moshe Idel, "We Have No Kabbalistic Tradition on This, " in *Rabbi Moses Nahmanides (Ramban): Explorations in His Religious and Literary Virtuosity* (ed. I. Twersky; Cambridge: Harvard University Press, 1983), 51–73.

33. Fine, *Physician of the Soul*, 285.

34. A. Z. Aescoli, *Sefer Hezyonot* (Jerusalem: Mosad Harav Kook, 1954). A second critical edition was published by M. M. Faierstein, *Sefer Hezyonot: Yomano shel R. Hayyim Vital*

(Jerusalem: Machon Ben Zvi, 2005). A much-abbreviated version of this work, which did not contain all of the possession stories, was published under the title *Shivhei Rabbi Hayyim Vital* (Ostraha, 1826).

35. Faierstein, *Jewish Mystical Autobiographies*, 236. Vital does not explain why Falcon was dismissed from the fraternity, only that he did something that greatly vexed Luria. We know from other sources that Luria and Vital after him strived to maintain the secrecy of Luria's teachings. Perhaps the distribution of his letter was a factor.

36. Morris M. Faierstein, "The *Dibbuk* in the *Mayse Bukh*," *Shofar* 30:1 (2011): 94–103.

37. Joseph Sambari, *Divrei Yosef* (ed. S. Shtober; Jerusalem: Machon Ben Zvi, 1994), 318–25.

38. Yosef Shelomo Delmedigo, *Ta'alumot Hokhmah* (Basel, 1629), 49b–50b.

39. Sara Zfatman. "The Story of an Evil Spirit in Koretz: A New Stage in the Development of a Popular Genre [Hebrew]," *Jerusalem Studies in Jewish Folklore* 2 (1982): 17–65. The dating of the pamphlet was based on the paper and typeface.

40. Zfatman, *Leave Impure One*.

41. Ibid., 241.

42. Ibid., 203–24.

43. An important study of the role of prophecy in Sabbateanism is Matt Goldish, *The Sabbatean Prophets* (Cambridge: Harvard University Press, 2004).

44. The most recent study of him and his *dybbuk* exorcisms is Yaron Ben-Naeh, "A Glimpse into a Hidden World: The *Dybbuk* Stories of Rabbi Eliyahu Hacohen of Izmir" [Hebrew], in *Fleeting Dreams and Possessive Dybbuks: On Dreams and Possession in Jewish and Other Cultures* [Hebrew] (ed. Rachel Elior, et al.; Jerusalem: Magnes Press, 2013), 305–23.

45. Gershom Scholem. "Rabbi Elijah ha-Cohen Ittamari and Sabbatianism [Hebrew]," in *Researches in Sabbataeanism* (ed. Yehudah Liebes; Tel Aviv: Am Oved, 1991), 453–77.

46. Rabbi Elijah Hacohen, *Midrash Eliyahu* (Izmir, 1759), 11d. Quoted in Yaron Ben-Naeh, "A Glimpse into a Hidden World," 311.

47. Morris M. Faierstein, "From Kabbalist to Zaddik: R. Isaac Luria as Precursor of the Baal Shem Tov," in *Studies in Jewish Civilization, Volume 13: Spiritual Dimensions of Judaism* (ed. L. J. Greenspoon and R. A. Simkins; Omaha: Creighton University Press, 2003), 95–104.

48. *In Praise of the Baal Shem Tov* (ed. and trans. D. Ben-Amos and J. R. Mintz; Bloomington: Indiana University Press, 1970), 34–35.

49. These Chasidic stories are described and analyzed by Gedalyah Nigal, *The Hasidic Tale* (Oxford: Littman Library of Jewish Civilization, 2008), 195–211.

50. See above, note 1.

Tasting Heaven: Wine and the World to Come from the Talmud to Safed

Vadim Putzu

INTRODUCTION

Until recently, in Italian family restaurants it was customary to find, hanging on the walls, a plaque that pictured two monks standing by a barrel, mugs in their hands. The picture was captioned with the saying: "In heaven there is no wine, so drink up while you are on earth!" In addition to encouraging patrons to have a drink while at the restaurant, this sign also teaches us that, according to Italian folk wisdom, one of the features that characterize the hereafter, as opposed to the present world, is its absence of wine. What is the situation as far as the Jewish tradition is concerned? Can wine help us distinguish between the *olam ha-zeh* and the *olam ha-ba*?

What follows is a short investigation of wine as it is represented and employed in relation to the world to come in kabbalistic literature and in some rabbinic texts. It will be argued that an analysis of the ways in which the rabbinic sages and, most prominently, renowned kabbalists (such as the authors of the *Zohar* [Book of Splendor], Joseph Karo, and Moses Cordovero) pictured and/or used wine gives us an intoxicating taste of their perspectives about this world and the hereafter alike. More specifically, the stage will be set by first showing how rabbinic descriptions of wine mirror, on the one hand, their authors' preoccupation with the *olam ha-zeh*: both winemaking and this-worldly existence require much toiling; the joys we can derive from them need to be regulated and confined to holy times; both can easily end up in degradation and sin. On the other hand, according to the rabbinic sages, the wine of the *olam ha-ba* is deprived of all of its negative aspects: it is easy to make, abundant, and gladdens without ever leading to sinful drunkenness—thus coming to represent the very delights that characterize existence in the world to come.

Kabbalists further contributed to the development of this picture by variously elaborating on the role of wine drinking for the sake of earning one's place in the hereafter. In this regard, the second and main part of this study contends that, while Karo's insistence on the importance of abstention and the Zoharic authors' recommendation to imbibe the symbolic wine of Torah signal their negative perception of this world, Cordovero's strategic

Italian popular plaque with wine-drinking monks. The text translates as: "In heaven there is no wine. Let us drink it while on earth!" Courtesy of Cristina Forest.

emphasis on the significance of preserving wine from Gentile contact for the sake of reaching the *olam ha-ba* reveals much about his overall plan for the *olam ha-zeh*.

THE PLACE OF WINE IN (PREMODERN) JUDAISM

The topic of wine in Judaism has, until recently, received little scholarly attention, especially for what concerns the medieval and early modern periods.[1] However, the current state of studies does not reflect the peculiarly important role of wine in Judaism and Jewish history. For our purposes, it is worthwhile to briefly highlight the ubiquitous presence of this beverage in various aspects of Jewish life in premodern times:

- As food, wine constituted one of the basic ingredients of the biblical[2] and the medieval meal,[3] providing an important caloric intake and reputedly stimulating appetite and digestion.[4]
- In the medical field, wine was widely employed and was credited with many beneficial properties,[5] including that of sanitizing drinking water.
- As an occupation, wine production and trade represented a significant activity from both a religious and an economic viewpoint.[6] Moreover, vintage and winemaking activities must have employed, at least for limited periods, most members of the Jewish community.[7]
- In the area of worship, wine was—and still is—an essential element of several rituals that characterize both the regularly recurring holy days (Sabbath, Passover, Purim, etc.) and some special lifecycle events (such as circumcision and marriage).[8]

Connected to this latter aspect in particular is the role that wine has performed, since biblical times, as an indicator of a specific socio-religious identity[9] and/or ethnicity.[10] In this sense, the act of (not) drinking (a certain type of) wine has served both to distinguish Jews from non-Jews,[11] and to establish an internal differentiation within the Jewish population itself.[12]

The important and conspicuous presence of wine in many dimensions of Jewish existence has also facilitated its use as a metaphor and a symbol, as is apparent already in the Tanakh. Ever since its first biblical attestations, this beverage is characterized by a fundamental symbolic ambivalence, inasmuch as it is associated with prosperity and beauty on the one hand, but also with debauchery and sin on the other.[13] As we shall see, this alternation between positive and negative connotations of wine as a symbol or metaphor can also be found in rabbinic literature and among kabbalists.

FOR A JEWISH CULTURAL ENOLOGY

The above-mentioned ubiquitous presence and important role of wine in multiple realms of premodern Jewish life, combined with certain general features of this beverage (variety of colors, aromas, and flavors; mind-altering effects; integration of natural and cultural components), conferred to it a distinctive status within Judaism. This has resulted in its prominent use as an ambivalent symbol throughout Jewish history.[14] Following from this recognition, the present study argues that the attitudes premodern Jews maintained toward wine provide a smaller-scale reflection of their perspectives on broader ideological and existential issues (in our case, their assessment of the nature and state of this world, and their expectations and plans for the hereafter). This is a contention that—within certain historical and geographical limitations—allows for an anthropology of wine within Judaism or, rather, for a Jewish cultural enology.[15] Accordingly, investigating the attitudes of Jewish authors toward wine may contribute to elucidating more fundamental elements in their mentalities, highlighting larger similarities and differences in their general religious and cultural outlooks.[16]

IS THERE WINE IN THE WORLD-TO-COME?

In the above-mentioned sign warning customers about the lack of wine in heaven, which used to camp in many Italian popular restaurants, this beverage is singled out and employed to characterize the afterworld in opposition to the present one. Here, Italian culture expresses its perspectives on this world and the hereafter by appealing to one of its most popular and central products—wine. Quite similarly, premodern Judaism, for which wine also held a very important role, used this beverage to depict the *olam ha-ba*, voicing its concerns for the *olam ha-zeh* in the process.

Jewish representations of the afterworld in vinous terms appear in many classic texts of rabbinic literature. For example, in the Talmud we find: "The world to come is not like this world. In this world there is the trouble of harvesting and treading [of the grapes], but in the world to come a man will bring one grape on a wagon or a ship, put it in a corner of his house and use its contents as [if it had been] a large wine cask, while its timber would be used to make fires for cooking. There will be no grape that will not contain thirty kegs of wine."[17] The rabbis' portrayal of the world to come through references to winemaking is one of leisurely existence and abundance. At the same time, this life of ease and plenty is presented as being radically different from the ordinary existence of the rabbinic sages in this world. From their depiction of the *olam ha-ba*, it appears that the rabbis of the Talmud perceived that the life they were living was marked by scarcity and uncertainty. One needed to do much toiling in order to achieve very little and could never be sure that she would succeed in reaping the fruits of her hard work.

The notion that, according to the rabbinic sages, our worldly existence is characterized by insecurity and risk can also be evinced from their descriptions of the effects of wine on those who drink it in the *olam ha-zeh* as opposed to what will happen in the *olam ha ba*. If, on the one hand, the Talmud states that, after the destruction of the Temple, the joys man can experience in this world can come only from the heart-gladdening effect of wine,[18] on the other hand, the rabbis variously declare that these same wine-induced pleasures need to be regulated and confined to holy times, inasmuch as they can all too easily lead one to degradation and sin.[19]

Some rabbinic texts explain the fact that the unavoidable threat of pleasure slipping into debauchery is an inherent trait of human existence in the *olam ha-zeh* by portraying the origin of the post-Edenic world as an act of (excessive) wine drinking. For example, one midrashic tradition attributes Adam and Eve's "original sin" to wine, as it claims: "That [forbidden] tree from which Adam ate was a vine, for nothing else but wine brings woe to man."[20] According to this text, the Tree of Knowledge of Good and Evil was a grapevine, and therefore wine was the substance responsible for interrupting the paradisiac life of man's progenitors in the Garden of Eden and for plunging them into the uncertain and dangerous condition that is this-worldly existence.

Interestingly, when presenting wine in the *olam ha-zeh* and the human condition its consumption has engendered in rather ambivalent terms, the rabbinic sages also envisage a radical reversal of this situation in the *olam ha-ba*. As one texts puts it: "The Holy One Blessed be He said: 'Since in this world wine is a problem to the world, in the future to come I will turn it into [a bearer of] joy.'"[21] Unlike ordinary wine, the wine of the world to come brings about all of the positive and none of the negative effects it ordinarily has on its drinkers. In this, this special beverage epitomizes the extraordinary existence—all joys, no problems—that awaits those who have earned their portion in the hereafter, and it is thus indicated as the eschatological reward for the righteous.

Indeed, according to various passages, those deserving to return to the Garden of Eden in the messianic age will drink "the wine which has been preserved in its grapes since the six days of Creation."[22] In dealing with wine and the afterworld, the rabbis establish a reverse parallel between the existence of mankind in its protological and eschatological state. Just as wine drinking drove the first humans out of the Garden, causing them to forfeit their Edenic condition for a this-worldly one (which the production and consumption of this beverage come to exemplify), the act of imbibing a unique vintage, stored in Eden since before the time of Adam and Eve's transgression, will characterize the otherworldly state of those living in the *olam ha-ba*.[23]

THE WINE OF TORAH

What is this extraordinary wine, preserved in its grapes since the six days of Creation, which awaits the righteous in the world to come? Considering the fact that, due to the technological limitations of the premodern period, wine could not be preserved for any length of time, it appears that the rabbinic sages did not conceive of this afterworldly drink as a variety—no matter how special—of the actual beverage, but rather used it to signify the delights that characterize existence in the hereafter.

Medieval Spanish kabbalists appropriated these rabbinic traditions and ideas about wine and the world to come, and they further contributed to developing the characterization of the "wine preserved in its grapes since the six days of Creation" as well as to defining the role of the actual beverage in either facilitating or impeding man's earning of their portion in the *olam ha-ba*.

As for the former contribution, both within the *Zohar*[24] itself and in other Hebrew writings associated with the Zoharic circle,[25] the special vintage kept in store for the righteous is described, much like in rabbinic literature, as the gladdening nourishment that typifies existence in the Garden of Eden and the world to come. Furthermore, building on the equivalence between wine, Torah, and secret that had been established by the rabbis,[26] these medieval Spanish kabbalists identified the heavenly liquid "preserved in its grapes since the six days of Creation" with the deepest scriptural secrets that will be revealed to the upright in the hereafter.[27] The picture of the kabbalistic *olam ha-ba* that emerges from this peculiar wine–Torah association is that of a scholar's paradise, where all the mysteries of the universe are finally unveiled and in which the righteous, for whom the ultimate delight is esoteric knowledge, can at last make sense of it all.

That afterworldly existence for the meritorious will involve engaging with (the wine of) Torah is confirmed by a Zoharic passage expounding on the Song of Songs, where good wine is contrasted with "another wine that is not good":

> Rabbi Yitzhak opened, saying: *Your mouth like choicest wine, flowing smoothly to my beloved* (Song 7:10). *Your mouth like choicest wine*—this is the wine of Torah that is good, for there is another wine that is not good,[28] but the wine of Torah is good for all, good for this world and good for the world that is coming. And this is the wine that pleases the Blessed Holy One more than all. And by virtue of

this, he who is saturated with the wine of Torah will awaken to the world that is coming and will merit to arise to life when the Blessed Holy One shall raise the righteous. Rabbi Yehudah said: *Rousing [dovev] the lips of sleepers* (Song 7:10)—for we have learned that even in that world he will merit to ply Torah, as it is written, *causing the lips of sleepers to move*.[29]

Here the *Zohar* views Torah as a wine that brings joy and intoxicates, arousing the drinker's senses when it is ingested: "The quest here is to be saturated with the wine of Torah, filled with the divine plenty, the flow of divinity, through learning or, more literally, through imbibing and internalizing words of Torah."[30] The "good wine" of Torah transforms human consciousness, awakening the learner to a state of mystical awareness of the divine dimensions of reality and of the world to come. The effect of inward transformation triggered by wine would almost suggest its use as a mystical tool, were it not for the fact that here we are dealing not with the actual beverage, but with a "drinkable" symbol of Torah.

Given that, as is apparent from other passages, the Zoharic authors viewed real wine as an all-too-dangerous beverage for the humans of this world,[31] it seems clear that the text above encourages the consumption of Torah, not actual wine, for the sake of deserving a spot in the afterworld. Why would the *Zohar* want to undermine wine consumption in this manner? While it has been proposed that the passage discussed above should be seen as an attack on medieval Andalusian Hebrew poetry and its glorification of promiscuous wine parties,[32] let us suggest here two alternative avenues of interpretation.

First, if we frame this statement within the intellectual context of thirteenth century Jewish Spain, then its invitation to replace wine with Torah could be viewed as an echo of the devaluation of the material in favor of the spiritual championed by philosophers such as Moses Maimonides (Rambam).[33] In this sense, acknowledging the complex influence of Maimonidean philosophy on the *Zohar*,[34] we could regard the aforementioned text as an appropriation of the Rambam's ascetic ideal of spiritual perfection and his quest for freedom from bodily needs and pleasures.[35]

Second, if we consider the immediate non-Jewish historical and socioreligious environment surrounding the likely author of the passage above, then its call to Torah for the sake of the hereafter over and against wine could function as a pronouncement in defense of the traditional Jewish values of education and scholarship vis-à-vis Christian doctrines and their supporters. At a basic level, to the extent that medieval Spanish Kabbalah can be seen as a particularistic reaction to philosophical universalism and its potential assimilationist threats,[36] the *Zohar*'s urging Jews to devote themselves to Torah instead of indulging with wine—the most popular social lubricant of the day—amounts to advocating for Jewish separateness and distinction, as well as to criticizing dangerous convivial interaction with Gentiles. At a more specific level, by insisting that it is the internalization of Torah, not the ingestion of wine—as Christians claim—that has salvific value (it gets you "high," awakening you to the afterworld), this Zoharic text might be polemicizing against the doctrine of the Eucharistic transubstantiation, which the Church officially adopted in the early thirteenth century.[37]

Overall, it appears from our analysis that the *Zohar*'s manifold strategy of discouraging actual wine consumption in this world for the sake of the *olam ha-ba* bespeaks a rather negative perception of the *olam ha-zeh* as a place where a Jew's existence is constantly threatened by desire, be it the craving for material and bodily pleasures or the attraction to esoteric knowledge and foreign ideas.

DRINKING IN AND OUT OF EDEN

As our summary investigation of the kabbalistic representations and uses of wine in relation to the world to come shifts from the medieval to the early modern period, the remainder of this study will consist of presenting, comparing, and contrasting the perspectives of Joseph Karo and Moses Cordovero, two central figures of the mystical renaissance that took place in Safed around the middle of the sixteenth century. As we focus on the differing ways in which these two kabbalists conceived of the role of wine drinking for the sake of earning one's place in the hereafter, it is imperative to keep in mind that Karo and Cordovero shared a peculiar common heritage and audience. Not only did they study together in Safed, but they were also both part of the wave of Jews who, after the expulsion from the Iberian Peninsula and the outward conversion of many to Christianity, decided to move to the land of Israel with the intention to return to Judaism and atone for their sins.

WHERE THERE IS WINE, THERE IS NO TORAH

Joseph Karo (1488–1575 c.e.) is one of the most senior characters among a number of important authors who were active in Safed around the middle of the sixteenth century.³⁸ Having abandoned the Iberian Peninsula in the wake of the expulsion, he lived in Egypt and Turkey before arriving in Safed in 1536/7. A towering figure in matters of halachah, Karo studied Kabbalah with his younger colleague, Solomon Alqabetz, and was also associated with Cordovero.³⁹ His kabbalistic ideas about wine and the afterworld are contained in *Maggid Meisharim* [Mentor of Uprightness], a mystical diary Karo apparently kept for most of his life.

From this work we learn that the author was visited by a *maggid*, a spiritual being who inspired him to lead a morally pure and ascetic life. Karo's *maggid* would appear at nighttime, when he would study the Mishnah, and require that the kabbalist divorce himself from ordinary life and all material sensations in order to focus his thought exclusively on Torah and commandments. The appearance of the *maggid* was contingent upon Karo's engagement in practices of self-mortification, which included sleep deprivation and, especially relevant for our purposes, abstention from eating and drinking to satiation.

Much like the *Zohar*, which suggests that in order to reach the *olam ha-ba* one should imbibe Torah instead of wine, Karo's *maggid* states:

> What you have done is not good, as you drank a lot tonight. And even if it was diluted, indeed by drinking much you weaken your body.... But if you will always beware from wine, you will be happy in this world, and the world to come will be good for you, for you will be a dwelling and a nest for Torah: always cleave to it without pause so as not to give room to the impure side to rule over you at all.⁴⁰

Going against Jewish (and non-Jewish) medical tradition, which maintained that wine is by and large beneficial to the human body, here Karo argues that this beverage actually weakens the body. In this sense, renouncing wine is good for man's existence in the *olam ha-zeh*, insofar as its avoidance serves as a medical recipe for happiness. Moreover, the author of this passage suggests that abstention from wine allows man to be filled with Torah, a condition that earns him a place in the world to come.

The fact that in this passage the "room" one makes in one's being through self-denial can then be filled by Torah presents us with yet another variation on the correspondence between wine and Torah already encountered in rabbinic and Zoharic materials. Instead of expressing the coincidence between the two entities, as was the case in the examples mentioned above, here the equivalence between wine and Torah is employed to suggest that they are in fact mutually exclusive. As a result, while in most cases this association results in a positive connotation for wine, here the correspondence functions as an opposition. While in the *Zohar* the effects that wine produces on its drinkers could still serve as positive descriptors for the experience of "filling up" on Torah, for Karo even as literary metaphor this beverage can function only as a negative equivalent to Torah.

Wine appears to be incompatible with Torah because of its connection with the side of impurity and, as we learn elsewhere in Karo's text,[41] with man's malevolent instinct. Accordingly, alongside other ascetic practices, avoiding wine helps man to subdue evil while making one's self fit for the divine. In this sense, our kabbalist's acts of self-denial for the sake of undermining his evil instinct constitute both a means of purification and an offering to God.

Here it should be noted that, according to Karo, it is this malevolent urge that drives mankind toward the satisfaction of their everyday needs, the fulfillment of their earthly desires, and the pursuit of material pleasures. Therefore, inasmuch as he views all objects (wine being an example) of these this-worldly needs, desires, and pleasures as receptacles for the forces of evil, Karo's perspective on the *olam ha-zeh* and on human existence therein appears decidedly negative. Moreover, his recommendations for earning one's portion in the *olam ha-ba*, which involve an intensely ascetic regimen intended to negate the material and human in favor of the spiritual and divine, toward ultimate self-sacrifice, can be seen as an example of Jewish response to the Spanish expulsion.

As scholars have argued,[42] Karo's life in Safed as a penitent longing for martyrdom must have been inspired by an overwhelming sense of guilt and a desire to make atonement to the point of self-sacrifice. As an exile from Spain himself, this kabbalist seems to have believed that the collective sins presumably committed by the Iberian Jews caused this catastrophe. Even more, he seems to have internalized his community's supposed responsibility for the expulsion to the point that he understood it as his own, a responsibility for which he had to atone.

A WINE THAT GLADDENS WITHOUT INTOXICATING

Despite the fact that, like Karo himself, Cordovero's family was almost certainly part of the Iberian Jewish diaspora, and even though the two studied together in Safed for many years, the latter's treatment of wine in connection to the world to come differs quite markedly from his older associate's. It is an indication, as will be demonstrated, of a different sort of response to the expulsion of the Jews from the Iberian Peninsula.

Unlike Karo, in his commentary on the *Zohar, Or Yaqar* [The Precious Light], Moses Cordovero (Ramak, 1522–1570 C.E.) does not recommend avoiding wine altogether in order to merit one's spot in the afterworld. Rather, in a lengthy section of this major work, the Ramak sets to schematize and organize the different views on this beverage in earlier Kabbalah.[43] He begins by distinguishing between a wine that, having been touched by Gentiles, intoxicates, and a gladdening wine that is untouched by non-Jews. In addition to bringing joy to man and the divine realm alike, the latter wine benefits the human limbs by strengthening them. From this point of view, Cordovero's attitude appears quite different from Karo's ascetic position. In fact, the author of *Or Yaqar* recognizes the positive medical effects that wine may have on the human body and appreciates especially its heating and arousing power, which stimulates coupling both in the *olam ha-zeh* and in the world above.[44]

However, for all these positive effects to occur, wine has to be preserved from Gentile contact—it has to be made holy by being kept separate. As a consequence, Cordovero emphasizes the importance of preserving wine from *goyim* [non-Jews]. In fact, being a material, this-worldly product, real wine is particularly prone to impurity and sin, since it can be touched by Jews and non-Jews alike. At the same time, this earthly beverage is connected to the divine realm of the *sefirot* [divine powers], which can thus be negatively impacted by "externals"—that is, non-Jews—touching kosher wine.

As a result, one's stringency and attention in preserving wine from Gentile contact determines, according to Cordovero, one's state of purity or sinfulness in this world, as well as her portion in the world to come.[45] In particular, those who keep kosher wine away from non-Jews increase holiness in the *olam ha-zeh* and are themselves preserved from evil and sin, thereby deserving—so to speak—an express lane pass to the *olam ha-ba* with no stops in gehenna [the Jewish version of hell]. In contrast, those who do not guard this beverage with enough care, and defile it, are subjected to the power of the evil inclination and put their portion in the world to come at risk.

On the face of it, Cordovero's attribution of tremendous consequences to the practices related to the preservation and defilement of kosher wine leaves us with the impression that *yayn nesekh* [prohibited libation wine] is an urgent and extremely serious issue in his mind. However, when one considers the socio-religious context in which the Ramak is operating—Islamic-ruled Safed—one may wonder whether he is reflecting an actual concern of his time and place or not. How likely were Jews to produce, consume, and/or trade wine with Gentiles (who would most likely be Muslims) in such an environment? Is Cordovero perhaps reflecting here the concerns of the societal realities represented in his sources—that is, thirteenth century Christian Spain—rather than his own? While I doubt that the latter question can be answered with any degree of certainty, one could still ask why the Ramak is charging with so much significance behaviors related to wine that were probably occurring sporadically at best in sixteenth century Safed.

If one continues to follow Cordovero's discussion of *yayn nesekh*, one gets the impression that, while his acknowledgment of the relationship of wine with evil inclination brings him close to Karo's negative stance about this beverage, his attitude in this matter is actually quite different from his senior associate's—being much more optimistic and constructive. In fact, in another passage, the Ramak specifies that, although wine kindles the forces of judgment embodied by the angel Samael, if it is preserved from Gentile contact, this beverage does not intoxicate and therefore does not arouse anger and sternness.[46] In this sense, as has been argued above, the act of keeping wine separate sanctifies it, thus nullifying its potentially negative effects. Furthermore, within a section in which he schematizes and orders the issues regarding the preservation of kosher wine, Cordovero emphasizes the exceedingly beneficial effects of keeping this beverage from non-Jews, while limiting the extremely negative consequences of failure to preserve it—defilement in this world and banishment from the world to come—only to those who actually drink Gentile wine. Drinking kosher wine in the company of non-Jews or even drinking Jewish wine defiled by Gentiles only delays, so to speak, one's journey to the world to come, making a pit stop in gehenna necessary for the sake of purification.[47]

As opposed to Karo's sole preoccupation with the negative qualities of wine, which can be minimized and redirected only through severe asceticism (and provided that the beverage is kosher), Cordovero's attitude seems more ambivalent with regard to the drink in general—including non-Jewish wine—and becomes an outright appraisal of preserved wine. In particular, according to the Ramak, it is the practice of keeping this beverage from non-Jews that has a highly positive, "sanctifying" function—rendering beneficial even the otherwise potentially dangerous effects of wine[48]—regardless of the limited consequences of dealing with Gentile wine and despite the (probably scarce) likelihood of interreligious wine exchanges in sixteenth century Safed. Cordovero seems to motivate his insistence on this matter by affirming that preserving kosher wine, even in cases when there is no risk of it being defiled by Gentiles, "adds holiness to the world below."[49]

In other words, by guarding Jewish wine from goyim, one keeps it separate and thus makes the beverage holy, increasing the amount of holiness in this world as a result. It is very possible that, by emphasizing the positive consequences of keeping kosher wine away from non-Jews, the Ramak is encouraging his coreligionists to uphold with stringency a certain set of halachic rules in a societal situation in which this can be done with relative ease. By magnifying the significance of Jewish legislation regarding wine, which demands separation from Gentiles, in a context where the overwhelming majority of non-Jews would not make use of this beverage anyway, Cordovero seeks to reinforce the religious identity of Safedian Jews by means of a traditional and fairly palatable tool.

If this interpretation is correct, then the Ramak's treatment of the issue of *yayn nesekh* may be inscribed within his project to consolidate Jewish life in the new center of Safed. As Moshe Idel has suggested,[50] Cordovero's basic goal is to "structure life in terms of mystical and religious meaning," seeking to "secure stability, to celebrate the mystical life as part of the traditional Jewish way of life." In this sense, the Ramak's call for engagement in the practice of preserving wine from Gentile contamination goes against ascetic tendencies (such as those manifested by Karo), which would suggest a retreat from the world and thereby constitute a potential threat to communal life and ritual.

Moreover, if, as Shaul Magid has suggested,[51] the majority of the audience for Safedian Kabbalah was made up of Iberian conversos [Jewish converts to Christianity] and/or their families, then the idea of a redeeming and soteric power that wine would symbolically possess would likely strike a familiar chord with "returning" Jews who must have been conversant with the Christian ritual of the Eucharist. By evoking a symbolic understanding of wine that would especially resound with conversos and reconfiguring its performance as a major expression of Jewish identity with salvific consequences, Cordovero could provide his followers with a significant yet manageable pathway into *teshuvah* [return to Judaism]. In light of these considerations, the Ramak's treatment of the topic of *yayn nesekh* may also be seen in terms of strategic use of a symbolic conception of wine for the sake of mobilizing and reshaping Jewish identities in an inebriating and convenient way.

In conclusion, Cordovero's peculiar perspective on the relationships between kosher wine and the world to come provides us with a window into his perception of the *olam ha-zeh* and of the task of a Jew's existence in it. Unlike Karo, for whom this world is irredeemably sinful, so that human life should be geared only toward the *olam ha-ba* through ascetic purification and ultimate self-sacrifice, Cordovero views the world he is living in as one that can and should be bettered and sanctified through man's positive action within it. Furthermore, for the Ramak one's bodily existence and active engagement in the material world provide the opportunity for securing a portion in the hereafter. While Karo's outlook on life in this world and the world to come, as it is expressed through his attitudes toward wine, betrays his experience of the expulsion of the Jews from the Iberian Peninsula as a catastrophe that could be atoned for only with extreme sacrifices, Cordovero's perspective on the same issues may be viewed as a different response to this historical event—one that centers on the opportunities that this-worldly existence in the land of Israel offered for penitents to return to a Jewish life, to expiate their sins, and to mend the *olam ha-zeh*.

To sum up the findings of our short survey, it appears that, unlike Italian popular culture hanging on restaurant walls, a number of rabbinic and kabbalistic traditions envision an afterworld in which wine—however intended—flows abundantly. On a more sobering note, medieval and early modern Jewish kabbalists urge human drinkers eager to secure a table at this intoxicating, out-of-this-worldly banquet either to imbibe exclusively kosher wine in their earthly lifetime or to avoid the beverage altogether and substitute it with Torah. Exemplifying cultural enology, our analysis of these varied Jewish views on wine in its relation to the world to come, however limited, has afforded us a window into their exponents' vision for the (ultimate) future, along with their outlook on the present. In this regard, the perspectives offered by the *Zoharic* author(s), Karo, and Cordovero in particular resonate especially well with the specific socio-historical conditions (i.e., thirteenth century Christian Spain or post-Spanish expulsion Safed) in which these kabbalists were operating.

ACKNOWLEDGMENTS AND PERMISSIONS

This essay is the offspring of a presentation given at the 28th Annual Klutznick-Harris-Schwalb Symposium on Jewish Civilization, "*Olam ha-zeh v'olam ha-ba*: This World and the World to Come in Jewish Belief and Practice," in Omaha. I wish to thank all my fellow presenters, and especially our host, Leonard Greenspoon, for partaking of food, drinks, and ideas over those two days in the true spirit of a symposium. Thanks also to John Strong for reading an earlier draft of this essay and for teaching me the American fraternity song "In heaven there ain't no beer / That's why we drink it here / And when we're gone from here / all our friends will be drinking all the beer." Its existence indirectly confirms my argument for a cultural enology and calls for an anthropology of beer in America.

NOTES

1. While the literature on wine in the Bible and in ancient Israel is extremely abundant and some important studies on this beverage in the rabbinic period do exist, when it comes to the Middle Ages and the early modern era, to my knowledge the only available scholarly titles are few and far between. See, for example, on vine-related terminology, Immanuel Löw, *Die Flora der Juden* (Vienna/Leipzig: Löwit Verlag, 1926), 1:48–189. On wine poetry in medieval Spain, see Dan Pagis, "'And Drink Thy Wine With Joy': Hedonistic Speculation in Three Wine Songs by Samuel Hannagid," in *Studies in Literature Presented to Simon Halkin* (in Hebrew; ed. E. Fleischer; Jerusalem: Magnes Press, 1973), 133–40; Raymond Scheindlin, *Wine, Women, and Death: Medieval Hebrew Poems on the Good Life* (New York: Oxford University Press, 1999); Michelle Hamilton, et al., eds., *Wine, Women and Song: Hebrew and Arabic Poetry of Medieval Iberia* (Newark: Juan de la Cuesta, 2004). On Jews and non-Jewish wine in medieval Ashkenaz, see Hayyim Soloveitchik, *Principles and Pressures: Jewish Trade in Gentile Wine in the Middle Ages* (in Hebrew; Tel Aviv: Am Oved, 2004); Hayyim Soloveitchik, *Wine in Ashkenaz in the Middle Ages: Yeyn Nesekh—A Study in the History of Halakhah* (in Hebrew; Jerusalem: Zalman Shazar Center, 2008). On Jewish perceptions and symbolic uses of wine, see Giulio Busi, *Simboli del pensiero ebraico* (Turin: Einaudi, 1999), 466–73, 660–62; Louis Grivetti, "Wine: The Food with Two Faces," in *The Origins and Ancient History of Wine* (ed. P. McGovern, et al.; Amsterdam: Gordon and Breach Publishers, 2000), 3–6, 9–16; Vadim Putzu, "*Il Leviatano . . . si digerisce con il vino*: Appunti sul simbolismo del vino in Menachem Azariah da Fano," *Materia Giudaica* 15–16 (2010–2011): 365–74; Neomi Silman, *Wine as a Symbol in Jewish Culture* (in Hebrew; Tel Aviv: Ha-Kibbutz ha-Me'uḥad, 2014). At present, the only near-comprehensive treatments of Jewish wine in the medieval and early modern period are Andreas Lehnardt, ed., *Wein und Judentum* (Berlin: Neofelis Verlag, 2014), 97–202, and Vadim Putzu, *Bottled Poetry/Quencher of Hopes: Wine as a Symbol and as an Instrument in Safedian Kabbalah and Beyond* (PhD diss., Hebrew Union College-Jewish Institute of Religion, Cincinnati, 2015).

2. For wine as daily nourishment, see Deuteronomy 8:8; 11:14; Proverbs 9:5; 1 Chronicles 12:41. See also, for example, Carey Walsh, *The Fruit of the Vine: Viticulture in Ancient Israel* (Winona Lake: Eisenbrauns, 2000), 1–7; David Jordan, "An Offering of Wine: An Introductory Exploration of the Role of Wine in the Hebrew Bible and Ancient Judaism through the Examination of the Semantics of some Keywords" (PhD diss., University of Sydney, 2002), 10–12; Nathan MacDonald, *What Did the Ancient Israelites Eat?: Diet in Biblical Times* (Grand Rapids: Erdsman, 2008), 27–28.

3. See *Zohar* 3:189b; Hayyim Soloveitchik, "Can Halakhic Texts Talk History?," *AJS Review* 3 (1978): 154; Soloveitchik, *Principles and Pressures*, 37–39; Hugh Johnson, *Vintage: The Story of Wine* (New York: Simon & Schuster, 1989); Tim Unwin, *Wine and*

the Vine: An Historical Geography of Viticulture and the Wine Trade (London: Routledge, 1991); John Cooper, *Eat and Be Satisfied: A Social History of Jewish Food* (Northvale: Jason Aronson, 1993), 100–101, 123; Ariel Toaff, *Love, Work, and Death: Jewish Life in Medieval Umbria* (London: Littman, 1996), 74–83; Jean-Louis Flandrin and Massimo Montanari, eds., *Food: A Culinary History* (New York: Columbia University Press, 1999); Yann Grappe, *Sulle tracce del gusto: Storia e cultura del vino nel Medioevo* (Bari: Laterza, 2006).

4. See BT *Berakhot* 35b; Moses Maimonides, *Treatise on Asthma* (ed. F. Rosner; Haifa: Maimonides Research Institute, 1994), 32–33; Fred Rosner, *Medical Encyclopedia of Moses Maimonides* (Northvale: Jason Aronson, 1998), 76, 168; Fred Rosner, *The Medical Aphorisms of Moses Maimonides* (Haifa: Maimonides Research Institute, 1989), 146, 313.

5. See BT *Shabbat* 129a; *Bava Batra* 58b; Rosner, *Medical Aphorisms*, 276, 297, 314; Rosner, *Medical Encyclopedia*, 20, 239.

6. See Soloveitchik, "Can Halakhic Texts Talk History?," 154; Soloveitchik, *Principles and Pressures*; Toaff, *Love, Work, and Death*, 74–83.

7. See Soloveitchik, "Can Halakhic Texts Talk History?," 171.

8. See Mishnah *Berakhot* 6:5–6. For post-rabbinic codifications of the rules about ritual use of wine, see Moses Maimonides, *Mishneh Torah, Sefer ha-Zemanim, Shabbat* 29; Maimonides, *Sefer ha-Maddah, Hilkhot Yesodei Torah* 9:1; Joseph Karo, *Shulḥan Arukh, Oraḥ Ḥayyim*, chs. 182 and 196.

9. According to Leviticus 10:9 priests should abstain from alcoholic beverages before entering the tent of meeting. This biblical prohibition against priests being drunk manifests a cultic distinction between the former and the rest of the population, just as the Nazirite, who is set apart from the rest of the community in order to consecrate himself exclusively to God, vows to abstain from the grape and all of its products, as well as from any kind of alcoholic drink, at all times (see Num 6:1–21, Judg 13:4 and 14). Rechabites also customarily abstain from wine (Jer 35), and so should kings too, lest under the influence they commit injustice (see Prov 31:4–5).

10. The complex rabbinic regulations concerning *yayn nesekh* [prohibited libation wine], which were first laid out in Mishnah *Avodah Zarah* 2:3–7 and 4:8–5:12, were originally intended to effect a clear-cut separation between the Jews and the nations. On the historical evolution of this legislation in the Middle Ages, see Soloveitchik, *Wine in Ashkenaz in the Middle Ages*.

11. Aside from the prejudice, epitomized in the popular Yiddish song *Shikker iz a goy*, which contrasts sober Jews with drunken Gentiles, one should nonetheless remark that Jewish imperviousness to drunkenness has been proverbial throughout history and has prompted observers, beginning with Immanuel Kant (see Morton Jellinek, "Immanuel Kant on Drinking," *Quarterly Journal of Studies on Alcohol* 1 [1941]: 777–78), to try to explain the "Great Jewish Drinking Mystery." This phrase describes a phenomenon, studied especially in the 1940s and 1950s (see, among others, Robert Bales, "Cultural Differences in Rates of Alcoholism," *Quarterly Journal for the Study of Alcoholism* 6 [1946]:

480–99; Donald Glad, "Attitudes and Experiences of American-Jewish and American-Irish Male Youth as Related to Differences in Adult Rates of Inebriety," *Quarterly Journal for the Study of Alcoholism* 8 [1947]: 406–72; Charles Snyder, *Alcohol and the Jews: A Cultural Study of Drinking and Sobriety* [Glencoe: Free Press, 1958]), whereby alcoholism was almost unheard of among observant Jews, despite their habitual drinking. Scholars (see especially Mark Keller, "The Great Jewish Drink Mystery," in *Beliefs, Behaviors, and Alcoholic Beverages: A Cross-Cultural Survey* [ed. M. Marshall; Ann Arbor: University of Michigan Press, 1979], 404–14) argued that training in the regular use of wine for ritual and other communal occasions (such as family meals) since childhood confers a sacred dimension on drinking this beverage (and possibly alcohol in general), which in turn generates strong feelings about the inappropriateness of inebriation and effectively eliminates the chances of alcoholism.

12. Interestingly, the rabbinic and medieval regulations concerning *yayn nesekh* have been employed in recent times as internal boundary markers, distinguishing "observant" Jews from non- or less observant ones. For these recent implications, see Silman, *Wine as a Symbol*, 130ff.

13. See, among others, Genesis 27:27–29 and 49:11–12, Deuteronomy 11:14 and 28:39, Jeremiah 48:33–34, Amos 5:11–12, Micah 6:15, Habakkuk 3:17, Zephaniah 1:13, Song of Songs 1:2–4, 2:4–5, 4:10, and 7:3–10.

14. On this aspect, see Busi, *Simboli*, 466–73, 660–62; Grivetti, "Wine: The Food with Two Faces," 3–6, 9–16; Silman, *Wine as a Symbol*. Wine has represented a peculiar cultural object not only in premodern Judaism, but also in a number of other civilizations, past and present. Scholars from various disciplines have expressed this same idea, emphasizing especially wine's symbolic dimensions; see for example, Nicola Perullo, "Wineworld: Tasting, Making, Drinking, Being," *Rivista di Estetica* 51 (2012): 10; Jean-Robert Pitte, *Le desir du vin à la conquete du monde* (Paris: Fayard, 2009); Roger Scruton, "The Philosophy of Wine," in *Questions of Taste: The Philosophy of Wine* (ed. B. Smith; New York: Oxford University Press, 2007), 1–18; Unwin, *Wine and the Vine*, 7–8.

15. Even though this essay focuses on rabbinic and kabbalistic perspectives on wine and the *olam ha-ba*, and thus is clearly limited in scope, I maintain that its fundamental argument about the epistemic value of studying attitudes toward wine can be successfully applied to other authors, currents, and historical manifestations of Judaism. While concentrating on halachic rather than on kabbalistic sources, Soloveitchik's work referenced above implicitly shares the same methodological assumption I have just laid out. For an example of "Jewish cultural enology" applied to a seventeenth century Italian author, see Putzu "*Il Leviatano . . . si digerisce con il vino*."

16. A very similar argument has been advanced by Grappe, who (in *Sulle tracce del gusto*, 159) maintains that in medieval Europe wine represented a cultural prism in which mentalities, practices, and customs were echoed. Writing from an even more general perspective, Unwin (*Wine and the Vine*, 62) has also contributed a similar observation by remarking that particularly when viticulture and wine had taken on religious significance,

their depiction in art and literature might reflect their ideological role. These authors' suggestions pave the way for extending our claim about the ideological import of attitudes toward wine from the particular case of premodern Judaism to religiously oriented civilizations in general.

17. BT *Ketubbot* 111b.

18. BT *Pesaḥim* 109a; *Taʿanit* 11a.

19. See especially *Leviticus Rabbah* 5:3 and 12:1 on the connection between wine drinking and sexual transgressions. For the notion that unregulated wine consumption may "put a man out of the world," see Mishnah *Avot* 3:11; BT *Berakhot* 29b, 40a, 63a; *Sanhedrin* 70a–b; *Numbers Rabbah* 10:4.

20. BT *Sanhedrin* 70a–b. See also *Genesis Rabbah* 19:5.

21. *Leviticus Rabbah* 12:5.

22. BT *Berakhot* 34b. See also *Sanhedrin* 99a.

23. On the idea that the fruit that brought sin into the world will become a healing in the afterworld, see Louis Ginzberg, *Legends of the Jews* (vol. 5; Philadelphia: Jewish Publication Society, 1969), 98n70.

24. See for example *Zohar* 2:147a; 3:40a; *Zohar Ḥadash* 64b.

25. This is the case, for example, in the works penned by Moses de Leon and Joseph Giqatilla. For the former, see Elliot Wolfson, ed., *The Book of the Pomegranate: Moses de Leon's Sefer Ha-Rimmon* (Atlanta: Scholars Press, 1988), 319. For the latter, see Joseph Giqatilla, *Shaʿarei Orah*, gate 9, sphere 2; Alexander Altmann, "Regarding the Question of the Authorship of *Sefer Taʿamei ha-Mitsvot* Attributed to Rabbi Yitshak Ibn Farkhi" (in Hebrew), *Kiryat Sefer* 40 (1965): 270–71.

26. See BT ʿ*Eruvin* 65a; *Sanhedrin* 38a; *Taʿanit* 7a; *Numbers Rabbah* 11:1, 13:15; *Leviticus Rabbah* 12:5; *Song of Songs Rabbah* 1:2, 1:19; *Tanḥuma, Shemini* 5; *Tanḥuma* (Buber), *Shemini* 7.

27. See *Zohar Ḥadash* 28a–b; *Tiqqunei ha-Zohar. Tiqquna* 28 (ed. Zhitomir, 72b); Wolfson, *Sefer ha-Rimmon*, 319–20.

28. What the *Zohar* identifies here as "not good" wine is not entirely clear. Context, however, suggests that the text could be referring to actual, undiluted wine as opposed to the symbolic "wine" that is Torah.

29. *Zohar* 3:39a. English translation in Nathan Wolski, *A Journey into the Zohar: An Introduction to the Book of Radiance* (Albany: SUNY Press, 2010), 89.

30. Wolski, *A Journey into the Zohar*, 99.

31. See for example *Zohar* 1:73a–b, 1:140b, 1:148a, 3:39a–41a. On a related note, drawing from the aforementioned rabbinic tradition, the Zoharic author identifies the deadly fruit Eve gave to Adam in the Garden of Eden with black treaded grapes. See *Zohar* 1:36a, 1:192a, 2:144a, 2:267b.

32. With reference to *Zohar* 3:39a, Wolski (*A Journey into the Zohar*, 111–12) claims that the author of this text must have been familiar with Andalusian Hebrew poetry and here comments—if not polemicizing directly—on it. While I do agree that here, as in most Zoharic passages, the author(s) use wine as a literary topos, without referring to the actual beverage, I find his claim quite hard to substantiate. In particular, I am not sure about the reason why a late thirteenth century author writing in a Christian environment would feel the urge to polemicize against customs that were celebrated—and supposedly practiced—in a very different (i.e., Muslim) environment at least two hundred years earlier.

33. See, for example, his *Guide of the Perplexed* 2:8, 3:27, 3:51, 3:54.

34. About this issue, see, for example, Moshe Idel, "*Sitre 'Arayot* in Maimonides' Thought," in *Maimonides and Philosophy* (ed. S. Pines and Y. Yovel; Dordrecht: Martinus Nijhoff, 1986), 79–91; Moshe Idel, "Maimonides and Jewish Mysticism," in *Studies in Maimonides* (ed. I. Twersky; Cambridge: Harvard University Press, 1990), 31–81; Moshe Idel, "Maimonides' Guide of the Perplexed and the Kabbalah," *Jewish History* 18 (2004): 197–226; Elliot Wolfson, "Beneath the Wings of the Great Eagle: Maimonides and Thirteenth-Century Kabbalah," in *Moses Maimonides (1138–1204)—His Religious, Scientific, and Philosophical Wirkungsgeschichte in Different Cultural Contexts* (ed. G. K. Hasselhoff and O. Fraisse; Würzburg: Ergon Verlag, 2004), 209–37; Elliot Wolfson, "Via Negativa in Maimonides and Its Impact on Thirteenth-Century Kabbalah," *Maimonidean Studies* 5 (2008): 363–412; Jonathan Dauber, *Knowledge of God and the Development of Early Kabbalah* (Leiden: Brill, 2012); Hartley Lachter, *Kabbalistic Revolution: Reimagining Judaism in Medieval Spain* (New Brunswick: Rutgers University Press, 2014), 32–36.

35. See, for example, his *Guide of the Perplexed* 2:33 and 2:48. See also 2:8, where Maimonides specifies that one should never drink for the purpose of pleasure, but rather feel grieved when satisfying this need.

36. On this idea, see for example Daniel Matt, "The Mystic and the *Mitsvot*," in *Jewish Spirituality* (ed. A. Green; vol. 1; New York: Crossroad, 1986), 374–76; Moshe Idel, *Kabbalah: New Perspectives* (New Haven: Yale University Press, 1988), 252–53; Harvey Hames, *The Art of Conversion: Christianity and Kabbalah in the Thirteenth Century* (Leiden: Brill, 2000), 25–81; 275–85; Lachter, *Kabbalistic Revolution*, 32–40; 91–93; 100–104; 132–33; 159–60.

37. In 1215, the Fourth Lateran Council used the word "transubstantiated" in its profession of faith to describe the change from bread and wine to body and blood of Christ that takes place in the Eucharist. See, for example, Miri Rubin, *Corpus Christi: The Eucharist in Late Medieval Culture* (Cambridge: Cambridge University Press, 1991). On the *Zohar's* polemics with the Eucharist, see Ellen Haskell, *Mystical Resistance: Uncovering the Zohar's Conversations with Christianity* (New York: Oxford University Press, 2016), 104–5. See also Jonathan Brumberg-Kraus, "Meat-Eating and Jewish Identity; Ritualization of the Priestly Torah of Beast and Fowl (Lev 11:46) in Rabbinic Judaism and Medieval Kabbalah," *AJS Review* 24 (1999): 227–62.

38. The most extensive work entirely devoted to Karo's life and thought is Zwi Werblowsky, *Joseph Karo: Lawyer and Mystic* (Philadelphia: Jewish Publication Society, 1977).

39. According to Werblowsky (*Joseph Karo*, 15–17), he was not accepted as a student by Isaac Luria though.

40. Joseph Karo, *Maggid Meisharim, Psalms*, ch. 19.

41. Joseph Karo, *2 Samuel*, ch. 10.

42. See especially Werblowsky, *Joseph Karo*, 57–65, 148–55; Lawrence Fine, *Physician of the Soul, Healer of the Cosmos: Isaac Luria and His Kabbalistic Fellowship* (Stanford: Stanford University Press, 2003), 71–73, 246.

43. Moses Cordovero, *Or Yaqar, Vayikra*, 17–22.

44. Moses Cordovero, *Vayikra*, 17. See also Moses Cordovero, *Terumah*, 100–101: wine consumption encourages intercourse among humans. Insofar as, according to most kabbalistic texts, human deeds in this world impact the dynamics among the *sefirot*, which populate the world above, this wine-inspired act of carnal union facilitates a similar process of unification and harmonization of the divine powers. In this sense, wine inspires coupling both below and above.

45. Moses Cordovero, *Shemini*, 166.

46. Moses Cordovero, *Terumah*, 100–101.

47. Moses Cordovero, *Shemini*, 166.

48. Moses Cordovero, *Terumah*, 100–101.

49. Moses Cordovero, *Shemini*, 166.

50. Moshe Idel, *Messianic Mystics* (New Haven: Yale University Press, 1998), 163–64.

51. See Shaul Magid, *From Metaphysics to Midrash: Myth, History, and the Interpretation of Scripture in Lurianic Kabbala* (Bloomington: Indiana University Press, 2008), 78–81.

Worlds to Come Between East and West: Immortality and the Rise of Modern Jewish Thought

Elias Sacks

There are many ways to describe the intellectual agenda of modern Jewish thought. We might tell a story about a growing emphasis on ethics, focusing on ways in which modern philosophers often grant morality a more central role in religious life than did premodern thinkers.[1] We might also tell a story about a newfound interest in history, arguing that many modern Jews stress themes such as the unceasing development of ideas and societies, the links between Jewish and non-Jewish history, and the importance of deriving Judaism's beliefs and relevance from the historical-critical study of Jewish sources.[2] Yet another option would be to focus on the classification of Judaism itself, exploring debates about "whether Judaism and Jewishness are matters of religion, culture, or nationality."[3] And there are still other possibilities, as well.[4]

In this article, I wish to recover the importance of another issue for the emergence of Jewish intellectual modernity: immortality. While it is clear that the notion of a messianic future is a central concern for many modern thinkers,[5] there is considerable disagreement about whether the idea of *olam ha-ba* or "world to come" in the sense of personal immortality—in the sense of the survival of the soul or some other aspect of the individual after the body's death[6]—plays a significant role in modern Jewish thought. A group of publications in the early 1960s suggested that debates about Jewish and non-Jewish access to the afterlife allowed philosophers to explore the role of reason and tolerance in the Jewish tradition,[7] and a number of studies have argued that nineteenth- and twentieth-century denominational literature, most notably works of liturgy, emphasizes personal immortality over themes such as bodily resurrection.[8]

By contrast, a starkly different view appears in the work of the historian and philosopher Hans Jonas, who famously began a 1961 lecture at Harvard Divinity School by invoking what he termed the "undeniable fact ... that the modern temper is uncongenial to the idea of immortality," especially to the "really substantive concept of immortality: survival of the person in a *hereafter*."[9] This position would reappear almost three decades later in the influential collection *Contemporary Jewish Religious Thought*, whose entry on "immortality"—written by Allan Arkush—argued that since the eighteenth century there has been no "major Jewish thinker . . . for whom the doctrine of a life after death was a consolation and not a source of some embarrassment."[10]

A middle position of sorts appears in a recent essay by Leora Batnitzky. Like the first group of interpreters, Batnitzky argues that "a commitment to immortality is central to modern Jewish thought" and that modern Jewish philosophers have largely rejected (or at least downplayed) bodily resurrection. But Batnitzky indicates that she is concerned less with immortality in the sense of the survival of the individual self and more with what she terms a "loose conception of immortality" or "immortality in a very general sense," namely, "the idea that the meaning of human life transcends human finitude or mortality." She focuses on what she describes as attempts "to refute materialist conceptions of human existence without committing to any particularly theological or traditionally metaphysical notion of immortality," and most of the thinkers she discusses are concerned with topics other than personal immortality—with the Jewish people's eternal survival, for example, or with the eternity of humanity's moral tasks.[11]

My goal is to show that what Jonas terms the "really substantive concept of immortality" does, in fact, play a key role in modern Jewish thought—indeed, that the survival of the soul after death is crucial to works well beyond denominational documents and liturgical texts. I will do so by exploring the Hebrew writings of two thinkers who are widely invoked but too little understood: the German-Jewish philosopher Moses Mendelssohn (1729–1786) and the Eastern European thinker Nachman Krochmal (1785–1840). Frequently portrayed as a leading figure in the late Enlightenment and as the founder of modern Jewish thought, Mendelssohn is known for his German writings on topics ranging from aesthetics to politics to metaphysics. Yet while these German works have long occupied scholars of philosophy and Judaism, Mendelssohn's extensive body of Hebrew writings is only starting to become an object of sustained study, and 2011 marked the first time that a broad selection appeared in English translation.[12] Krochmal has received even less attention, especially among English-speaking audiences. A teacher, businessman, and communal leader born in what is now Ukraine, he is remembered as one of modernity's most significant Eastern European Jewish philosophers, and his unfinished Hebrew magnum opus—*The Guide of the Perplexed of the Time* [*Moreh Nevukhei Hazeman*]—is an early Jewish attempt to wrestle with developments such as biblical criticism and historicist thinking. However, despite some signs of renewed interest, his philosophy has rarely been subject to scrutiny in North America, and his *Guide* is still largely unavailable in English.[13]

This essay will draw on these neglected Hebrew works to reassess the role of personal immortality in the rise of Jewish modernity. More specifically, I will argue that the emergence of modern Jewish thought involves a high-stakes soteriological debate between East and West—that one of modern Jewish philosophy's early episodes is a debate between Krochmal and Mendelssohn about immortality and the nature of Judaism. I will begin with Krochmal, showing that he casts Judaism's affirmation of an afterlife as the product of long-standing debates among postbiblical Jews who disagreed about whether the soul is immortal. I will then suggest that Krochmal's view is best read as a critique of a type of position that he associates with Mendelssohn, whose Hebrew writings are concerned less with showing that immortality was contested among postbiblical Jews and more with establishing that this doctrine is affirmed by the Bible itself. I will conclude by arguing that the Mendelssohn-Krochmal clash is, in part, a dispute about the nature of the Jewish tradition. Whereas Mendelssohn's claims are part of a broader project of presenting Judaism as a vehicle of rationally accessible eternal truths affirmed by the Bible, Krochmal's position helps ground a different vision of this tradition—a vision of Judaism as a phenomenon whose doctrinal content emerges through the efforts of postbiblical human beings. For these foundational philosophical voices in Jewish modernity, the world to come serves as a crucial terrain for formulating—and contesting—theories of Jewish existence.

A preliminary remark is in order. Readers familiar with Mendelssohn's thought will not be surprised to find him invoked in an essay on immortality. His fame in his own era was due, in part, to a celebrated 1767 treatise—a rewriting of Plato's *Phaedo*—that defends the demonstrability of immortality and was quickly translated into five languages.[14] Nevertheless, for many commentators, Mendelssohn's work signals the end of a concern with personal immortality among modern Jewish philosophers. When Arkush suggests that after the eighteenth century "the doctrine of a life after death was . . . a source of some embarrassment," he takes Mendelssohn to be the "last major Jewish thinker" for whom this was not the case.[15]

Similarly, Neil Gillman, one of the readers who focuses on the role of immortality in modern denominational literature, moves from his treatment of Mendelssohn not to a survey of other philosophical perspectives but rather to topics such as "modern liturgical reforms," returning to philosophical voices primarily when discussing renewed interest in bodily resurrection among late twentieth-century Jews.[16] By contrast, I seek to complicate this picture and recover a trajectory of philosophical thinking about immortality as a significant element in the emergence of Jewish intellectual modernity. Rather than signaling the end of a philosophical embrace of the survival of the soul, Mendelssohn's writings constitute the first stage in a debate, extending from Germany to Eastern Europe, that treats this belief as an opportunity to construct visions of the Jewish tradition.

KROCHMAL

Krochmal's *Guide* is a wide-ranging text, dealing with topics including metaphysics, Jewish law, and biblical criticism as part of an effort to address "perplexities" plaguing nineteenth-century Jews. Unfinished at the time of its author's death in 1840, the manuscript was edited by a leading German scholar, Leopold Zunz, and eventually published in 1851.[17] The key section for us is the *Guide*'s discussion of Ecclesiastes, a biblical book that presents itself as the words of "Koheleth, son of David, king in Jerusalem," traditionally identified as King Solomon.[18] This insistence on Solomonic authorship was challenged by eighteenth- and nineteenth-century biblical critics such as Johann Gottfried Eichhorn, and Krochmal devotes a section of the *Guide* to defending this critical perspective. Ecclesiastes, he argues, was written long after Solomon's reign by a Jewish nobleman who oversaw a group of scholars, and the book's post-Solomonic provenance was already well known to the rabbis of late antiquity.[19]

Krochmal's initial comments explore Ecclesiastes' concluding verses:

> A further word: Because Koheleth was a sage, he continued to instruct the people. He listened to and tested the soundness of many maxims. Koheleth sought to discover useful sayings and recorded genuinely truthful sayings. The sayings of the wise are like goads, like nails fixed in prodding sticks. They were given by one Shepherd. A further word: Against them, my son, be warned! The making of many books is without limit and much study is a wearying of the flesh. The sum of the matter, when all is said and done: Revere God and observe His commandments! For this applies to all mankind: that God will call every creature to account for everything unknown, be it good or bad. (Eccl 12:9–14)

Commentators have long noted that these words read more as an epilogue appended to Ecclesiastes than as an integral part of the book. Krochmal suggests that the opening of this passage was written by the book's post-Solomonic author,[20] but he argues that the final lines were written not by that individual, but rather by a later group of scholars involved in the process of compiling the biblical canon. It is worth quoting Krochmal's words at length:

> Behold, it seems to us that those verses at the end of the book of Ecclesiastes—"the sayings of the wise are like goads," etc., until the end of the book—are verses of sealing and completion not for this book (for what would be the reason for and sense in Solomon, or whoever wrote this book, warning against producing further books beyond this book of his?), but rather for the collection of the books of the Writings [the third section of the Hebrew Bible] as a whole. It seems that the men of the Holy Assembly of that time—which was closer to the time of the initial arrival of the Greeks and the priest Jaddua or Simon I—sealed and closed the compilation of the third part of the Holy Scriptures with these verses.... They further completed their words of sealing with ethical teaching: "The sum of the matter, when all is said and done," etc. They did this in order to remind [readers] that the purpose of all the study and reading of books is reverence for the Lord and observing His commandments, in accordance with the verse: "The beginning of wisdom is reverence for the Lord" [Ps 111:10].[21] And with the statement "God will call every creature to account," etc., they were affirming the final judgment in the world to come, since many denied this at that time, as is known from the Sadducees.[22]

According to Krochmal, the final verses quoted above were written by the compilers of the canon not as a conclusion to the book of Ecclesiastes, but rather as an epilogue to the entire third section of the Hebrew Bible—as "verses of sealing and completion not for this book ... but rather for the collection of the books of the Writings as a whole." The idea here is that Ecclesiastes was originally the concluding book of the final division of the Bible[23] and that these lines were intended to serve as the closing words of that section—and, by extension, the canon as a whole.

I am interested less in the historical accuracy of this claim and more in the argument Krochmal builds on its basis. Consider his declaration that "with the statement 'God will call every creature to account,'" the compilers of the canon "were affirming the final judgment in the world to come, since many denied this at that time, as is known from the Sadducees." He is suggesting that this epilogue to the Bible was composed, in part, as an intervention in debates in antiquity. On this interpretation, many ancient groups denied "the final judgment in the world to come," and the compilers of the canon responded by placing a reference to this judgment in *olam ha-ba* at the end of the Bible as a whole, reminding readers that God "will call every creature to account."

If we read this comment against the backdrop of earlier sections of the *Guide*, it becomes clear that the reference to "the world to come" is crucial—that Krochmal sees these lines as an intervention not simply in debates about a "final judgment," but rather in debates about the very existence of a "world to come" in which such a judgment can occur. More precisely, he takes these lines to be an intervention in debates about whether the soul endures after the death of the body. He suggests that the tensions he has in mind are similar to those involving the ancient sect known as the Sadducees, and he stresses earlier in the *Guide* that this group clashed with another sect, the Pharisees, over whether the soul survives death.

According to Krochmal, the Pharisees "believe that there exists within souls the power of eternal life, and that beneath the earth there is reward and judgement for everyone who proceeds through life to righteousness or wickedness: the lot of the latter is eternal imprisonment, whereas the former are given the power to live and return to life."[24] Drawn from the historian Josephus, the picture here is of a sect that affirms the survival of souls after the death of bodies: for Krochmal's Pharisees, the souls of the wicked survive and are subjected to "eternal imprisonment," while the souls of the righteous also endure but are returned to resurrected bodies. Krochmal repeats this point less than a page later, writing that the Pharisees hold that "the soul does not fall under the sway of death: the souls of the righteous return to their bodies, and the souls of the wicked are afflicted with torment without end."[25]

By contrast, he continues, the Sadducees "deny the eternity of the soul," "teach that souls disappear with bodies," and clash with the Pharisees "on the principle that is the main one of them all: the belief in the eternity of the soul and the resurrection of the dead being found in the Torah."[26] Krochmal again emphasizes the survival of souls after death: whereas the Pharisees affirm this principle, the Sadducees deny this idea, along with the idea that the Bible takes at least some of those immortal souls to return to resurrected bodies. For the *Guide*, this issue stands at the very heart of the Pharisee-Sadducee controversy, serving not as a peripheral concern but rather as "the principle that is the main one of them all." When Krochmal links the final lines of Ecclesiastes to the disputes involving the Sadducees about a "world to come," then, he is presenting these verses as an intervention in debates about personal immortality, suggesting that the compilers of the biblical canon were so troubled by widespread denials of this doctrine that they inserted an affirmation of the soul's survival into the closing words of Scripture.

Krochmal casts these final lines not simply as an intervention in ancient debates, but as part of a string of ultimately successful interventions in those debates—as part of a constellation of efforts that eventually established belief in the afterlife as an accepted element of the Jewish tradition. Consider, again, his claim that the compilers of the canon "were affirming the final judgment in the world to come, since many denied this at that time [*bazeman hahu*], as is known from the Sadducees." Elsewhere in his writings, Krochmal stresses that the Sadducees did not prevail in their debates with the Pharisees. He introduces these clashes by stating that in most cases "the approach of the early Pharisees to belief and deeds . . . is in its substance and appearance the approach of our sages, may their memories be for a blessing, in all the works of the Oral Torah that we possess," suggesting that it was this sect, rather than its Saducean rival, that shaped the subsequent development of Jewish life.[27] Krochmal repeats this point later in his discussion, insisting that many of "the words of the Pharisees are words of our tradition" and that key "beliefs and practices . . . were supported in the hands of individuals among their men"[28]—that the Pharisees played an important role in securing the place of various principles in the Jewish tradition. Moreover, he identifies the notion of an afterlife as one of the Pharisaic ideas accepted by later Jewish thinkers, referring in his correspondence to the rabbis' insistence in the Mishnah that "all Israel has a share in the world to come"[29] and to treatments of immortality by medieval Jewish philosophers such as Maimonides.[30] Krochmal's view is thus that immortality eventually became an accepted part of the Jewish tradition despite opposition from groups such as the Sadducees. When he discusses the composition of Ecclesiastes' final verses by suggesting that "many denied" immortality "at that time," then, the phrase "at that time" seems significant. Krochmal seems to be alluding to the idea that denials of immortality were eventually overcome—to be suggesting that although "many denied" this belief at that time, this was not the case in later times, since the efforts undertaken by groups such as the compilers of the biblical canon and the Pharisees were ultimately successful.

Finally, while Krochmal alludes to the idea that denials of immortality were eventually overcome, his comments regarding Ecclesiastes indicate that, on his interpretation, this result was not achieved until well after the emergence of the Bible. The key, once again, is his use of the Sadducees as an example of how "many denied" immortality in the ancient world. Discussing this sect earlier in the *Guide*, he states that it did not emerge until "after the final sealing of the Holy Writings."[31] By invoking this group immediately after describing the efforts of the compilers of the biblical canon to affirm immortality, then, he is indicating to his readers that those efforts did not prevent future disputes about life after death—that groups such as the Sadducees would still emerge and "deny the eternity of the soul." He is indicating, that is, that the status of immortality as an accepted element of the Jewish tradition is a decidedly postbiblical achievement—that the production of the biblical canon failed to firmly embed the notion of *olam ha-ba* into the fabric of Jewish life and that it was therefore the efforts of postbiblical groups, such as the Pharisees, that ultimately secured the place of this doctrine in Judaism.

Indeed, Krochmal seems to carefully avoid clarifying the degree to which the Bible should be read as endorsing the eternity of the soul. Although he states that verses quoted above—the epilogue appended to Ecclesiastes and the biblical canon—affirm "the final judgment in the world to come," he rejects the idea that the body of Ecclesiastes itself advances this doctrine,[32] and his account of the Sadducee-Pharisee clash suggests that the rest of the Bible does not address this topic with sufficient clarity to forestall theological uncertainty. After all, he claims, this exegetical point figured prominently in the controversies between these sects, who disagreed on "the eternity of the soul and the resurrection of the dead being found in the Torah."

The issues at stake in Krochmal's treatment of Ecclesiastes now begin to emerge. Invoking the existence of debates in ancient Judaism about the immortality of the soul, he suggests that it was the efforts of groups involved in these debates that secured the place of this belief in Jewish life, and he emphasizes that this result was not achieved until long after the Bible emerged. The *Guide*'s discussion of Ecclesiastes thus provides readers with a history of immortality in the Jewish tradition. Krochmal casts Judaism's affirmation of an afterlife as the product of long-standing debates among postbiblical Jews who disagreed about whether the soul is immortal. He argues that the notion of a world to come continued to be contested even after the biblical canon took shape and that it was only the efforts of later, postbiblical groups that established this doctrine as an accepted element of the Jewish tradition.

KROCHMAL AND MENDELSSOHN

Krochmal soon turns to other Jewish interpretations of Ecclesiastes, invoking "our early sages who labored to interpret" this book as well as later figures who struggled with its plain sense:

> May blessings rest upon the heads of the interpreters focused on the plain sense of Scripture who preceded us—among them, in particular, the master Moses the son of Menahem, may his memory be for a blessing—who made every effort to elucidate and interpret [Ecclesiastes] internally so that it does not contradict true belief. . . . But was this, in fact, the opinion and desire of the book? This is a question that earlier generations never asked. In the present time, however, the path of inquiry drives us to this question.[33]

The reference to "Moses the son of Menahem" attempting to "elucidate" Ecclesiastes is a reference to Mendelssohn and his Hebrew commentary on that book. Published in 1770, this work includes a verse-by-verse commentary on the text of Ecclesiastes, along with an introduction that discusses the nature of this biblical book and of scriptural exegesis more generally.[34] Krochmal offers a critical evaluation of Mendelssohn's exegetical work, citing him as an example of a thinker who "made every effort to elucidate and interpret" Ecclesiastes "so that it does not contradict true belief," but who failed to ask a question to which "the path of inquiry drives us" in "the present time": namely, "was this, in fact, the opinion and desire of the book?" What is Krochmal claiming?

Consider the description of Mendelssohn as attempting to show that Ecclesiastes "does not contradict true belief." His commentary expresses concern that Ecclesiastes' early chapters contain "difficult words that seem, heaven forfend, as if they are opposed to belief in providence and immortality, which are fundamental principles of the true religion," and he declares that he is even more troubled by later sections that "seem, at first glance, to be even more difficult and further from the fundamental principles of the true religion."[35] His worries revolve around lines such as these:

> And, indeed, I have observed under the sun: Alongside justice there is wickedness, alongside righteousness there is wickedness. I mused: "God will doom both righteous and wicked, for there is a time for every experience and for every happening." So I decided, as regards men, to dissociate them [from] the divine beings and to face the fact that they are beasts. For in respect of the fate of man and the fate

> of beast, they have one and the same fate: as the one dies so dies the other, and both have the same lifebreath; man has no superiority over beast, since both amount to nothing. Both go to the same place; both came from dust and both return to dust. Who knows if a man's lifebreath does rise upward and if a beast's breath does sink down into the earth? I saw that there is nothing better for man than to enjoy his possessions, since that is his portion. For who can enable him to see what will happen afterward? I further observed all the oppression that goes on under the sun: the tears of the oppressed, with none to comfort them; and the power of their oppressors—with none to comfort them. (Eccl 3:16–4:1)

However we might understand these verses today, it is not difficult to see how a reader such as Mendelssohn could interpret them as denials of doctrines such as immortality. These lines declare that "there is nothing better for man than to enjoy his possessions" because we "return to dust" and material life is our only "portion," a statement that could be read as a rejection of the idea that there is some incorporeal substance that endures after the body's death.

Another passage that is troubling for Mendelssohn reads as follows:

> For he who is reckoned among the living has something to look forward to—even a live dog is better than a dead lion—since the living know they will die. But the dead know nothing; they have no more recompense, for even the memory of them has died. Their loves, their hates, their jealousies have long since perished; and they have no more share till the end of time in all that goes on under the sun. Go, eat your bread in gladness, and drink your wine in joy. . . . Enjoy happiness with a woman you love all the fleeting days of life that have been granted to you under the sun—all your fleeting days. For that alone is what you can get out of life and out of the means you acquire under the sun. Whatever it is in your power to do, do with all your might. For there is no action, no reasoning, no learning, no wisdom in Sheol, where you are going. I have further observed under the sun that the race is not won by the swift, nor the battle by the valiant; nor is bread won by the wise, nor wealth by the intelligent, nor favor by the learned. For the time of mischance comes to all. (Eccl 9:4–11)

These lines suggest that even the lowliest living animal ("a live dog") enjoys an advantage over the noblest deceased creature ("a dead lion"), for while "the living know they will die . . . the dead know nothing." These lines might be interpreted as a claim that while living creatures possess some degree of awareness (albeit awareness of their impending doom), death marks the end of all awareness and a passage into nonexistence.³⁶

One of the central claims in Mendelssohn's commentary is that he has discovered a way to show, contrary to appearances, that Ecclesiastes affirms doctrines such as immortality:

> Not all that is said in [Ecclesiastes] is, in truth, the opinion of King Solomon, may peace be upon him. Rather, he sometimes speaks as one engaged in give-and-take regarding a matter, asking and responding in the manner of syllogistic thinkers who search for the truth by means of the intellect. These thinkers arrive at what they seek only if they attend to contradictory arguments, raise all sorts of doubts, straighten out the matter with proper scales and balances, and carefully consider and approach the lines of reasoning, one after another, until they separate the true from the false, and the correct from the doubtful. . . . We see that the author of this book wrote in the manner of searching and give-and-take.³⁷

Mendelssohn casts Ecclesiastes as a philosophical dialogue, as a book written "in the manner of syllogistic thinkers who search for the truth" by engaging "contradictory arguments." On this view, Ecclesiastes presents arguments in favor of various doctrines as well as arguments against those doctrines, leading readers to ascribe "truth" to whichever set of arguments seems stronger. Applied to immortality, this means that "not all that is said . . . is, in truth, the opinion of King Solomon"—that verses such as the ones quoted above, which seem to deny this doctrine, do not reflect the opinions of Ecclesiastes' author, but rather function as hypothetical arguments against this belief that set the stage for its ultimate affirmation. Indeed, lest readers miss Mendelssohn's focus, he emphasizes his concern with personal immortality, stating that he addresses "the immortality of the soul" and the idea "that souls remain after death,"³⁸ along with perspectives that posit the "destruction" and "annihilation of the soul."³⁹

Some examples will prove helpful. On various occasions, Mendelssohn suggests that the author of Ecclesiastes issues statements that seem to reject immortality not in order to undermine this doctrine, but rather in order to reveal the problematic consequences that follow from its denial and to thereby provide readers with a reason to avoid such a posture and instead affirm the eternity of the soul. Consider Mendelssohn's discussion of Ecclesiastes 3–4:

> After I reflected on this entire section from beginning to end, it seemed to me that the significance of the verses is that the most

> correct and powerful proof for the immortality of the soul and reward in the world to come is the one on the basis of injustice in this world. [Consider the verses from] "Alongside justice there is wickedness," etc., [to] "the tears of the oppressed, with none to comfort them," etc. [Eccl 3:16–4:1]. For one who believes in the existence of God and His providence cannot escape one of these two options: either he will believe that souls remain after death, and that afterwards there is a time of judgement for every deed, either good or evil; or he will ascribe, heaven forefend, iniquity and injustice to the holy God.[40]

According to Mendelssohn, Ecclesiastes 3–4 may seem to deny immortality, but it does so in order to highlight a "proof for the immortality of the soul and reward in the world to come . . . on the basis of injustice in this world." By stating that we "return to dust" while repeatedly invoking the "wickedness" and "oppression" we see around us,[41] this text reminds us that someone who denies immortality will have to come to grips with the pervasiveness of evil in this world and that such an individual will ultimately be forced to "ascribe, heaven forefend, iniquity and injustice to the holy God." While those who "believe that souls remain after death" can affirm that perpetrators of evil are punished (and the victims of evil compensated) in an afterlife, someone who denies immortality will be forced to conclude that God has created nothing other than a world riddled with evil and suffering, choosing to produce a cosmos in which wickedness goes unpunished and righteousness unrewarded. Unless we are prepared to ascribe this sort of behavior to the deity, then, our only option is to reject denials of immortality and embrace this doctrine. Unless we are willing, that is, to cast God as a cruel entity unconcerned with the well-being of creatures and values such as justice, we must take the deity to have created not only a universe replete with evil and suffering, but also a compensatory afterlife for immortal souls.

Mendelssohn adopts a similar strategy when discussing material such as Ecclesiastes 9, declaring that "with the help of God, may He be Blessed, I have also arrived at and found a way . . . to resolve every difficulty in those sections and interpret the words of the wise king in a manner that does not contradict, heaven forfend, but rather strengthens the fundamental principle[s] of the true religion."[42] For example, juxtaposing the statement in Ecclesiastes 9:4 that "a live dog is better than a dead lion" with the claim in Ecclesiastes 4:2 that we should count "those who died long since more fortunate than those who are still living,"[43] Mendelssohn suggests that these verses are supposed to illuminate another problematic consequence that follows from denying immortality:

> The distinctive mark of this worthless opinion is that it distorts the ways of the intellect and inquiry and brings those who affirm it, in great perplexity, to a point where they do not know whether to prefer life or death. For if the one who denies immortality sees the evil deed performed under the sun, it is possible that he will abhor life. . . . For many evils and sorrows trouble him, but nothing offers comfort. . . . But if he responds to himself that there is no evil greater than the complete absence and destruction [of the soul], then the ways of the intellect will compel him to prefer a life of suffering and grief over death and the destruction of the soul.[44]

On this reading, Ecclesiastes includes lines that valorize life (such as 9:4) alongside verses that praise death (such as 4:2) in order to indicate that individuals who deny immortality cannot coherently decide which option to prefer. While such individuals might conclude that life should be preserved at all costs because the only other option is "death and the destruction of the soul," they might also conclude that injustice and suffering are so pervasive, and the absence of divine justice so glaring, that nonexistence is preferable to remaining in a world of "evils and sorrows."

Moreover, Mendelssohn continues, this is not the only perplexity that will plague someone who denies immortality:

> Sometimes he will say to himself "do whatever it is in your power to do, for there is neither justice nor accounting" [based on Eccl 9:10]; at other times, he will despair of doing anything great or small, and he will say "the race is not won by the swift," etc. [Eccl 9:11], as is explained in the ninth section of this book. Therefore, his thoughts will frighten him and, as an instrument of torture, cast his soul from panic to fear: there will always be strife in his heart. . . . An individual will be rescued from this perplexity only by the belief in immortality and in reward in the world to come.[45]

On this reading, verses such as Ecclesiastes 9:10 and 9:11 are supposed to show that individuals who deny immortality cannot coherently make decisions about how to behave. After all, such individuals will be unable to decide whether they should "do whatever it is in [their] power to do" and disregard moral norms on the grounds that there is no final judgment, or whether they should "despair of doing anything great or small" and avoid participation in worldly affairs on the grounds that human life is transitory and human accomplishments fleeting. Unless we are prepared to live with these forms of incoherence, then, the only solution is to reject attacks on immortality and affirm this doctrine.

Krochmal's argument now takes shape. When the *Guide* invokes Mendelssohn's attempt to interpret Ecclesiastes "so that it does not contradict true belief," the reference is to the types of arguments outlined above—to Mendelssohn's attempt to show that this biblical book affirms rather than rejects doctrines such as immortality. Krochmal goes further, however, and claims that while Mendelssohn is a type of thinker who failed to ask whether "this [was], in fact, the opinion and desire of the book . . . the path of inquiry drives us to this question" in "the present time." The reason that Mendelssohn strives to show how Ecclesiastes "does not contradict true belief," the *Guide* charges, is that he never seriously contemplates the genuine possibility of such a contradiction, assuming instead that biblical books must affirm doctrines such as immortality. By contrast, Krochmal claims to avoid that assumption and ask what the available evidence actually shows. He indicates, in other words, that his treatment of Ecclesiastes and immortality should be understood as a critique of Mendelssohn. He casts his position as an attempt to avoid the type of approach adopted by his German-Jewish predecessor: while Mendelssohn seeks to show that immortality is affirmed by a biblical book such as Ecclesiastes, Krochmal contends that an honest assessment of the evidence points in a different direction, revealing that the Bible does not address this topic with sufficient clarity to forestall theological uncertainty, that this doctrine continued to be contested long after the canon took shape, and that it was the efforts of groups such as the Pharisees that firmly embedded the soul's eternity into the landscape of Jewish belief.

This confrontation with Mendelssohn seems to so occupy Krochmal's attention, in fact, that he implicitly takes aim at his predecessor on multiple occasions, repeatedly targeting the type of position associated with Mendelssohn (albeit without mentioning him again by name). As the *Guide*'s treatment of Ecclesiastes proceeds, Krochmal not only declares that this biblical book "does not engage in philosophy,"[46] but also denies that "the book's style of inquiry points to its composition at a time when the philosophy of the Greeks had already been disseminated among us in the land of Israel."[47] Indeed, he suggests in an earlier paragraph, "even if we concede that the book's opinion does not accord with all the sayings mentioned therein, and that its words follow the approach of human investigation exclusively, proceeding by offering all parts of a contradiction for the sake of ultimately leading to the opinion of faith—behold, we do not know how and by what means that good opinion is established and affirmed by [the author], and he mentions nothing regarding this in his book."[48]

THE RISE OF MODERN JEWISH THOUGHT

It might be tempting to dismiss Krochmal's critique of Mendelssohn as a relatively insignificant episode in the history of Jewish philosophy. After all, the argument might run, what we have here is little more than a dispute about the interpretation of one biblical text and the history of one theological doctrine.

Consider, however, the element of Mendelssohn's argument singled out in Krochmal's *Guide*: the insistence that Ecclesiastes affirms rather than rejects immortality. One of the claims that recurs throughout Mendelssohn's writings is the idea that immortality is an "eternal truth"—an eternally valid principle accessible through rational reflection.[49] As noted above, his 1767 rewriting of the *Phaedo* defends the demonstrability of this doctrine, seeking to "adapt the metaphysical proofs" for immortality offered by Plato "to the taste of our time."[50] Similarly, Mendelssohn's best known treatment of Judaism—his 1783 treatise *Jerusalem, or on Religious Power and Judaism*—suggests that we encounter eternal truths in the statement that God is "the necessary, independent being, omnipotent and omniscient, that recompenses men in a future life"[51] or that God "rules the entire universe . . . and discerns men's most secret thoughts in order to reward their deeds . . . if not here, then in the hereafter."[52] When Mendelssohn insists that Ecclesiastes affirms immortality, then, he is arguing that a key eternal truth is present in the Bible.

This is not a trivial claim for the German-Jewish thinker. *Jerusalem* places rationally accessible eternal truths such as immortality, as well as God's existence and providence,[53] at the heart of Jewish life, famously claiming to "recognize no eternal truths other than those that are not merely comprehensible to human reason but can also be demonstrated and verified by human powers," and to "consider this an essential point of the Jewish religion."[54] He elaborates:

> Although the divine book that we received through Moses is, strictly speaking, meant to be a book of laws containing ordinances, rules of life and prescriptions, it also includes, as is well known, an inexhaustible treasure of rational truths and religious doctrines which are so intimately connected with the laws that they form but one entity. All laws refer to, or are based upon, eternal truths of reason, or remind us of them, and rouse us to ponder them.[55]

Judaism is presented here as a tradition whose "divine book . . . includes . . . an inexhaustible treasure of rational truths" and whose laws "refer to . . . eternal truths of reason, or remind us of them, and rouse us to ponder them." That is, Mendelssohnian Judaism is a vehicle of rationally accessible eternal truths affirmed by the Bible, a tradition whose laws lead adherents to reflect on principles that can be discovered through reason but are also articulated in the biblical text[56]—a tradition that requires practices, such as prayer or the celebration of holidays, that remind adherents of rationally accessible and biblically expressed ideas such as God's existence and providence. The idea here seems to be, at least in part, that much of Jewish law can be traced to biblical provisions (or, at least, to rabbinic interpretations of biblical provisions), that the Bible also affirms rationally derivable principles such as God's existence, and that this connection between norms and a textual "treasure" of eternal principles results in the former calling attention to the latter. Put more simply, if adherents trace laws to a biblical text that invokes eternal truths, these individuals are likely to associate these norms with those principles, and the performance of actions required by one is likely to bring to mind the other.[57]

It is important to be clear about Mendelssohn's position here. He is neither uninterested in changes in Jewish life over time nor unconcerned with the activities of postbiblical Jews. On the contrary, I have argued elsewhere that history is one of the central concerns animating his thought. While he takes Jewish law to generate reflection on rationally accessible eternal truths affirmed by the Bible, he also holds that these principles have been understood in different ways at different points in time. For instance, while he claims that Judaism's adherents find themselves reflecting on principles such as divine providence, he also insists that shifts in philosophical and scientific models have led these individuals to understand the nature of this divine governance in different ways in different eras, with medieval Jews influenced by Aristotelianism taking God to be concerned only with the fates of species and modern Jews influenced by other philosophical frameworks taking God's care to extend to the fates of individual creatures.[58] Similarly, Mendelssohn is deeply interested in postbiblical groups such as the rabbis of antiquity, taking rabbinic exegesis to play a crucial role in securing the authoritative grounding of much of Jewish law—to establish that many norms governing Jewish life are rooted in the text of the Bible.

Nevertheless, despite this interest in historical change and in postbiblical groups such as the rabbis, it remains the case that, from Mendelssohn's perspective, the core doctrinal content of Judaism is already affirmed by the

Bible. Postbiblical Jews may play an important role in Judaism and understand principles such as providence in different ways at different points in history, but according to *Jerusalem* it is the presence of these principles in Scripture—the existence of "an inexhaustible treasure of rational truths and religious doctrines" in "the divine book that we received through Moses," and the resulting link between these truths and the norms governing Jewish practice—that leads individuals to reflect on such content, taking up biblical ideas such as the notion that God governs the cosmos and attempting to understand what that governance involves.[59]

The crucial point for our purposes is that the position outlined in *Jerusalem* relies on precisely the type of claim Mendelssohn advances in his Ecclesiastes commentary. If he wishes to present Judaism as a vehicle of eternal truths affirmed by the Bible, it will be crucial for him to show that such truths are, in fact, present in that work. That is, it will be crucial for him to show that biblical books such as Ecclesiastes endorse principles such as immortality, strengthening rather than contradicting "the fundamental principles of the true religion." It will be particularly important to advance this claim with respect to the eternity of the soul, for one of the recurring attacks on Judaism advanced by Mendelssohn's Enlightenment contemporaries was the claim that this notion is absent from the Hebrew Bible. According to this accusation, while texts such as the New Testament accept the concept of an afterlife, the Hebrew Bible lacks any such notion, and Judaism—a tradition built on the Hebrew Bible, rather than the New Testament—is therefore either (at best) an inferior religion or (at worst) no religion at all.[60] Mendelssohn's treatment of immortality in his Ecclesiastes commentary thus plays an important role in his thought, providing evidence for a presupposition on which his portrayal of Judaism depends: he takes Judaism to be a vehicle of eternal truths affirmed by the Bible, and his commentary helps establish that such truths are actually endorsed by the biblical text.

Strikingly, Krochmal's claims about Ecclesiastes and immortality play a similar role in his philosophy. The *Guide*, we will recall, casts Judaism's affirmation of an afterlife as the product of debates among postbiblical Jews who disagreed about whether the soul is eternal. The implication is that Judaism is a phenomenon whose doctrinal content emerges through the efforts of postbiblical human beings—that Judaism's beliefs develop over time because of the activities of the tradition's adherents. While Krochmal acknowledges that groups such as the compilers of the canon affirmed immortality, he emphasizes that such voices have not always been dominant: according to the *Guide*, immortality was a contested doctrine, and it was only the efforts of postbiblical groups that established this belief as an integral element of the Jewish tradition. Indeed, we saw him claim that various "beliefs and practices . . . were supported" not simply by the biblical text, but rather "in the hands of individuals among" the Pharisees.

Far from constituting a peripheral element of Krochmal's thought, this vision of Judaism as a tradition that develops over time by means of human efforts appears elsewhere in the *Guide*. One of this book's primary concepts is the "spiritual" or *ruhani*, understood as a dimension of existence distinct from (albeit discernable in) the physical world and manifest with particular clarity in human beings and cultures. For example, a nation's "spiritual inheritances" include elements such as its "laws, ethical teachings, linguistic concepts, [and] books of science."[61] Drawing on this conception of the *ruhani*, Krochmal argues that Judaism's central metaphysical claim is that God should be understood as "the absolute spiritual," as the source and totality of spiritual manifestations such as human cognition and culture. What Judaism treats as divine is the totality of spiritual phenomena: while other nations accord supremacy to entities such as a god of war or a god of beauty and thus each emphasize one subset of spiritual manifestations, Judaism takes God to in some sense encompass all such phenomena, from art to ethics.[62]

Nevertheless, Krochmal denies that this view of God was always a widely accepted element of the Jewish tradition. After introducing this understanding of the divine, he offers the following account of its history within Jewish life: "Even the Israelites who stood at Mount Sinai and heard [this conception of God] did not attain it, in the purity of its truth, in their multitude and totality until around the time that the exiles returned from Babylonia, that is to say, until the passage of one thousand years from the giving of the Torah."[63] Krochmal's claim is that even if the events at Mount Sinai involved some exposure to a key understanding of God, this view of the divine neither enjoyed widespread acceptance, nor was fully grasped, until the return from the Babylonian exile and "the passage of one thousand years from the giving of the Torah."

In fact, he stresses, it was the actions of later generations of Jews that established this conception of God as an integral part of Jewish life:

> The time would come when the spiritual orientation of the nation would be strengthened until it arrived at a point that had not been achieved by the prophets of old. All of this occurred in every place of exile, not in the way of signs and wonders by means of revealed

miracles, and not even by means of the force of arms or the strength of the sword . . . but rather exclusively by means of quiet well-being and spiritual arousal among the elders and the people.⁶⁴

On Krochmal's interpretation, it was not "signs and wonders by means of revealed miracles," but rather the efforts of "the elders and the people," that ensured that "the spiritual orientation of the nation would be strengthened" by the time following the Babylonian exile—that enabled the understanding of God as the absolute spiritual to become more firmly rooted and widely disseminated over time. For example, members of the Jewish community would "reflect" on and seek to "comprehend" religious matters, arriving at a deeper understanding of the divine and thereby leading their nation to "arriv[e] at a point that had not been achieved" in earlier times.⁶⁵

This account of Jewish views on God resonates strongly with the *Guide*'s account of Jewish views on immortality. In both cases, an idea that initially enjoys only limited affirmation eventually becomes an accepted part of the Jewish tradition due to human efforts. Krochmal's claims about immortality thus constitute an element of a broader argument about the nature of Judaism, providing further evidence for, or another example of, the idea that this tradition's doctrinal content has developed over time through human efforts. Just as Mendelssohn's treatment of immortality helps secure his vision of Judaism, so too do Krochmal's arguments about immortality help ground his portrayal of this tradition.

The significance of the Krochmal-Mendelssohn dispute should now be clear. Earlier, we saw that Krochmal's reading of Ecclesiastes offers an account of the place of immortality in the Jewish tradition and that he casts this account as a critique of a type of position associated with Mendelssohn. While the German-Jewish thinker attempts to show that the eternity of the soul is already affirmed by the Hebrew Bible, his Eastern European successor insists that the Bible does not address this topic with sufficient clarity to prevent future conflict and that this doctrine achieved acceptance only as a result of debates among postbiblical Jews. We have now seen that these accounts of immortality are crucial to broader philosophical projects that animate these thinkers. Whereas Mendelssohn's reading of Ecclesiastes as a philosophical defense of this doctrine helps ground his picture of Judaism as a vehicle of rationally accessible eternal truths affirmed by the Bible, Krochmal's narrative of biblical uncertainty and communal debate strengthens his own image of this tradition as a phenomenon whose content emerges through the efforts of postbiblical human beings.

When Krochmal engages Mendelssohn, then, what we have is not simply a debate about the afterlife, but a debate about the very nature of Judaism. Krochmal is presenting an account of immortality that helps establish the conception of Judaism that he wishes to advance, and he is criticizing a Mendelssohnian account of immortality that is crucial to a competing vision of this tradition. When he criticizes Mendelssohn for taking immortality to be affirmed by Ecclesiastes and highlights the existence of ongoing debates about this doctrine, Krochmal is rejecting a key building block in the Mendelssohnian construction of Judaism and highlighting a piece of evidence for his own understanding of this tradition. For these foundational philosophical voices, then, *olam ha-ba* becomes a crucial terrain for formulating—and contesting—theories of Jewish existence. Immortality provides an arena in which the German-Jewish founder of modern Jewish thought and one of Eastern Europe's most significant Jewish philosophers generate competing understandings of the Jewish tradition.

Jonas may be correct that for some thinkers, "the modern temper is uncongenial to the idea of . . . the survival of the person in a *hereafter*." Yet this judgment offers only a partial picture of the concerns that shape modern Jewish philosophy. An exploration of Hebrew texts such as Mendelssohn's Ecclesiastes commentary and Krochmal's *Guide* suggests that immortality should figure prominently in the stories we tell about the emergence of Jewish intellectual modernity, for one of the early episodes in modern Jewish thought turns out to be a high-stakes soteriological debate between East and West. When it comes to Jewish philosophy, we might say, "the modern temper" emerges among thinkers who, operating in very different settings across Europe, embrace the eternity of the soul and treat it as a starting point for delving into the nature of Judaism itself. Wrestling with the status of immortality in the past, Mendelssohn and Krochmal seek to forge visions of the Jewish tradition for the present.

NOTES

1. See, e.g., Nathan Rotenstreich, *Jewish Philosophy in Modern Times: From Mendelssohn to Rosenzweig* (New York: Holt, Rinehart, and Winston, 1968).

2. See, e.g., Ismar Schorsch, *From Text to Context: The Turn to History in Modern Judaism* (Hanover: University Press of New England, 1994); Yosef Hayim Yerushalmi, *Zakhor: Jewish History and Jewish Memory* (Seattle: University of Washington Press, 1996).

3. Leora Batnitzky, *How Judaism Became a Religion: An Introduction to Modern Jewish Thought* (Princeton: Princeton University Press, 2011), 1.

4. For example, we might understand modernity as a "condition"—as a constellation of factors, such as "the differentiation between public and private spheres, the weakening of religious governing structures, and the democratization of knowledge in Jewish society"—that generated ideologies ranging from Chasidism to the Haskalah [the Jewish Enlightenment] to Zionism. See Eliyahu Stern, *The Genius: Elijah of Vilna and the Making of Modern Judaism* (New Haven: Yale University Press, 2013), 8.

5. One well-known example is Hermann Cohen. See, e.g., his *Reason and Hope: Selections from the Jewish Writings of Hermann Cohen* (trans. Eva Jospe; Cincinnati: Hebrew Union College Press, 1971). Another example is Jacob Taubes. See, e.g., his *The Political Theology of Paul* (trans. D. Hollander; ed. A. Assmann et al.; Stanford: Stanford University Press, 2004); *From Cult to Culture: Fragments Toward a Critique of Historical Reason* (ed. C. E. Fonrobert and Amir Engel; Stanford: Stanford University Press, 2010).

6. Understood in this sense, immortality is distinct from, but in principle compatible with, the idea of bodily resurrection. That is, if immortality denotes the idea that the soul or some other part of the self endures after death, it is possible that this soul (or other part of the self) could either remain in an incorporeal state or be returned to a resurrected body. Indeed, it could be the case that some souls return to bodies while other souls do not: this position, for instance, will be ascribed by one of the thinkers we explore, Nachman Krochmal, to the Pharisees. On the relationship between immortality and resurrection in Jewish thought, see the sources in notes 8–11 below.

7. See Jacob Katz, *Exclusiveness and Tolerance: Studies in Jewish-Gentile Relations in Medieval and Modern Times* (Oxford: Oxford University Press, 1961), 169–81; Steven Schwarzschild, "Do Noachites Have to Believe in Revelation? (A Passage in Dispute between Maimonides, Spinoza, Mendelssohn and H. Cohen): A Contribution to a Jewish View of Natural Law," *Jewish Quarterly Review* 52:4 (1962): 297–308; Steven Schwarzschild, "Do Noachites Have to Believe in Revelation? (Continued)," *Jewish Quarterly Review* 53:1 (1962): 30–65.

8. See, e.g., Neil Gillman, *The Death of Death: Resurrection and Immortality in Jewish Thought* (Woodstock: Jewish Lights Publishing, 1997), 189–214; Gillman also highlights what he takes to be renewed interest in resurrection among late twentieth-century thinkers (215–41). Jakob Petuchowski calls attention to similar issues, although he suggests that a narrative in which modern Jews—or in which specific groups of modern Jews, such as the Reform movement—entirely reject resurrection represents "an over-simplification": see Jakob Petuchowski, "'Immortality: Yes; Resurrection: No!' Nineteenth-Century Judaism Struggles with a Traditional Belief," *Proceedings of the American Academy for Jewish Research* 50 (1983): 133. Jon Levenson presents a similar narrative, while also noting that some modern Jews stress what they take to be the "this-worldliness" of Judaism: see Jon Levenson, *Resurrection and the Restoration of Israel: The Ultimate Victory of the God of Life* (New Haven: Yale University Press, 2006), 1–22.

9. Hans Jonas, "Immortality and the Modern Temper," in *Mortality and Morality: A Search for the Good after Auschwitz* (ed. L. Vogel; Evanston: Northwestern University Press, 1996), 115, 117.

10. Allan Arkush, "Immortality," in *Contemporary Jewish Religious Thought: Original Essays on Critical Concepts, Movements, and Beliefs* (ed. A. Cohen and P. Mendes-Flohr; New York: Free Press, 1987), 480–81. Steven Nadler has argued that a rejection of personal immortality is central to the work of (and opposition to) Baruch Spinoza: see Steven Nadler, *Spinoza's Heresy: Immortality and the Jewish Mind* (Oxford: Oxford University Press, 2001).

11. See Leora Batnitzky, "From Resurrection to Immortality: Theological and Political Implications in Modern Jewish Thought," *Harvard Theological Review* 102:3 (2009): 279–96; the quotes appear on 295 and 279.

12. On the neglect of Mendelssohn's Hebrew writings, see, e.g., David Sorkin, "The Mendelssohn Myth and Its Method," *New German Critique* 77 (1999): 7–28. For some examples of recent works that explore this material, see Edward Breuer, *The Limits of Enlightenment: Jews, Germans, and the Eighteenth-Century Study of Scripture* (Cambridge: Harvard University Press, 1996); David Sorkin, *Moses Mendelssohn and the Religious Enlightenment* (Berkeley: University of California Press, 1996); Carola Hilfrich, *"Lebendige Schrift": Repräsentation und Idolatrie in Moses Mendelssohns Philosophie und Exegese des Judentums* (Munich: Fink, 2000); Andrea Schatz, *Sprache in der Zerstreuung: Die Säkularisierung des Hebräischen im 18. Jahrhundert* (Göttingen: Vandenhoeck & Ruprecht, 2009); Gideon Freudenthal, *No Religion without Idolatry: Mendelssohn's Jewish Enlightenment* (Notre Dame: University of Notre Dame Press, 2012); Grit Schorch, *Moses Mendelssohns Sprachpolitik* (Berlin: de Gruyter, 2012); Elias Sacks, *Moses Mendelssohn's Living Script: Philosophy, Practice, History, Judaism* (Bloomington: Indiana University Press, 2017). For the selection of English renderings, see my translations in Moses Mendelssohn, *Moses Mendelssohn: Writings on Judaism, Christianity, and the Bible* (trans. Allan Arkush, Curtis Bowman, and Elias Sacks; ed. Michah Gottlieb; Waltham: Brandeis University Press, 2011).

13. My point, of course, is not that there has been no scholarship on Krochmal. But he has received far less attention than other leading modern Jewish philosophers, especially among North American scholars. For some older works, see, e.g., Simon Rawidowicz, introduction to *Kitvei Rabbi Nachman Krochmal* (2nd ed.; ed. Simon Rawidowicz; Waltham: Ararat, 1961), 17–225; Steven Schwarzschild, "Two Modern Jewish Philosophies of History: Nachman Krochmal and Hermann Cohen" (PhD diss., Hebrew Union College, 1955); Jacob Taubes, "Nachman Krochmal and Modern Historicism," *Judaism* 12:2 (1963): 150–64. Some more recent studies include Jay Harris, *Nachman Krochmal: Guiding the Perplexed of the Modern Age* (New York: New York University Press, 1991); Andreas Lehnardt, "Die Entwicklung von Halakha in der Geschichtsphilosophie Nachman Krochmals," *Frankfurter judaistische Beitrage* 29 (2002): 105–26; Yehoyada Amir, "The Perplexity of Our Time: Rabbi Nachman Krochmal and Modern Jewish Existence," *Modern Judaism* 23:3 (2003): 264–301; Yossi Turner, "Ma'amad Haru'ah Betefisat Hahistori'a shel Rabbi Nachman Krochmal," in *Derekh Haru'ah* (2 vols.; ed. Yehoyada Amir; Jerusalem: Hebrew University and Van Leer Institute, 2005), 1:289–323; Eliezer Schweid, *A History of Modern Jewish Religious Philosophy: Volume 1: The Period of the Enlightenment* (trans. L. Levin; Leiden: Brill, 2011), 267–334; Lawrence Kaplan, "Saving

Knowledge," *Jewish Quarterly Review* 106:2 (2016): 138–144. One sign of a renewed interest in Krochmal is the publication of a new Hebrew edition of the *Guide*: Nachman Krochmal, *Moreh Nevukhei Hazeman* (ed. Yehoyada Amir; Jerusalem: Carmel, 2010). Another sign is the appearance of a German translation: Nachman Krochmal, *Führer der Verwirrten der Zeit* (2 vols.; trans. Andreas Lehnardt; Hamburg: Meiner, 2012).

14. On this work, see Alexander Altmann, *Moses Mendelssohn: A Biographical Study* (Tuscaloosa: University of Alabama Press, 1973), 140–79.

15. Arkush, "Immortality," 480–81.

16. See Gillman, *The Death of Death*, 190–241. Gillman does discuss the philosopher Mordecai Kaplan during this treatment of denominational literature, but he does not describe Kaplan's conception of immortality as a belief in the survival of a soul. Quoting a statement by Kaplan that "insofar as the good we do while we live bears fruit after we are gone, we have a share in the world to come," Gillman writes that "that is about as much immortality as Kaplan is prepared to concede" (210). Batnitzky does call attention to one post-Mendelssohnian philosopher who endorses personal immortality (and not simply, say, the eternity of the Jewish people or moral tasks): Samson Raphael Hirsch. See Batnitzky, "From Resurrection to Immortality," 289–90.

17. See the sources in note 13 above.

18. This description appears in Ecclesiastes 1:1. Unless otherwise noted, I follow the New Jewish Publication Society translation of the Bible throughout this essay.

19. See Harris, *Nachman Krochmal*, 172–83.

20. Krochmal, *Moreh Nevukhei Hazeman*, 148. All translations of Krochmal are mine.

21. I alter the New Jewish Publication Society translation of this verse.

22. Krochmal, *Moreh Nevukhei Hazeman*, 139–40. Krochmal also cites 2 Maccabees as evidence.

23. Ibid., 140.

24. Ibid., 73.

25. Ibid., 74.

26. Ibid., 75–76.

27. Ibid., 72.

28. Ibid., 74.

29. Krochmal, Letter 13, in *Moreh Nevukhei Hazeman*, 435.

30. Krochmal, Letter 1, in *Moreh Nevukhei Hazeman*, 415.

31. Krochmal, *Moreh Nevukhei Hazeman*, 75.

32. Krochmal suggests that beyond the epilogue appended by the compliers of the canon (and perhaps one or two other verses), "we did not find a verse that clearly agrees with

truth and with faith." Similarly, he takes a line that might seem to endorse immortality—Ecclesiastes 12:7, which states that "the dust returns to the ground as it was, and the lifebreath returns to God who bestowed it"—to refer to God's absolute power over human beings. See ibid., 145.

33. Ibid., 143.

34. On this commentary see Sorkin, *Moses Mendelssohn*, 35–45. For other references to or uses of Mendelssohn in the *Guide*, see, e.g., Amir, "The Perplexity of the Time," 294n26, 295n35.

35. Moses Mendelssohn, *Sefer Megilat Kohelet*, in *Gesammelte Schriften Jubiläumsausgabe* (ed. F. Bamberger, et al.; 24 vols.; Stuttgart-Bad Cannstatt: F. Frommann, 1971–), 14:154. References to this edition of Mendelssohn's work appear as *JubA*. Unless otherwise noted, translations of Mendelssohn are mine.

36. See also ibid., 14:193.

37. Ibid., 14:154.

38. Ibid.

39. Ibid., 14:193. As indicated above, he is also concerned about perspectives that deny providence.

40. Ibid., 14:154.

41. The quotes are from Ecclesiastes 3:20, 3:16, and 4:1, respectively.

42. Mendelssohn, *Sefer Megilat Kohelet*, in *JubA*, 14:155.

43. Ibid., 14:151–52.

44. Ibid., 14:152.

45. Ibid.

46. Krochmal, *Moreh Nevukhei Hazeman*, 145.

47. Ibid., 146.

48. Ibid., 142.

49. On eternal truths, see Moses Mendelssohn, *Jerusalem, or on Religious Power and Judaism* (trans. Allan Arkush; Hanover: University Press of New England, 1983), 90–94; the German is *JubA*, 8:157–61.

50. Moses Mendelssohn, *Phädon, or on the Immortality of the Soul* (trans. P. Noble; New York: Peter Lang, 2007), 42; the German is *JubA*, 3.1:8.

51. Mendelssohn, *Jerusalem*, 97; the German is *JubA*, 8:164.

52. Mendelssohn, *Jerusalem*, 98; the German is *JubA*, 8:164–65.

53. On God's existence and divine providence as additional eternal truths, see the lines quoted in the previous paragraph. See also Mendelssohn, *Jerusalem*, 63; the German is *JubA*, 8:131.

54. Mendelssohn, *Jerusalem*, 89; the German is *JubA*, 8:156–57.

55. Mendelssohn, *Jerusalem*, 99; the German is *JubA*, 8:165–66.

56. Mendelssohn's insistence that the Bible outlines rationally accessible principles has often been obscured by his denial that revelation communicates indispensable eternal truths that are not rationally derivable. Nevertheless, Mendelssohn repeatedly affirms that the Bible presents—we might say repeats—truths that are *also* accessible through reason. See Michah Gottlieb, "Aesthetics and the Infinite: Moses Mendelssohn on the Poetics of Biblical Prophecy," in *New Directions in Jewish Philosophy* (ed. A. Hughes and E. Wolfson; Bloomington: Indiana University Press, 2010), 326–53; Michah Gottlieb, *Faith and Freedom: Moses Mendelssohn's Theological-Political Thought* (Oxford: Oxford University Press, 2011), 56–58.

57. See Sacks, *Moses Mendelssohn's Living Script*, 29, 44–59. Mendelssohn may also have in mind additional mechanisms through which Jewish law yields reflection, such as requirements to invoke God during rituals: see Freudenthal, *No Religion without Idolatry*, 135–59.

58. Mendelssohn's position, in other words, is that although there is only one correct understanding of a principle such as providence, this view has not always been affirmed, with alternate perspectives gaining acceptance—and being rejected—over time. What is "eternal" about an eternal truth is thus the validity of its proper understanding, rather than its interpretation throughout history.

59. On these issues, see Sacks, *Moses Mendelssohn's Living Script*.

60. See, e.g., Allan Arkush, *Moses Mendelssohn and the Enlightenment* (Albany: SUNY Press, 1994), 133–58.

61. On "spirit" and "the spiritual," see Krochmal, *Moreh Nevukhei Hazeman*, 29–39; the quotation appears on 35. See also, e.g., Harris, *Nachman Krochmal*, 70–88; Amir, "The Perplexity of Our Time," 281–89; Yehoyada Amir, "Leksikon Munahim Umivhar Hafnayot Lemekorot Mikrai'im, Liturgi'im, Umidrashi'im," in Krochmal, *Moreh Nevukhei Hazeman*, 59–60; Schweid, *A History of Modern Jewish Religious Philosophy*, 302–34.

62. See Krochmal, *Moreh Nevukhei Hazeman*, 29–39.

63. Ibid., 39.

64. Ibid., 52.

65. Ibid., 51–52. More specifically, Krochmal suggests that members of the Jewish community would "gather, write down, and copy all that remained to them of the holy books. They would reflect on them and comprehend them, clearly and with reason." That is, using the Bible as a starting point for theological reflection, Judaism's adherents would eventually go further and arrive at a deeper understanding of the divine through rational reflection.

Emmanuel Levinas's Messianism and the World to Come: A Gnostic-Philosophical Reading of Tractate *Sanhedrin* 96b–99a

Federico Dal Bo

In this essay I address Emmanuel Levinas's[1] notion of "messianism," as it is presented in his long commentary on six pages from Tractate *Sanhedrin* of the Babylonian Talmud: *bSanh* 96b–99a.[2] I maintain that Levinas commented on these talmudic pages for a specific purpose: to complete his critique of the phenomenological notion of "world," substituting for it a religious notion of the "world to come" by which we can determine the ethical parameter to live "in this world." I assume that Levinas's reading has been heavily influenced by gnostic-philosophical notions derived from his previous monumental philosophical monograph, *Totality and Infinity*.[3] As a consequence, I also assume that Levinas's reading might have succeeded in addressing, in religious terms, the question of a "difficult freedom," just as the title of his commentary anticipates. Instead, he produced a hermeneutically imbalanced commentary on some very famous talmudic pages. More specifically, I maintain that Levinas provides a strict selection of the talmudic portions to comment on, whereas he neglects important, specific theological-political presuppositions and eventually imposes a normalized—if not generic—notion of "religion" that is finally "supplemented," in Derrida's sense, by a set of metaphysical notions.[4]

In order to prove this, my paper is divided in four sections, as follows: a first exposition of Levinas's gnostic-philosophical presuppositions, a general appreciation of his commentary on the Talmud, the examination of a specific portion of his commentary on "messianism," and finally the exposition of the "supplementary" nature of Levinas's argumentation.

LEVINAS'S "GNOSTIC"-PHILOSOPHICAL CRITIQUE TO HUSSERL'S NOTION OF "WORLD"

Levinas's reading of Tractate *Sanhedrin* follows shortly after the publication of his monumental philosophical monograph *Totality and Infinity*, eloquently subtitled *An Essay on Exteriority*. This monograph was written in 1961, more than thirteen years after Levinas's post-phenomenological inquiries on time.[5] Its aim was to criticize Husserl's as well as Heidegger's phenomenological notions of "world" and "horizon." Levinas founded his critique on a number of premises: (1) the rejection of Continental and specifically post-Romantic German ontology, (2) the evaluation of the notion of "infinite," (3) the exaltation of the notion of "ethics," and (4) the conception of "justice" as the most fundamental ontological attitude.[6] With respect to this set of assumptions, Levinas designated with the term "exteriority" exactly a dimension of "reality" that would exceed the boundaries of German ontology and lay claim to a "righteous"—or "ethically" and "juridically" based—confrontation with "the Other," whether the latter would be identified with "the others" as fellow human beings [*autrui*] or with God Himself [*Autre*], "the absolutely other is the Other [*l'absolument Autre, c'est Autrui*]."[7]

Levinas assumes that the "alterity" of "the Other" [*Autre*] should be understood both as the alterity of "the others" [*autrui*] and as "alterity" of the Most High. Under this premise, he evidently measures the degree of "alterity" in terms of everyone's "familiarity" with the "world," which he inhabits in the midst of "things" that are held out to the grasp of the hand. The grade of "estrangement" is then measured upon the "intimacy" of "dwelling": "To exist [*exister*] henceforth means to dwell [*demeurer*]. To dwell is not the simple fact of the anonymous reality of being cast into existence as a stone one casts behind oneself; it is a recollection, a coming to oneself, a retreat home with oneself as in a land of refuge, which answers to hospitality, an expectancy, a human welcome."[8]

In the present circumstance, it is not possible to catalogue Levinas's quite problematic use of spatial metaphors—such as "dwelling," "habitation," and "exteriority"—that render his efforts at "escaping" metaphysics problematic if not only tentative. It is sufficient to turn our attention to the ambiguous nature of "dwelling" in a "world": on the one hand, the act of "dwelling" in a "world" constrains the individual within a "horizon" and fundamentally alienates him, by preventing him from ethically committing with "the others"; on the other hand, the act of "dwelling" permits everyone to possess the sufficient, minimal degree of intimacy and interiority that is needed for "escaping" the boundaries of the "horizon" and for ethically connecting with "the others."[9] Levinas here resolves this paradox by introducing an eschatological tone that emerges at the end of *Totality and Infinity* and opposes the "logic of violence that dominates the present."[10]

This notion of "logic" is to be understood here in its strongest sense as a reference to Hegelian "science of logic," which in turn is conceived as a sort of philosophical commentary on the Gospel of John and its assumption that "history" eminently is the development of God's "Word" [*Logos*] in space and time.¹¹ In concert with Hegel, Levinas also exhibits in *Totality and Infinity* similar tones and argumentations. More specifically, he constantly maintains a theological undertone when playing with the keystones of the Hebrew Scripture: God's revelation as "Word," the Revelation of God's "Visage," the commandment "Do not murder," and so on. There is little doubt that *Totality and Infinity* is a philosophical paraphrase of Hebrew Scripture, especially the books of Genesis and Exodus, where the divine enters impetuously into the human "world" and fundamentally dismisses its authorities and anthropological boundaries.

Levinas here assumes a genuinely "gnostic" attitude and maintains that the "world"—together with its tools, finalities, and horizons—is deeply alien to the ethical-juridical dimension of the "divine"; therefore, Levinas concludes that the world's normative validity shall be "suspended," or "put into brackets," by the transcendent impetuousness of the divine. This act of "suspension" is obviously reminiscent of Husserl's notion of *epoché*, but is produced again by emphasizing the act of "dwelling" in someone's "own" home, where one retires from the anonymity of the "world," its horrifying "neutrality," or its indifference to the divine sense for justice. Therefore, the individual who decides to "dwell" in his "own" home enters his interiority and suspends—or delays—his "enjoyment" of the "world."¹²

This important variation of Husserl's phenomenological notion of "suspension" determines, in Levinas's eyes, the discovery of the existence of "consciousness" as the most intimate and retired dimension of the self. And yet this also involves the suspension of "violence"—inherently connected to the commitment with the world, its ontological injustice, and ethical ambiguity. In this regard, the "introversion" into the self at the expense of someone's commitment into the world truly is a messianic act. Exactly how, Levinas himself will not fail to emphasize, a few years after publishing *Totality and Infinity*, in his commentary on Tractate *Sanhedrin*. And yet Levinas's ethical metaphysics neither adheres to neoplatonic assumptions nor rejects the "inner logic" of late post-Romantic German philosophy in principle. The assumptions of *Totality and Infinity* are rather more refined. Levinas mobilizes a large set of "Hebrew" concepts against unethical "desolation"—a blank vacuity void from human presence—which would be the ultimate outcome from a strict ontological thought: "the Being of the existent is a *Logos* that is the word of no one."¹³

The introduction of these "Hebrew" concepts involves Husserl's notion of "world" as well as Heidegger's notion of "ontology." More specifically,

Levinas rejects the phenomenological assumption of "world," in so far as it claims that the given "horizon" is epistemologically exhaustive and maintains that there is "nothing" beyond the events by which phenomena appear in the world. At the same time, Levinas rejects Heidegger's onto-theology that is implicit in his translucent event of "truth"—either *aletheia* or *Unverborgenheit*—and maintains that the "nothingness" beyond the "horizon" is not "the Being" [*Sein*] veiled by the realm of "the beings" [*die Seinende*]; this "nothingness" rather is the emergence of the "Visage"—an event that is ontologically and ethically challenging: "the Other is not the incarnation of God, but precisely by his face, in which he is disincarnate, is the manifestation of the height in which God is revealed.[14]"

The emergence of the "Face" [*Visage*] calls the individual to a number of ethical and ontological challenges that Levinas enumerates in *Totality and Infinity* in terms of a specific "philosophical anthropology": eros, love, friendship, family bounds, and so on. The dimension of "justice" is frequently evoked as a sort of "metaphysical quality," but it is not really appreciated in its social and political specificities. These are indeed much more taken into account in Levinas's later commentary on Tractate *Sanhedrin*. Its speculative relevance had already been anticipated in a short quotation in *Totality and Infinity*, while mentioning the importance of "feeding" anyone, regardless of his ethical, juridical, and social affiliation.[15] It is this sense for justice that Levinas attributes to Tractate *Sanhedrin* and that might have fascinated him while finishing *Totality and Infinity* and persuaded him of the necessity of writing a commentary on this text.

Is it possible that Tractate *Sanhedrin* might offer an insight into a "world-to-come" essentially different and distant from the many flaws of "this world"? What was then "messianism" for Levinas?

LEVINAS'S READING OF TRACTICE *SANHEDRIN* 99B–99A

Levinas's interest in Tractate *Sanhedrin* had never been occasional. Over a period of years Levinas commented four times on it on four different occasions and in four different contexts.[16]

It is difficult to determine the reasons for such an interest with respect to other talmudic tractates. At first, one could maintain that Tractate *Sanhedrin* is a famous and well-studied talmudic text, and it would then be surprising if Levinas had not studied it intensively together with "Monsieur Chouchani" (a mysterious, still unidentified talmudic genius, who used to live as a tramp and who introduced Levinas to Talmud in a series of private lessons, from 1947 to 1951).[17] Besides, Tractate *Sanhedrin* speaks about "justice" both in abstract and practical terms; indeed, it prescribes what crimes have to be punished with the death penalty but it also examines the ways by which to deliver it upon wrongdoers. Finally, Tractate *Sanhedrin* also includes a famous section on "messianism" that is not to be found elsewhere in rabbinic literature. Before examining the congruence of these pages with Levinas's philosophical investigations, it is necessary to provide readers with a brief description of the talmudic section examined in his "messianic" texts."

From a formal point of view, the talmudic section from Tractate *Sanhedrin* 96b–99a is a long nonjuridical, narrative appendix (*haggadah*) that is annexed to the previous discussion on the institution of prophecy, on the correct punishment for a false prophet, and specifically on the opinion that the son of the wicked Haman might teach Scripture.[18] These six pages are written exclusively in Hebrew—with the exception of the first two lines written in Aramaic (*bSanh* 96b)—and therefore should be accounted as an early, possibly Palestinian external source [*baraita*] that had been discarded from the Palestinian Talmud for probable reasons of "political prudence" toward the Roman government, whereas it was included in the Babylonian Talmud due to the relatively more relaxed religious policy in the Sassanid Persia.[19] Therefore, these six pages devoted to messianism are an exceptional document that has possibly been redacted in several layers and finally organized into a discrete number of topics: (1) the generation of the Messiah (*bSanh* 97a), (2) the notion of "truth" (*bSanh* 97a), (3) a first investigation on the time of the messianic advent (*bSanh* 97a–b), (4) the notion of the "righteous ones" in every generation (*bSanh* 97b), (5) the notion of "repentance" (*bSanh* 97b–98a), (6) a second investigation on the time of the messianic advent (*bSanh* 98a), (7) the times before the messianic advent (*bSanh* 98b), (8) the identity of the Messiah (*bSanh* 98b), and (9) the duration of messianic times (*bSanh* 99a).

Levinas's reading of these very complex pages is quite selective. Levinas completely neglected the historical reasons for redacting these pages, their linguistic and theoretical nature as well as most of the topics already reported above. Levinas has rather focused his attention especially on four themes: (1) the duration of messianic times (*bSanh* 99a), (2) the notion of "repentance" (*bSanh* 97b–98a), (3) the time before the messianic advent (*bSanh* 98b), and (4) the identity of the Messiah (*bSanh* 98b), as it can be summarized in the following chart.

Topics of the sugya	Levinas's commentary
(1) the generation of the Messiah (*bSanh* 97a)	
(2) the notion of "truth" (*bSanh* 97a)	
(3) the time of the messianic advent I (*bSanh* 97a–b)	
(4) the notion of the "righteous ones" (*bSanh* 97b)	
(5) the notion of "repentance" (*bSanh* 97b–98a)	✓
(6) the time of the messianic advent II (*bSanh* 98a)	
(7) the times before the messianic advent (*bSanh* 98b)	✓
(8) the identity of the Messiah (*bSanh* 98b)	✓
(9) the duration of messianic times (*bSanh* 99a)	✓

Levinas expounds these four selected topics more than once in a nonlinear perspective and appears to discourse several times on the same issue, as if he were digging deeper in search of an ethical-philosophical meaning of the text. In particular, Levinas proposes a different segmentation of the text according to six paragraphs that rearrange the whole narrative section: (1) the notion of messianism, (2) the ethical conditions for the messianic advent, (3) the contradictions of messianism, (4) the overcoming of messianism, (5) the question about the identity of the Messiah, and (6) the correlation between messianism and universalism.

It is evident that Levinas's rearrangement of the textual material does not follow the thematic sequence of the original text. At first one could object that a nonjuridical, narrative text can easily be dismounted and rearranged differently; thus, one could even maintain that Levinas has indeed clarified the thematic consistency of a long talmudic section that would hardly have been expounded otherwise.

On the contrary, my argument is that Levinas has deliberately imposed a philosophical reading with a specific purpose: mobilizing a supposedly "Hebrew" concept of "world" over against a phenomenological-ontological one. In other terms, Levinas intended to employ the talmudic notion of "the world to come" as a correction to the phenomenological notion of "world." More specifically, my assumption is that Levinas is interested in Tractate *Sanhedrin* especially because of his need for a speculative alternative to post-Romantic German phenomenology. The break of the phenomenological notion of "world" in *Totality and Infinity* had implied the necessity of coming to terms with the eschatological notion of "the world to come" because the latter would oppose the former in many respects: (1) the nature of an eschatological event would oppose the ontological uniformity of the ordinary "world," (2) the messianic claim for absolute justice would oppose Western, ethically neutral societies, and finally (3) the emergence of a personal intimacy with "ethics" would oppose the contemporary anonymity of social and political practices.

For brevity's sake it is not possible to review each of these very important oppositions between "this world" and "the world to come" in Levinas's commentary. Therefore it would be sufficient to take into account the most decisive one: the opposition between the anonymity of "this world" and the intimacy of "the world to come." Levinas makes the notion of "messianism" coincidental with a specific condition of the self due to a particular interpretation of a short talmudic inquiry about the identity of the Messiah:

> What is his [the Messiah's] name? The House of Rabbi Shila said: His name is Shilo, since it is written: "until Shiloh will come" (Gen 49:10). The House of Rabbi Yannai said: His name is Yinnon, since it is written: "his name will endure for ever . . . his name is Yinnon" (Ps 72:17). The House of Rabbi Hanina said: His name is Hanina, since it is written: "where I will not give you Haninah [i.e., mercy]" (Jer 16:13). (*bSanh* 98b)

At first, Levinas admits that the question of the identity of the Messiah clearly has specific historical and cultural anti-Christian inclinations. Yet Levinas dismisses quite easily these historical implications and emphasizes that these answers imply that "the pupil-teacher relationship" has a messianic value.[20] Accordingly, he comments on them and comes to this surprising conclusion:

> I venture to propose an interpretation of this text that is less special. . . . The Messiah is the Prince who governs in a way that no longer alienates the sovereignty of Israel. He is the absolute interiority of government. Is there a more radical interiority that the one in which the Self [*moi*] commends itself? Non-strangeness, *par excellence* is ipseity. The Messiah is the King who no longer commands form outside. . . . The Messiah is Myself [*moi*]; to be Myself is to be the Messiah.[21]

This is probably one of the most eloquent passages that gives evidence of Levinas's practical use of talmudic literature for philosophical purposes.

On the one hand, Levinas clearly intends to propose an "ethical" vision of the "world to come" that is inherently different from the ordinary "world," which is circumscribed by anonymity and negligence. On the other hand, Levinas here manipulates the talmudic source—whose intentions probably are ironical with respect to Christianity and apologetical with respect to the rabbinic establishment—and rephrases it in strict philosophical-phenomenological terms. What is here relevant is that Levinas indulges in this "egocentric" interpretation of the messianic condition and at the same time ignores the obvious theological-political setting of this text, which is easily demonstrated by the first lines, written in Aramaic, from the talmudic passage:

> Rav Nachman said to Rabbi Itzhaq: Have you heard when "the son of the fallen" [*bar nafley*] will come? Whence is [the expression] "the son of the fallen"? He said to him: Messiah. Do you call him, the Messiah, "the son of the fallen"? He said to him: isn't it written: "Today I will raise up the tabernacle of David that has fallen [*ha-nofelet*]" (Amos 9:11)? (*bSanh* 96b–97a)

These few words in Aramaic do not only introduce the extraordinary talmudic discussion in Hebrew on "messianism," but also provide the interpretative key to it by alluding to a number of theological presuppositions through a complex word play. Scholars usually agree that the Aramaic expression *bar nafley* [the son of the fallen] is indeed both a translation and an interpretation of the Greek expression *uios nefelon* [the son of clouds] that would allude to the cosmological advent of the eschatological figure of the "son of man" in the book of Daniel as well as to its rephrasing in the gospel of Matthew.[22] Rabbi Nachman might have been making a pun on the Greek description of Jesus as the Messiah and claiming for the intrinsic "Jewishness" of the Messiah himself: a descendent from the House of David who will restore the "tabernacle of David" or restore the theological-political prominence of Israel. And yet Levinas ignores these very important connotations.

As a consequence, the claim to be the Messiah in Levinas's interpretation is deprived of its theological-political significance and is rather forced into a philosophical perspective: the "individualism" by which each prominent rabbi calls himself a Messiah and therefore exalts the ideals of rabbinic education is reinterpreted if not rephrased in terms of phenomenological "ipseity."

What are the consequences of this method by which nonphilosophical material is rephrased in philosophical terms?

LEVINAS'S TALMUDIC HERMENEUTICS AND HIS PHILOSOPHICAL INTERPRETATION OF THE TEXT

Levinas's talmudic hermeneutics seems to reflect the interpretative method that he was probably taught by "Monsieur Chouchani." This implied a sort of thematic conflation of "legal" and "nonlegal" texts under the assumption that both juridical and narrative texts should be examined from the same points of view: as texts susceptible of being interpreted in "ethical"-"metaphysical" terms. In order to appreciate the impact of this hermeneutical method on the thematic and textual integrity of the Talmud, I will specifically focus on Levinas's treatment of the notion of "repentance." Levinas's argumentation is very complex. For clarity's sake I will first report the essential points of his interpretation. Only later do I analyze it in detail and expose its metaphysical and "supplementary" character.

First, Levinas describes the debate between two talmudic authorities, Samuel and Rav Hiyya bar Abba in the name of Rabbi Johanan, on the notion of "repentance" and only then takes side with one of them (*bSanh* 99a):

> For Samuel, on the other hand, something foreign to the moral individual exists, something which must first be suppressed before the messianic era can come. The Messiah is, first and foremost, this break. For the lucid conscience in control of its intentions, the coming of the Messiah carries an irrational element or at least something which does not depends on man, which comes from outside: the outcome of political contradictions. . . . It matters little whether this outside is the action of God or a political revolution that is distinct form morality.[23]

From the glosses on the importance of "ethics" and "self-commitment" with justice, it is quite evident that Levinas is hiding behind the words of Samuel and offering a specific critique, in talmudic terms, to the phenomenological notion of "world." Levinas is maintaining here that the ordinary "world" cannot be the true source for "messianism" in so far as the latter implies a deep reconfiguration of morals and ethics. The "world" can provide only a sort of "socialist utopia," as expressed in the words of Rav Hiyya bar Abba, but it cannot really launch an epoch-changing event like the messianic one. This is impossible for an essential reason: "messianism" implies an ethical as well as metaphysical break into the ontological "horizon" of the ordinary "world," whereas any political utopia implies the belief that salvation can eventually originate from within the "world" itself.

Yet Levinas is not satisfied with this first examination of the dispute between Samuel and Rav Hiyya bar Abba in the name of Rabbi Johanan.

Therefore, he examines also a similar discussion that takes place between Samuel and Rav, his usual opponent in the Talmud, on the notion of "repentance." After examining several alternatives in identifying who is the individual who is said to be mourning for Israel (*bSanh* 97b–98a), Levinas summarizes the terms of this dispute as follows: "The two theses propounded by Rab and Samuel seem clearer: . . . either morality . . . will save the world or else what is needed is an objective event that surpasses morality and the individual's good intentions."[24]

Levinas's argumentation goes further by resuming an earlier discussion on "repentance" between Rabbi Eliezer and Rabbi Jehoshua (*bSanh* 97b) in order to support his main assumption that messianism intrinsically involves an extramundane irruption of the divine into the human history. Therefore, Levinas assimilates the discussion between Rabbi Eliezer and Rabbi Jehoshua to the two previous ones.

For now we can stop at this point of the discussion and proceed with a first evaluation of Levinas's interpretation. As far as Levinas's reading is fascinating, it imposes a subtle manipulation of the talmudic text, regardless of its original aims and composition. In the original text of Tractate *Sanhedrin*, the discussion on the notion of "repentance" is introduced in the middle of two larger textual sections on the time when the Messiah is going to come. The discussion on the notion of "repentance" (*bSanh* 97b–98a) specifically divides the first investigation on the time of the messianic advent (*bSanh* 97a–b) from the second one (*bSanh* 98a). The apparent reasons for this redactional choice are quite obvious: providing a two-step discussion on the same issue of the time of the messianic advent by inserting a new parameter—the moral quality of the individuals who will be living at the time of the messianic advent itself.

Yet Levinas's treatment of these two discussions is much less philologically and hermeneutically accurate than would at first appear. My assumption is that Levinas manipulated the talmudic source and "supplemented" it with a specific "ethical" argumentation with particular consequences that imposed specific theological-political costs to his interpretation of the text. In order to appreciate this, it is necessary to resume Levinas's interpretation and to compare it with the original talmudic source.

LEVINAS'S SUPPLEMENTING THE TALMUD

The most important difference between the original page and Levinas's arrangement of this text is the segmentation of the textual material. The original passage from Tractate *Sanhedrin* offers a very specific sequence of the textual portions on which Levinas comments: at first, the debate between Rabbi Eliezer and Rabbi Joshuah (*bSanh* 97b) that anticipates the debate between Samuel and Rav (*bSanh* 97b–98a), and then—after a long cosmological section on the secular cycles of the messianic times (*bSanh* 98a–99a)—the debate between Samuel and Rav Hiyya bar Abba in the name of Rabbi Yohanan (*bSanh* 99a). This disposition follows both chronological and thematic criteria: on the one hand, it is clear that the Amoraic debate between Samuel and Rav (*bSanh* 97b–98a) resumes the Tannaitic debate between Rabbi Eliezer and Rabbi Jehosuha (*bSanh* 97b); on the other hand, it is clear that the debate between Samuel and Rav (*bSanh* 99a) concludes the long narrative talmudic section on messianism (*bSanh* 96b–99a) and, more specifically, resumes the previous discussion on the notion of "repentance," after a parenthetical discussion on the cosmological evidence of messianic times (*bSanh* 98a–99a).

Levinas apparently pays attention neither to the complex texture of these talmudic passages nor to the progression from the Tannaitic to the late Amoraic times. On the contrary, he deeply changes the order for reading in two ways: first, he analyzes the debate between Samuel and Rav Hiyya bar Abba (*bSanh* 99a) before the debate between Samuel and Rav (*bSanh* 97b–98a); he then encapsulates the early debate between Rabbi Eliezer and Rabbi Jehoshua (*bSanh* 97b) within the larger frame of the two debates between Samuel and Rav Hiyya bar Abba, on the one hand, and between Samuel and Rav, on the other hand. The inversion of the talmudic material in Levinas's commentary can easily be displayed in the following chart.

Development of the sugya	*Levinas's sequence*
debate Rabbi Eliezer/Rabbi Jehoshua (*bSanh* 97b)	debate Samuel/Rav Hiyya bar Abba (*bSanh* 99a)
debate Samuel/Rav (*bSanh* 97b–98a)	debate Samuel/Rav (*bSanh* 97b–98a)
debate Samuel/Rav Hiyya bar Abba (*bSanh* 99a)	debate Rabbi Eliezer/Rabbi Jehoshua (*bSanh* 97b)

It is precisely this "dislocation" of the early Tannaitic debate that plays a very specific role in Levinas's exegesis. Levinas moves aside the early debate between Rabbi Eliezer and Rabbi Johoshua with a specific purpose: supplementing his argument about the indisputable extramundane nature of the messianic event. I emphasize here Derrida's notion of "supplement" that designates, in deconstructive terms, an "inessential extra added to something complete in itself."[25] Accordingly, Levinas at first ignores, then dislocates, and finally resumes the debate between Rabbi Eliezer and Rabbi Jehoshua in order to reiterate an exegetical point—the value of "repentance"—on which he had already commented twice: once while reviewing the debate between Samuel and Rav Hiyya bar Abba (*bSanh* 99a) and once while reviewing the debate between Samuel and Rav (*bSanh* 97b–98a). What is relevant here is not the simple different disposition of textual material, rather the effect that Levinas intended to produce by offering a different segmentation of the text. Levinas is not simply reading the original text in reverse order; he is also imposing a hermeneutical dynamics into it so that he can support his own reading of the notion of "repentance" as well as prevent a specific accusation against his main assumption that messianism would be the "outbreak"—if not an "evasion"—from the ordinary "world."

This passage is very subtle. Let us view once again the structure of the original talmudic text, Levinas's commentary, and the "supplement" that he finds for his interpretation.

At first, the original talmudic text offers a progressive line of thoughts that goes as follows in three fundamental steps:

(1) the Tannaitic debate between Rabbi Eliezer and Rabbi Joshuah (*bSanh* 97b) introduces the alternative between a conditioned and unconditioned salvation by the Messiah: Rabbi Eliezer maintains that salvation will depend on an economical exchange of good deeds, a sort of metaphysical *do ut des*; on the contrary, Rabbi Johoshua believes in a sort of divine "grace" that will save everyone, regardless of his crimes.

(2) These opinions are then expanded into the later Amoraic debate between Samuel and Rav (*bSanh* 97b–98a), who respectively argue for an unconditioned messianic advent as an "external event" and for a conditioned event that fundamentally depends on a specific moral, social, and political commitment of the individuals.

(3) After a digression on the cosmological cycles of messianic times (*bSanh* 98a–99a), the previous discussions culminate in the debate between Samuel and Rav Hiyya bar Abba (*bSanh* 99a) on the very nature of the messianic advent: Samuel thinks of the messianic advent as the irruption of "the Other," whereas Rav insists on the moral, social, and political presuppositions to this event. A short sacerdotal coda to the discussion ends the six pages on messianism with an eloquent invocation to Paradise and the Garden of Eden.

Levinas rejects this original arrangement of the text, as already remarked. He starts his commentary from the very last lines of the text on the metaphysical mystery of the end of times, but he is mostly troubled by the possibility that these "messianic texts" might resemble some form of Christianity: "The commentator [the Maharsha][26] was probably shocked by the idea of redemption which is obtained by the sole effect of suffering and without any positive virtue being required, something that reeks of Christianity [*a un fort relent chrétien*]."[27]

Therefore, he inverts the order of reading the long talmudic text and begins with the discussion between Samuel and Rav Hiyya bar Abba (*bSanh* 99a), passing then to the discussion between Samuel and Rav (*bSanh* 97b–98a), and finally ending with the Tannaitic debate between Rabbi Eliezer and Rabbi Jehoshua (*bSanh* 97b).

It is exactly at this point that Levinas exhibits the logic of the "supplement." This fundamentally consists of holding two contradictory assumptions at the same time and yet maintaining that the one actually sustains, or supplements, the other one.

On the one hand, Levinas claims that the debate between Rabbi Eliezer and Rabbi Jehoshua should not be interpret in terms of a divine "grace": "Precisely, *because evil is not simply a 'backsliding,' but a profound illness in being, it is the sick person who is first and principal worker of his own healing*. This is a unique logic [*singulière logique*], and the opposite of the logic of grace. I can save you on condition that you return unto me."[28]

On the other hand, Levinas claims that the debate between Rabbi Eliezer and Rabbi Jehoshua does actually support a "gracious" form of salvation although this divine intervention is rather described as "brutal"—somehow spelled out in "uncivilized terms": "Rabbi Joshua's final argument consists in brutally [*brutalement*] affirming the deliverance of the world by a fixed date, whether or not men deserve such deliverance."[29]

This little linguistic detail is particularly relevant because it actually exposes the logic of "supplement" at work here. Levinas intends to keep away from any interpretation of the text that might suggest some theological congruity between Judaism and Christianity, but he cannot help remarking twice—on the basis of two simultaneous discussions—that the messianic advent breaks up the ordinary "horizon" of the "world." The logic of "supplement" can be seen at work especially when Levinas implicitly applies to these texts his notion of "religion," as he elaborated on it in his *Totality and Infinity*: "We propose to call 'religion' the bond [*lien*] that is established between the same [*Même*] and the other [*Autre*] without constituting a totality. . . . For the relation between the being here below and the transcendent being that results in no community of concept or totality—a relation without relation [*relation sans relation*]—we reserve the term religion."[30]

The logic of "supplement" exactly intervenes in order to prevent the reader from understanding this phenomenologically neutral definition of "religion" in Christian terms. Levinas intends to avoid the suspicion that this powerful vision of "grace" might be misunderstood as a Christian belief. Particularly eloquent is the empirical, almost trivial expression that he uses: "something that reeks of Christianity [*a un fort relent chrétien*]."[31] This little slip of the pen lowers the religious debate to the level of dispute between Judaism and Christianity, betraying the suspicion that Levinas's notion of "religion" intends to be not only "phenomenologically" but also "morally" if not even "physiologically" pure from contaminations—from something that actually "reeks" as a popular form of religion.

What are the consequences of this kind of reading? The particular segmentation that Levinas imposes on the talmudic text and especially his interest in avoiding any "contamination" with a popular understanding of the notion of "repentance" have specific costs: the suppression of theological-political nuances in favor of a "metaphysical" appreciation of the notion of "messianism." This "philosophical reduction" is not infrequent in Levinas's commentaries on the Talmud and reflects both the hermeneutical method taught by "Monsieur Chouchani" and his own commitment to reviewing phenomenology. Just as his *Totality and Infinity* appears as a philosophical rephrasing of the biblical books of Genesis and Exodus, so does his commentary on Tractate *Sanhedrin* appear as a "philosophical reduction" of traditionally Jewish literature and specifically of the religious doctrine of messianism. Levinas's neglect of the theological-political connotations of this text might then appear inadequate if not paradoxical, but it is rather the consequence of philosophical and phenomenological approach to the text.

ACKNOWLEDGMENT

I would like to thank Prof. Dr. Tal Ilan (Free University Berlin) for reading a first draft of this paper.

NOTES

1. Emmanuel Levinas (1906–1995) was an important French philosopher of Lithuanian origins. Most of his philosophical work, written in French, was inspired by Edmund

Husserl's phenomenology, Martin Heidegger's "existentialism," and, later, by rabbinic literature—especially the Talmud. Levinas's philosophical education began at Strasbourg University in 1924, where he knew the French philosopher Maurice Blanchot and later became one of the very first French intellectuals to have studied Husserl and Heidegger. After World War II, he began teaching at the University of Poitiers in 1961, at the Nanterre campus of the University of Paris in 1967, and at the Sorbonne in 1973, from which he retired in 1979. Scholarship on Levinas is immense and, as maintained by Peter Atterton and Matthew Calarco, it virtually divides into three "waves:" (1) a "traditional" one, mostly represented by "phenomenological" commentaries on *Totality and Infinity*; (2) a "deconstructive" one, mostly represented by Derrida's reception of Levinas's *Totality and Infinity* and its followers; (3) a sociopolitical one, represented by most recent scholarship. On this, see P. Atterton and M. Calarco, eds., *Radicalizing Levinas* (New York: SUNY Press, 2010). For a recent general exposition of Levinas's thought, see M. L. Morgan, *The Cambridge Introduction to Emmanuel Levinas* (Cambridge: Cambridge University Press, 2011).

2. E. Levinas, "Messianic Texts," in *Difficult Freedom. Essays on Judaism* (ed. E. Levinas; London: Athlone, 1990), 59–96 (henceforth, DF).

3. E. Levinas, *Totality and Infinity: An Essay on Exteriority* (Pittsburgh: Duquesne University Press, 1969) (henceforth, TI).

4. I obviously follow Derrida's famous critique of *Totality and Infinity* as it was presented in his early essay, Jacques Derrida, "Violence and Metaphysics," in *Writing and Difference* (Chicago: University of Chicago Press, 1978), 79–102.

5. I am referring here to Levinas's short text, *The Time and the Other* (Pittsburgh: Duquesne University Press, 1987 [1948]), in which he turns his attention to an ontology—later called "transcendence" or "metaphysics"—that no longer conforms to the guidelines of Husserl's and Heidegger's post-Romantic phenomenology and opens to a different "existential analytics."

6. For a comprehensive commentary on this complex text, see J. R. Mensch, *Levinas's Existential Analytic: A Commentary on Totality and Infinity* (Evanston: Northwestern University Press, 2015). See also this excellent monograph, E. Severson, *Levinas's Philosophy of Time: Gift, Responsibility, Diachrony, Hope* (Pittsburgh: Duquesne University Press, 2013).

7. Levinas, TI, 39.

8. Ibid., 156.

9. This fundamental ambiguity is a recurrent theme in Levinas's scholarship and especially in his commentaries on the Talmud. I have recently analyzed this ambiguity in Levinas's commentary on the institution of the "cities of refuge." See F. Dal Bo, "Between the 'City of Man' and the 'City of God': Levinas on the Biblical Institution of the 'Cities of Refuge' in Talmudic Literature (b *Makk* 9b–10a)," *Zeitschrift für Politisches Denken/ Journal for Political Thinking* 1:8 (April 2016): 74–92 (online edition: http://www.hannaharendt.net/index.php/han/article/view/345/474).

10. Levinas, TI, 177.

11. The resonance between Hegelian "logic" and the Gospel of John has been investigated in detail in two relatively recent monographs that respectively assume a "trinitarian" structuration of the epochal divine and its articulation both in a binary and triadic "logic": C. O'Regan, *The Heterodox Hegel* (New York: SUNY Press, 1994), and N. Adams, *Eclipse of Grace: Divine and Human Action in Hegel* (London: Wiley-Blackwell, 2013).

12. Levinas's notion of *jouissance* obviously resonates with Lacan's, especially when they both insist on the dimension of "femininity" on the wayside of ethics. See in particular S. Harasym, *Levinas and Lacan: The Missed Encounter* (New York: SUNY Press, 1998), 42–46 and especially 90–96.

13. Levinas, TI, 299.

14. Ibid., 79.

15. There is indeed a short talmudic quotation in *Totality and Infinity* (201): "'to leave men without food is a fault that no circumstances attenuates; the distinction between the voluntary and the involuntary does not apply here,' says Rabbi Yochanan. " Levinas claims this quotation is from *bSanh* 104b, but there is no evidence that such a passage actually exists. Rabbi Eliezer Chrysler (in the talmudic portal *Kollel Iyun ha-Daf*) has recently suggested that Levinas's quotation was apparently an elaboration of different statements from the folios 103b–104a of Tractate *Sanhedrin*: namely, Rabbi Yohannan's ruling that inadvertently failing to feed anyone who is in need shall be accounted as a deliberate negligence (*bSanh* 103b) and the *Gemara* support of this view on account of Rav Yehudah in the name of Rav (in *bSanh* 104a). Levinas's inaccuracy in reporting the quotation from the Talmud should not be judged lightly but rather be accounted as a sign of his talmudic hermeneutics, fundamentally based on the "elaboration" of textual passages rather on their actual "interpretation." The consequence of this hermeneutical approach will be evident in the following pages.

16. Levinas will comment on *bSanh* 96b–99a (the text analyzed presently here) in the 1963 text *Difficult Freedom*; on *bSanh* 36b–37a in the 1968 *Four Talmudic Readings*; on *bSanh* 67a–68a in the 1977 text *From the Sacred to the Saint*; and in 1988 on *bSanh* 99a–b in his *The Hour of the Nations*.

17. Monsieur Chouchani (?–1968?), most probably a French adaptation of Shushani, "a person from Shushan," was a sobriquet for a still unidentified Jewish individual, who appeared to have an encyclopedic knowledge and who taught a small and select number of distinguished students in postwar France, including E. Wiesel, E. Levinas, and other prominent intellectuals. For an investigative report on this enigmatic individual, see S. Malka, *Monsieur Chouchani: L'énigme d'un maître du XXe siècle* (Paris: Lattès, 1994); see also E. Wiesel, "The Wandering Jew," in *Legends of Our Time* (New York: Avon Books, 1968), 121–42, and E. Wiesel, "The Death of My Teacher," in *One Generation After* (New York: Random House, 1970), 120–25. See also the website dedicated to him: http://www.chouchani.com/.

18. The Aramaic commentary on the mishnaic ruling against a false prophet (*mSanh* 11:5ss) is to be found in the folios *bSanh* 89a–96b. The "little Apocalypse" (G. Stemberger) on "messianic times" is joined after the juridical discussion on the Mishnah.

19. The different impacts of Roman and Persian government on Palestinian and Babylonian Jewry respectively has been examined by P. Schäfer with particular attention to the anti-Christian sentiments expressed against Jesus in Tractate *Sanhedrin*. See P. Schäfer, *Jesus in the Talmud* (Princeton: Princeton University Press, 2009). For a much more detailed investigation into the Persian setting of the Babylonian Talmud, see especially S. Secunda, *The Iranian Talmud: Reading the Bavli in Its Sasanian Context* (Philadelphia: University of Pennsylvania Press, 2013).

20. Levinas, DF, 85.

21. Ibid., 89.

22. The Aramaic expression *bar nafley* probably reflects the Greek expression *uios nefelon* [son of clouds] that would be a deformation or possibly an abridgment of the Greek verse *uios tou anthropou erchomenos epi ton nefelon tou ouranou* [the Son of Man coming on the clouds of the sky] from the Gospel of Matthew (Matt. 24:30) that in turn is an elaboration on the book of Daniel (Dan 7:13). This would imply that Rav Nachman—provided that he is the author of this expression—was aware that the Gospel of Matthew had described Jesus as "the son of man coming on the clouds of the sky." With respect to this, Rav Nachman's Aramaic version, *bar nafley*, would provide both the purpose of referring polemically to Jesus and the effort of associating the Messiah with David, who will raise the House of Israel. For a classical identification of these congruences, see H. Strack and P. Billerbeck, *Kommentar zum Neuen Testament aus Talmud und Midrasch. Das Evangelium nach Matthäus*, (Munich: Beck, 1956), vol. 2, 956–59; see also C. A. Newsom, *Daniel: A Commentary* (Louisville: John Knox Press, 2014), 246.

23. Levinas, DF, 64–65.

24. Ibid., 72.

25. This is the definition of J. Culler, *On Deconstruction: Theory and Criticism after Structuralism* (Ithaca: Cornell University Press, 1982), 103.

26. Rabbi Shmuel Eliezer Edeles (later called Maharsha, the acronym for *Morenu Ha-Rav Shmuel 'Edeles* [Our Master Rabbi Shmuel Edeles], 1555–1631 c.e.) belongs to the first generation of the *Aharonim* [the last ones, from the sixteenth century c.e. on] of the commentators on the Talmud. He was a prominent commentator on the Talmud in Lubin and other Polish cities. His *Hiddushey Maharsha* [Edeles' Novellae] are usually published in every edition of the Talmud. See D. Bonami, "The Theological Ideas in the Hiddushey Aggadot of Maharsha" (PhD diss., Jewish Theological Seminary, 1976).

27. Levinas, DF, 70.

28. Ibid., 75.

29. Ibid., 77.

30. Levinas, TI, 40 and 80.

31. Levinas, DF, 70. See above.